ALDERBURY
and
WHADDON

A MILLENNIUM MOSAIC
of People Places and Progress

THE ALDERBURY & WHADDON

LOCAL HISTORY RESEARCH GROUP

ALDERBURY
and
WHADDON

A MILLENNIUM MOSAIC
of People Places and Progress

THE ALDERBURY & WHADDON
LOCAL HISTORY RESEARCH GROUP

First published by the
Alderbury & Whaddon Local History Research Group,
Hawthorns, Old Road, Alderbury, Wiltshire,
United Kingdom.

ISBN 0-9538004-0-7

Front cover:
The front cover, based on a design by June Brind,
shows the decorative sign that the parish council is erecting to mark the
millennium. It will stand in the middle of the village on the green at
Waleran Close, almost on the boundary between Alderbury and Whaddon.
It depicts the Fountain memorial made using pillars from the ruins of
Ivychurch Priory. Between the pillars is Alderbury Church. The artist's
impression of a Victorian brick kiln commemorates the former Whaddon
Brickworks, flanked by the signs of the two inns; the Green Dragon at
Alderbury and the Three Crowns at Whaddon. The old plough represents
agriculture, the principal occupation of villagers until recent times.
Bluebells symbolise the Clarendon Forest which centuries ago surrounded
the village. Hidden in the picture are two amusing touches
for children to discover.

Village sign reproduced by permission of Alderbury Parish Council.

Designed in France, by Frances Marr.
Printed and bound in Great Britain by
Salisbury Printing, Salisbury, Wiltshire.

The Alderbury & Whaddon Local History Research Group

The Alderbury & Whaddon Local History Research Group formed in 1998,
as a group of enthusiastic amateur historians who had
determined to write a village history for the Millennium.

Richard Atkinson
June Brind
Veronica Dodkins
Peter Hammond
Mary Hinchcliff
Brian Johnson
Peggy (Eastman) Ling
Christine Marr
Bernice Range
Pat Sheppard
Margaret Smale

Additional contributions by
George Bayford
Patricia Boyle
Gracie Bungey
Michael Clarke
Gregory Cooper
Ellie Green
Colin Hastings
Mike Hiley
Christina Hunt
Gale Hunt
Graham Hunt
Flora Lampard (deceased)
Colin MacKenzie
Frank Moody
Barbara Riches
Betty Scammel
Don Tomblin
Mary Wharton (deceased)
Bridget Wort
Rosemary Witt

Memories contributed by
Tom Dowty
Gordon Eastman
Stanley Gray
George Hatcher
Vera James
Henry Maidment
Mary Milner (deceased)
Frank Moody
Len Moody (deceased)
Muriel Northeast
Will Northeast
Edith Sargent
Vivien Taylor
Brenda Wort

ACKNOWLEDGEMENTS

We are grateful for the assistance provided by the following:

The Millennium Festival Awards for All for their generous financial support

Andrew Christie-Miller for acting as Independent Referee in support of the History Group's Millennium Award application

Wiltshire Record Office, Trowbridge

Wiltshire Building Record, Trowbridge

The Local Studies Section, Salisbury Public Library

Barbara Griffiths, British Telecom Archives, London

Roy Canham, Wiltshire County Council Archaeology Section, Trowbridge

Michael Marshman, County Local Studies Library, Trowbridge

The Rt Hon. The Earl of Radnor for the use of the 1765 map of Alderbury

Nancy Steele, Archivist, Longford Castle by kind permission of The Rt Hon. The Earl of Radnor

Catherine Peters and Richard J Smith for providing access to a copy of the memoirs of Harriet Collins, and Faith Clarke for permission to quote from it

Rosemary Collis for use of her grandfather, Tom Prewett's autobiography

Graham Clarke for detailed information on the Lewis family

John Bament for local housing research material

Frances Marr for design and layout

We are grateful to the following for permission to publish illustrations

Village sign reproduced by courtesy of Alderbury Parish Council
Alderbury Band (Frontispiece, Figure 12.2): courtesy of Henry Maidment
Map of Alderbury 1809 (Figure 1.2): Alderbury Parish Council
Ye Old Post Office Cottage (Figure 10.1): courtesy of Will Northeast
High Street c.1885 (Figure 10.6): Alan Sutton Publishing
Brick-making at Whaddon (Figure 10.14): courtesy of Michael Crook
Alderbury Junction (Figure 11.4): courtesy of Edwin Wilmshurst
Reading Room and Women's Institute (Figure 14.2): courtesy of Tony Howe
Alderbury Cottage (Figure 15.1): courtesy of Donald C Whitton
and David Robson, photographer, Salisbury
Alderbury Forge (Figure 15.3): courtesy of Henry Maidment
Back cover photograph taken by Ray Dodkins

CONTENTS

LIST OF ILLUSTRATIONS

PREFACE

This book comprises a number of unattributed articles written by individual members of the Alderbury and Whaddon Local History Research Group, notes on local groups and societies submitted by their representatives, and reminiscences.

Our aim has been to provide a wide-ranging history of Alderbury and Whaddon, authoritative yet readable, at an affordable price. Although we have researched comprehensively we have had to be selective in both content and depth of detail of items included. We have therefore tried to avoid the detailed reproduction of information contained in publications easily available and have limited our references to our parish neighbours Longford Castle and Clarendon to those matters which have impinged on our local history.

We have striven for accuracy in the factual content of articles, and sought to differentiate between fact and legend. We have not included detailed references to sources but have provided a list of publications found to be useful. Where we have stated, or implied, that information is not known this should not be taken to imply that information does not exist, but only that it is not known to the writers. Reminiscences have, in the main, been printed as submitted.

We hope that the book will provide a useful guide to the history of Alderbury and Whaddon and will provide a stimulus for continuing discussion and research. The data accumulated in its preparation will be preserved and expanded, as the Group will continue to meet, research, and publish further local history documents.

Alderbury, 2000.

1
INTRODUCTION

Figure 1.1

The Old School

House, shown

from Old

Vicarage Lane

In some ways local historians are like archaeologists – pushing and prodding among the debris of their chosen field. They search for the bits and pieces of evidence which, when fitted together, will create a picture from the past, as in some ancient mosaic.

It is true that the picture can never be complete. Some fragments of the mosaic are clear and colourful. A few require more polish and definition; a number have burned or crumbled to dust and are lost forever. Others lie scattered or concealed, awaiting the discovery that may fill a vital gap in the jigsaw that encapsulates the story of Alderbury and Whaddon.

The heritage of our past is evident in the present. The labours of our predecessors can be witnessed here and now: in the hedges and the highroads, the buildings and the byways, the farms and the fields, the ditches and the deer leap.

Readers may detect the many hands that have shared in the compilation of this book. Some belong to contributors who have gladly given of their knowledge or searched their memories. Most belong to the Local History Research Group, for whom the hours of research, discussion and writing have been a labour of love.

What sort of picture emerges from the mosaic? It is one of two separate communities merging into one: of a static, inward-looking society becoming mobile and venturing out into the world; of dependence on agriculture becoming one of independence through technological change: and of a surging population growth, bringing people from far and wide to settle here. The picture shows that village life still continues. It is different from the past, but satisfying.

Figure 1.2

Alderbury Parish·1809

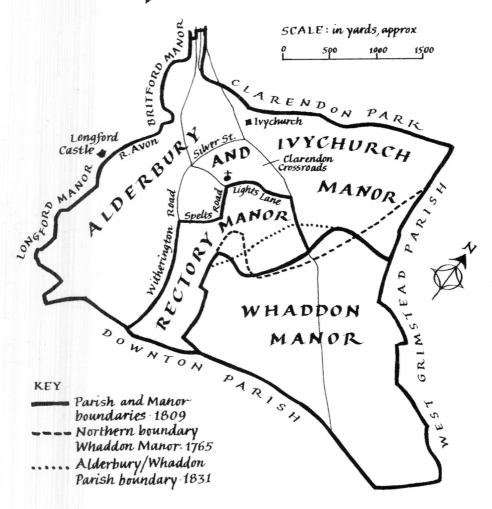

SCALE: in yards, approx

0   500   1000   1500

KEY

▬▬▬ Parish and Manor
boundaries·1809
‑ ‑ ‑ Northern boundary
Whaddon Manor·1765
······ Alderbury/Whaddon
Parish boundary·1831

2

THE VILLAGE TODAY

Aspects of Alderbury and Whaddon

Leaving Salisbury in a southerly direction, passing Petersfinger, the land rises as it reaches Alderbury. Once separate from Whaddon, which like Alderbury lay on the old turnpike road, the two villages have now coalesced to form a linear development. The villages lie to the east of the River Avon, bordering the Clarendon estate, with the Longford estate to the other side, more of which later.

After departing from the modern road to Southampton and passing the last few houses at Petersfinger, one is greeted by an unusual looking house at the junction of the main road and Shute End Road. This house, with its peculiar turret and ornate finish is Saint Marie's Grange, located at the edge of the Alderbury parish boundary. The house is noteworthy not only for its novel architecture, but because of the architect himself; it was designed by, and built for the famous Victorian architect Augustus Welby Northmore Pugin.

The parish of Alderbury today is bounded by two great estates, Clarendon Park (home to the Christie-Miller family) and Longford Park (family seat of the Earls of Radnor). Both of these estates have had significant influence on the development of the settlements into the villages we see today. It is the royal connection with Clarendon that has led to much of Alderbury's early mediaeval history being recorded in sources such as the Calendar Patent Rolls. In more recent times, the Longford Estate has played a greater part in recording events.

Turret,

St Marie's

Grange

As the traveller progresses closer to the village, passing the boundary marker showing the ancient division between Laverstock and Alderbury, Old Road on the left leads to the site of the ancient Augustinian priory, Monasterum Ederosum. More commonly known as Ivychurch Priory, this dates from the late twelfth century. The few remnants of the ruins which remain today are probably the oldest surviving indicators of the early settlement in the parish. Some of the stones are incorporated in the Fountain on the village green. On the site there now stands a private house and the only significant remains of the ancient priory can be seen in the garden in the form of a fragment of an archway. A few other remains can be found in the museum in Salisbury.

Once a great forest, the estate of Clarendon dates back to before the time of Domesday, when William the Conqueror visited in 1072. Then a simple hunting lodge, it was to become a royal palace by 1189, with a grand hall for the king to greet his guests and royal suites, guest rooms and the

Figure 2.1
Remains of
Ivychurch
Priory
(Monasterum
Ederosum)

supporting dining halls, kitchens, wine cellars and sundry other rooms. In 1164, the Council which met there produced the now famous Constitutions of Clarendon, which Thomas Becket at first refused to endorse because they limited the power of the Church. In those far-off halcyon days, it must have been hard to envisage the difficulties which would emerge in subsequent times. By the late thirteenth century, Clarendon had fallen out of royal favour. At this time, there were also allegations of misuse of their position by royal officials at Clarendon. Throughout the fourteenth century, this decline continued, interrupted only when royal patronage increased momentarily as a means of escaping the great plague of London. By 1574, when Queen Elizabeth I visited, Clarendon Palace was no longer suited to housing the royal party although it is not clear whether this was due to its being too small for Elizabeth's large entourage or because it had begun to deteriorate. Gradually, the old palace fell into ruin and in 1737, a new house was built by a subsequent owner, Peter Bathurst, MP for Salisbury. It was purchased by the present owners, the Christie-Miller family, in 1919.

Once past Ivychurch, Old Road sweeps past the forge and forks to encompass the village green. One fork passes the old post office to rejoin the main village road at Clarendon crossroads. The other passes the Green Dragon public house to rejoin the modern road opposite Silver Street, one of the oldest parts of Alderbury. Silver Street runs down to the Witherington Road, passing one of the village's few springs, so important in the days before a piped water supply. On the far side of the field is the parish church, which commands a picturesque position with views to Longford Park.

Alderbury is now an ecumenical parish, with a long history as a place of religious worship. We have already been introduced to Ivychurch Priory.

14

The history of the parish church, St Mary's, has been well documented, but there have been several other places of worship in the parish. Some, such as the Wesleyan Chapel at Folly Lane and the Roman Catholic Church at Clarendon cross-roads, (where new houses are now to be found), have now gone. Evidence of the Quakers has also now vanished. Others, such as St Mary's Hall and the Primitive Methodist Chapel in Whaddon (now the Chapel of the Holy Family, used by the Roman Catholics) continue to serve the community. The church is, in most of the villages of rural England, the single most long-lived symbol of continuity, surviving in much the same form over many hundreds of years. Even when the physical nature of the building changes (as in Alderbury), its purpose remains constant. It therefore provides a direct and meaningful link with the past, a factor which even those for whom it has no importance will accept.

There are those who believe Alderbury to have been the site of a Saxon minster, although there appear to be no recorded archaeological finds to support this. However, Domesday (1086) does mention a church in Alderbury. It is believed to have occupied the site of the present church, which has an ancient yew tree by its door.

Yew trees were ancient signs of religious worship and have been of significance since pagan times, a modern-day reminder of early man's pantheism. Symbols both of life (owing to their very considerable

Figure 2.2

The ancient

yew tree, by St

Mary's Church

*Figure 2.3
Certification
of the age of
the Alderbury
yew tree*

THE CONSERVATION FOUNDATION

COUNTRY LIVING

YEW TREE CAMPAIGN

This is to certify that
using all the data we have to hand,
the age of the yew tree at

ALDERBURY

is *1500* years

Please do all you can
to help prolong the life of this
venerable member of your local community

George Trevelyan
Sir George Trevelyan

Allen Meredith
Allen Meredith

Robert Hardy
Robert Hardy

David Bellamy
David Bellamy

longevity) and of death (through their poisonous berries and leaves), yews can be found in churchyards across Britain. Sadly, that in Alderbury can no longer be described as attractive. The heart of the tree has long since decayed and the bole has been supported by staves and iron collars for many a year. It is evident from the remaining parts of the bole that had the tree survived with its trunk completely intact, it would have been of tremendous girth. It is, in any case, the oldest resident!

Experts generally agree on an age of some 1,500 years and there is a certificate to this effect, (reproduced in Figure 2.3), in the porch to the church. This age puts the date of its germination at around the latter part of the fifth century. To put this into context, the Roman presence in Britain had just ended and it is highly probable that the tree was alive at the time when the Roman villa at East Grimstead was in use. Certainly, events in Britain in the period between the Roman occupation and the coming of St Augustine in 597 are shrouded in mystery. At the time of Augustine's arrival, Britain was a deeply pagan country, bearing support for the theory that the planting of the tree in Alderbury had its particular origins in pagan rites. In 1992, the Parochial Church Council applied for permission to fell the tree as it had decayed so much that it was in danger of falling. This led to a survey of the tree and its condition, as part of a concerted campaign to save it. The noted botanist David Bellamy gave his support, as did the London-based Conservation Foundation and the tree was eventually saved, being subject to no more than a little judicious surgery to thin the crown and remove dead wood. A cutting from the old tree, planted adjacent to it by the Rev. Christopher Pooley, is now 15 feet tall.

To the west of Alderbury and Whaddon lies Longford Park, home since 1717 to the Earls of Radnor and their ancestors. This estate has had an enormous influence on the village over the past 400 years and although this has waned considerably in modern times the estate is nevertheless still influential in certain areas. Much of the land on which present dwellings are built once belonged to the estate and indeed many of these dwellings were once estate cottages. This accounts for the two cottages at the end of Junction Road having numbers whereas all other houses in the road do not, being known by their names only. The two cottages in question were estate properties and the numbers relate to their numbers on the estate's lists. There are other examples. Many houses in the village still have a clause in their deeds requiring them to be offered first to the estate if they are put up for sale, and although Longford Castle is actually outside the parish boundary being situated in Britford, much of its land lies within Alderbury. Historians owe much to the Longford Estate as the present Earl has deposited huge numbers of family papers in the County Records Office, many of which relate to the routine business of the village in times past.

Longford Castle was originally built by the wife of Sir Thomas Gorges in 1578. The Bouverie family eventually purchased the estate in 1717. A number of modifications began, including much rebuilding. This was completed in the mid-nineteenth century, by the Earl of Radnor and the castle has remained substantially the same since then.

17

The village has seen a number of changes over recent years. There has been much construction and a number of housing estates have been built, including over 250 houses on Whaddon Common (built by George Wimpey in the late 1970s and early 1980s) and 50 at Oakwood Grove built in the late 1980s. Smaller numbers have been added during the 1990s on the site of the old Yeates' garage (now Pepperbox Rise), at The Sandringhams and at Silver Wood. A badly-needed new school was built at a cost of some £800,000, opening its doors in 1993. There has continued to be infill building over the years and this is likely to continue although in the last years of the millennium, many of the villagers were fighting the prospect of large scale construction on both sides of Junction Road.

Over the years, a number of shops and trades have come and gone. Today, the village has two shops, the Spar shop in Canal Lane and the Londis shop, which is also the Post Office. Both provide the wide range of services which have become necessary to the survival of rural shops in modern times. However, the days of the Salisbury Cooperative store in Alderbury High Street and its earlier use as a shop are sadly over. We have mentioned the forge in Alderbury, which continues to this day; that at Whaddon has gone and the site opposite the post office now houses The Garden Machinery Centre, a repair shop for lawn mowers and the like. The village does, however, have a significant number of other businesses, including car repair, four-wheel drive vehicle sales, two public houses and, at the time of writing, some 15 small units on a business park at Whaddon. These are located close to the site of the defunct Whaddon brickworks. Adjacent to the business park is a camping and caravan site.

Today, Alderbury and Whaddon hold much for their denizens and both have a long history with which residents old and new alike can identify. They have a wide-ranging age distribution, from infants to nonagenarians and although many people commute to work-places further afield, the villages have retained their independence, resisting all attempts to turn them into mere suburbs of nearby Salisbury.

3

GEOLOGY, LANDSCAPE AND THE NATURAL ENVIRONMENT

The legacy of past millennia

The view from the northern edge of Dean Hill is a spectacular panorama of south-east Wiltshire. Undulating woodland sweeps away to fields on the high horizon, while to the west the Great Ridge and the Vale of Wardour mark the valleys of the River Wylye and the River Nadder. The spire of Salisbury Cathedral rises above trees, a silent witness to the almost hidden city. Alderbury Hill, a promontory at the foot of the steep slope, is so densely wooded that the villages of Alderbury and Whaddon are scarcely visible. A peaceful, rural landscape is hiding the upheaval of the recent geological past – but the clues are there.

About 90 million years ago – a mere fraction of geological time – a great thickness of chalk of some 300 metres was raised above the sea across southern England. Salisbury Plain is the western limit of this new land. Over the next 70 million years dramatic events with far-reaching effects were slowly but inexorably happening: the Atlantic Ocean was widening, the North Sea area was sinking, and in the far south, the Alpine mountain range was being raised. The continent – later to become Europe – was slowly drifting northwards. All this created great forces which compressed and stressed the chalk of southern England into long west-to-east ridges.

Figure 3.1

Dean Hill and the Great Ridge were formed in this way about 35 million years ago. They are not the highest points of the ridges. The summits were most easily worn away and, as in the Vale of Wardour, what we see today are the remnants of their sides.

From the earliest time of the raising of the ridges, the rivers draining the higher points of the chalk on Salisbury Plain – the future Avon, Till, Wylye, Nadder and Ebble, all flowed directly

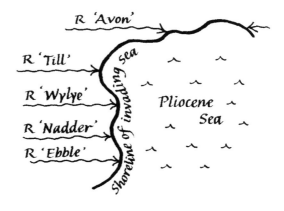

19

Development of the Avon drainage system

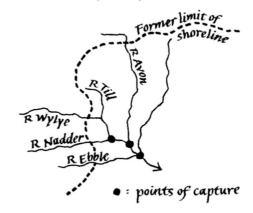

Figure 3.2

● : points of capture

Probable eastward flowing drainage system

Figure 3.3

Present-day river and ridge system

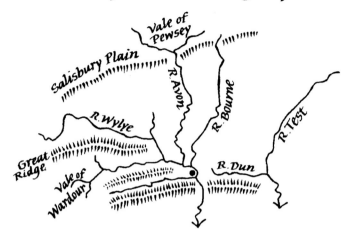

Figure 3.4

eastwards, most probably to join a river which would become the River Thames. Then more earth movements tilted the land from north to south, and the sea invaded, covering the extreme south east of Wiltshire (Figure 3.1). The tilt of the land gave the most northerly rivers more cutting power and as the sea was by then receding, they were able to break through the ridges to flow southwards. The River Avon, with the steepest gradient and greatest power, captured the other eastward flowing rivers (Figure 3.2) on its way to a new coastline.

It is probable that at one time the River Avon joined the rivers Nadder and Ebble to flow as one river across the present site of Alderbury Hill. It ran along the valley now occupied by the Dun to drain into the River Test (Figure 3.3). Evidence for this is found in the Plateau Gravels on Alderbury Hill, which contain pebbles from the Greensand of the Nadder valley – these could not have arrived there any other way. Similar pebbles have been found along the River Test. The size of the Dun valley also suggests that it once contained a larger river.

For many millions of years, and in two distinct periods, the sea covered the chalk in south east Wiltshire, dropping pebbles, sand, and mud, and smoothing out the ridges. The tilting of the land continued and eventually the River Avon, made more powerful by the steepening gradient, broke through the Dean Hill ridge to flow directly southwards to the sea, making a new broader valley to the west of Alderbury (Figure 3.4).

Geological sketch section across Alderbury Parish

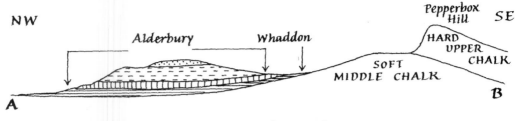

Vertical Scale approx. 1 cm : 50 metres   Linear Scale approx 1 : 50,000

Geology of Alderbury and surrounding parishes

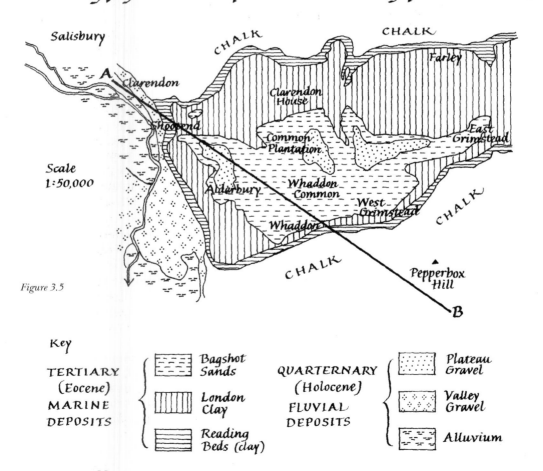

Figure 3.5

Scale 1:50,000

Key

TERTIARY (Eocene) MARINE DEPOSITS
- Bagshot Sands
- London Clay
- Reading Beds (clay)

QUARTERNARY (Holocene) FLUVIAL DEPOSITS
- Plateau Gravel
- Valley Gravel
- Alluvium

The seas finally drained away some two million years ago, leaving a geological feature not found elsewhere in Wiltshire. As the material of the sea bed was taken southwards, much of it was dropped again in the Hampshire Basin, covering the region that is now the New Forest. But some was trapped by Dean Hill, and spread across the Dun Valley, making the undulating surface that is seen today. An even smaller amount of the most recent material was caught between Dean Hill and the River Avon, to form the unique feature of Alderbury Hill.

The sorting of material from a shoreline by the sea is commonly seen – pebbles are left at the high tide line, then sand, and finally, if the tide recedes far enough, mud. This is exactly the sequence of marine deposits at Alderbury, shown in Figure 3.5.

The geology of Alderbury and its surrounding parishes is also shown in Figure 3.5. The divisions are not always perfectly clear, as all beds contain seams of sandy clay and flinty pebbles. The rocks have never been covered and so have not been compressed and hardened. They remain unconsolidated, except that the muds have been pressed into clay by the overlying gravel and sand. This is not a rewarding sequence for fossil hunters. There are no fossils in situ in the Plateau Gravel and Bagshot Sand. Some gastropods and bivalves may be found in the London Clay, particularly at Clarendon, and fragments of oyster shells and worm clusters in the Reading Beds.

In the last million years Alderbury Hill has been moulded into the height and shape it is today – a narrow ridge about three and a half km long and one km at its widest. From Shute End it rises by a fairly steep slope of 1:20 to reach a summit of over 100m at Clarendon cross roads. The slope down from this point to Whaddon is only slightly less steep. Beyond Whaddon the ridge joins the chalk terrace at the foot of Whiteparish Hill.

On the western side, a straight slope drops sharply down from the summit to the water-meadows and the Avon valley. The average gradient is 1:12 – as anyone walking up Tunnel Hill, School Hill and Lights Lane will know! Not so very long ago the River Avon flowed at the foot of the slope, cutting it away and steepening it. Southwards, at Whaddon, the western slope is more gentle, being further from the eroding river, and here springs have moved the sand away to form a broad hollow.

On the east, the lower slopes have been modified by the railway and road cuttings, but it is still possible to see two valleys – one of them now dry with one side obscured by the bypass, and the other a broader valley carrying a head-stream of the River Dun. This is probably the route of the River Avon before it cut through Dean Hill.

In the recent past the gravel and sand outcrops at the top of the hill have been shaped into a very irregular terrain by surface water or streams. This is best seen from the by-pass. At the present day there are no streams of any significance on the eastern side, but on the west a small stream has divided the hill top by cutting a very deep cleft as it has worked its way through the sandstone, down the steep slope to the Avon. This is best seen from a bus!

23

Overall Alderbury Hill is not spectacular, but it is a very unusual geological feature, and although there may be similar deposits in the New Forest, there is nothing like it elsewhere in Wiltshire.

Another remarkable feature of Alderbury Hill and the land to the east, is that it is so densely wooded. This is largely due to the soils which have developed over several thousand years. On gravel and sand, water drains quickly to the clay below, carrying nutrients downward. So the natural soil, although fine, light and easy to work, is acid and infertile, with very few micro-organisms and earthworms. As some local residents will know, in certain places where the clay is not far below, it may become waterlogged at times of heavy rainfall.

Lesser

Skull - cap

(Scuttellaria

minor)

The neutral to acid loam of the hilltop and upper slopes is ideal for oak and hazel, which together with ash, field maple, and beech have formed extensive woodland. Not far away at Clarendon similar woodland became a hunting forest of the kings of England, but in and around Alderbury it was mainly used as hardwood coppice, where the hazel was regularly cut. Although some conifers grew amongst the hardwoods – as they still do – there were more extensive stands of pine, fir and birch on the acid soils of Alderbury and Whaddon Commons. Together, both Commons used to be Wiltshire's only extensive areas of heathland, with acid-tolerant plants of heather, gorse, bilberry, and thorn and birch scrub. Some plants, such as the marsh cinquefoil, sundew, lesser skull cap, and dwarf willow, were found here and nowhere else in Wiltshire.

Much of this heathland ecosystem has now been lost. Some was disturbed by the development of the railway and later the bypass, and birch coppice has been replaced by the conifer plantations of Common Plantation and Nightwood Copse. Settlement has also gradually encroached. In the 1930s some smallholdings were established on the Salisbury to Southampton road, and over the years the Commons have continued to disappear under housing developments.

The farmed land in Alderbury is on the infertile sandy slopes, or on the richer but heavier clay of the lower slopes and river valley, both of which are under permanent pasture. Arable farming is confined to Whaddon, where the soils are alkaline and more fertile, with a mix of sand, clay, and chalk. From the earliest times this has been primarily an agricultural settlement, its name meaning 'wheat hill' or 'wheat lands'. The mediaeval open fields were worked on the westerly slopes, and today the majority of farms in the parish are located here.

Flora and Fauna – A Memory of Whaddon

Mary Milner (née Waters; 1908-99) came with her parents to live at Longford Farm House on the Longford Estate in 1924, when she was aged 16. In 1927 the family moved to Haven Court in Clarendon. In 1932 she married Ron Milner in Alderbury church, the service being taken by Dr Wand, who later became Bishop of London.

With a £700 mortgage guaranteed by her father, the couple built a house on Ron's 12 acres of land situated on the north side of Grimstead Road, Whaddon. They named the house 'Briar Heath'.

It was very hard for young couples during the 1930s Depression. Ron kept poultry and to make some money they bought a Morris Cowley two-seater which they converted into a van. Mary delivered the trussed fowl, home-made cakes, eggs and honey to the homes of her Salisbury clientele. The couple left Alderbury in 1934 to become tenant farmers in Idmiston. Her parents, Joseph and Kathleen Waters, her parents-in-law and, eventually, her husband in 1978, were buried in Alderbury Churchyard.

A great lover of nature and a keen photographer with her trusty Box Brownie camera, Mary kept an album of photographs taken at 'Briar Heath'. She still belonged to the RSPB in her ninetieth year. Following correspondence, an interview was recorded at her nursing home in Dinton. Sadly she died in 1999. The following description of the wildlife around 'Briar Heath' is taken from one of her letters.

Ron's 12 acres was bordered on the back by the old canal. On its bank was a small wood, mostly Fir and Pine trees and here in the evenings we used to see woodcock. Great spotted woodpeckers nested each spring; also meadow pipits and woodlarks used to soar up from the trees singing. A fair amount of heather grew there from which our beees made a vast amount of honey. There were also gooseberry bushes and briar rose bushes with sweet smelling foliage and with blooms that were a far more beautiful shade of pink than the more common dog rose. We also had a small clear-running stream and a pond. Each spring mallards and moorhens used to nest.

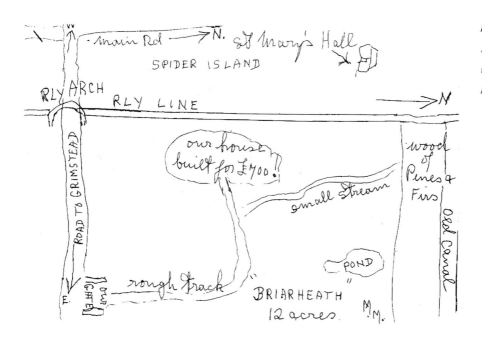

Figure 3.6

Mary Milner's

map, showing

Briar Heath

Growing in the grass behind the house were the finest cowslips I have ever seen. On the opposite side of Grimstead Road was a small copse where each spring nightingales used to sing. Every night we used to hear nightjars "chirring". They used to nest on the ground among the heather. The two eggs and the body of a sitting bird were so well-camouflaged that we were only able to find them because we knew they were there. A pair of stonechats used to build their beautifully constructed cup-shaped nest containing five eggs barely a foot above ground. Robins, blackbirds thrushes, chaffinches, hedge sparrows and linnets – all the more common birds were there in abundance. In fact, with such varied flora and fauna those 12 acres would have made a good nature reserve.'

Mary's map, at Figure 3.6, shows where Briar Heath was situated in 1933. The railway shown has been dismantled.

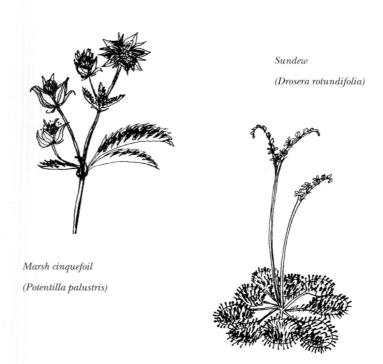

Sundew

(Drosera rotundifolia)

Marsh cinquefoil

(Potentilla palustris)

26

4

EARLY ORIGINS AND HISTORY TO DOMESDAY

Early beginnings

It was cold; the traveller stood on the hill-top looking across the valley below, wondering if he would be well received by the small settlement. Hwœt-denu (the valley of the wheat) lay before him and was only a short journey away now. Night was drawing in and to be left in the open once darkness fell would be dangerous. He drew his furs around himself as the cold began to penetrate, adjusting his sword. He took comfort in the weight of his shield and spear and resolved to seek shelter for the night. After all, hadn't his people been at peace with Cynewalc, King of Wessex, since before the death of his father, Cynegils? He had an iron buckle filled with glass cloissones to give, should a gift be necessary to ease his passage, for urgent business in the north beckoned him and delay would mean that the warrior would have failed in his mission. He could feel the outline of the buckle in his pouch. It was valuable, made in lands afar and he would rather not have to part with it.

And so it might have been. For in reality there is little in the archaeological record relating to the villages of Alderbury and Whaddon and to help to form a picture of life in ancient times, it is necessary to draw on a knowledge of surrounding settlements. These are shown in Figure 4.1.

Alderbury and Whaddon are ancient village settlements, with evidence of occupation since at least Mesolithic times. In keeping with this heritage, the village names also have a long history. The name 'Alderbury' is believed to be derived from Æthelware byrig, meaning Æthelwearde's fortified place. (Æthelwearde is a female name). 'Byrig' is the derivative of the old English 'burh', a word applied to prehistoric earthworks, Iron Age camps and later, to Saxon defence works. The name Æthelware byrig is known to have been in use in 972 AD, although by 976 AD, it had become Ædeluuaraburth. In Domesday (1086), it is recorded as Alwarberie and Alwaresberie, possibly after Alward the Priest. The name went through a number of changes through mediaeval times, including Ailwardesberie (1195), Alwardesburie (1288), Alrebury (1341) and Alewardbury (1476). In the 'Longford Manuscript', believed to have been written in the late seventeenth century, the village name is said to be derived from 'Ailwardus', a man of great possessions as appears by virtue of a charter of Henry II confirming the lands of the Church of New Sarum. This adds credence to the use of the name 'Alewardbury'. It is a short step from these latter versions to the modern name.

27

Whaddon has similarly been through a number of changes, traceable from ancient times. The earliest known name is believed to have been derived from the old English Hwœt-denu meaning 'valley where the wheat is grown'. As the area is substantially flat, it may be an early corruption of denu for valley. By Domesday the name was recorded as Watedene. Like Alderbury, it then went through a number of corruptions, including the following: Hwatedene (1109), Watden (1242), in Waddone (1243), and in Watdene (1273). The name Whaddon first appeared in 1316.

Prehistory: 10,000 BC to 50 BC

In times of prehistory, once the ice began to withdraw, pine trees and oaks spread across the landscape and man began to settle in the countryside. Mesolithic, or middle stone-age man (10,000-4,000 BC) began to inhabit the valleys, fishing in the rivers and hunting in the forests.

The river gravels are a rich source of archaeological finds and the few surviving prehistoric artifacts of significance to Alderbury and Whaddon have been found in gravel deposits. Most are shaped flint tools, celts and socketed bronze tools such as a sickle or chisel. These, however, are too few in number to permit any real analysis although they have been preserved and can be found in the various museums of the region. The only large Mesolithic site in Wiltshire was found at Downton below excavations of a Neolithic site (4,000-2,000 BC) at Castle Meadows, carried out in 1956.

Alderbury itself does, however, have some signs of early settlement. At The Lynchets, there is evidence of an enclosed settlement, probably from the late bronze age or early iron age. This is the earliest known settlement within the boundary of today's parish.

The Romans: 50 BC to 450 AD

There are few traces of Roman artifacts being found within the boundaries of Alderbury and Whaddon. However, it is almost certain that there would have been strong Roman influence in the area, as Roman roads are to be found in many of the adjoining parishes and many of the surrounding towns were of major significance to the Roman occupation. For example, there was a major Roman presence at Rockbourne, only ten or so miles away and there is a well established Roman road passing near the adjoining villages of Pitton and Farley, on its way from Salisbury to Winchester. By 60 BC, the whole of southern England (with the exception of the area to the west of Exeter) was under Roman rule.

There have been a number of finds which indicate the presence of the Romans. These include sherds of Romano-British pottery found near Hole Farm and two brooches from the same period. There was also a corridor-type Roman villa to the east of the present parish boundary in Grimstead. It has been shown to comprise a well appointed farmhouse with hypocaust, three bath-houses and sundry outbuildings. It is considered by Sumner,

Sites of Historic Interest

Figure 4.1

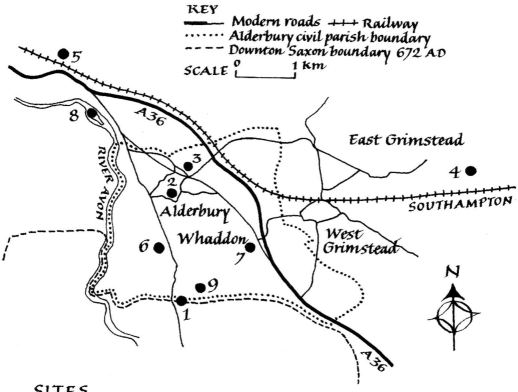

KEY
— Modern roads +++ Railway
...... Alderbury civil parish boundary
- - - - Downton Saxon boundary 672 AD
SCALE 0 |_____| 1 km

SITES

1· Saxon burial (possible warrior or thane) at the Lynchets
2· Probable Saxon settlement at site of present church
3· Ivychurch (site of Augustinian priory)
4· Site of Roman Villa at Grimstead, mid-late 3rd century
5· Saxon burial ground, Petersfinger
6· Possible Iron Age or Romano-British settlement
7· Possible mediaeval settlement, Whaddon
8· St Kitts Island, possible site of mediaeval mill
9· Enclosure, possible late Bronze Age or early Iron Age

who conducted the excavations, to be of higher standing than the better known remains at Rockbourne. Unfortunately, no visible traces now remain due to modern farming techniques, mainly ploughing. Excavated in 1914 and 1915, it revealed 59 coins from the period of Gallenius (Emperor 253-268) through to Valentinian I (Emperor 364-375). Only seven, however, were fourth century, suggesting a date for the villa of the second half of the third century. There was also what was possibly a Centurial stone. Artifacts found included a silver spoon, bronze ornaments, an iron stylus, fragments of glass vessels and various types of pottery, including Samian, New Forest ware and red rosette stamped ware. All of this points to a building of some importance and is a reflection of the Roman occupation in the area.

In the following years, from about 300 onwards, the south of Britain was subject to intermittent raids by the Saxons. The Romans finally withdrew in 400 and by the year 442, the Saxons had become rulers.

The Saxons: 450 AD to 1087 AD

Moving forward in time, the area to the south of Salisbury has long been known to be of importance as a Saxon settlement and it is to this that we must turn for an impression of life in Alderbury and Whaddon in Saxon times. The Saxon settlement at Downton was extensive and stretched from where Grim's Ditch crosses the modern A354 road in the west, to Bramshaw in the east. These lands were ceded by King Cynewalc to Winchester Cathedral some time before 672, a transfer recorded in a twelfth century cartulary by the monks of St Swithun's Priory at Winchester. These lands may have followed the river Avon for part of their eastern boundaries but it is probable that any settlement in the Alderbury and Whaddon area at that time would have been under the influence of the Downton chieftain. Certainly, some of the lands were associated with the modern parish boundary as the ancient Saxon boundary was known to bisect Witherington Ring to the east of The Lynchets, (an old stockaded area of entrenchments), following the old Pack Path road. What is probably the most significant Saxon find within the modern boundary was unearthed at The Lynchets, to the SW of Treasurer's Dean Wood. In 1874, one of Lord Radnor's keepers was out with his ferrets when one became stuck in a rabbit hole. On digging it out, the keeper discovered a skeleton. Next to it was a two-edged sword, with an inscribed pommel. A spear head, the remains of a shield and other artifacts all point to a warrior and the burial was typical of a Saxon thane and warrior of some worth. Certainly, the burial contained works of mixed metals, including bronze, iron and silver. The Saxon Chronicles teach that in 519, the Saxon Cerdic advanced from Cerdicesore (near Southampton) to defeat the Britons at Cerdicsford (now Charford) and in 527, Cerdic and his son Cynric defeated the Britons at Cerdics leah (Cerdics field). Thus, The Lynchets burial was considered the first grave to be found on the spot where Cerdic fought one of his decisive battles – on the edge of the parish of Alderbury!

There is also evidence that the Saxons had a settlement within what is now the parish of Alderbury. A number of earthworks have been found at the northern end of the village and notably, near to the site of the present St Mary's church. These are recorded as not having been surveyed, although the WI History of Alderbury records that: '*Many Saxon remains were found when the road up from Longford Lodge to the Church school was straightened out instead of curving round by Alderbury House. This must have been in the last half of the nineteenth century as it is recorded that the remains were all re-buried in the present churchyard under Canon Hutchings' supervision*'.

Village folk-lore talks about 'the long man', a skeleton of some two metres or more found at this time, but it has not been possible to trace any archaeological record relating to this. Further research may bring this to light. It is, however, interesting to note that Wiltshire Notes and Queries states that the skeleton at The Lynchets was considered to belong to a tall man, the length of the leg bones initially being taken as that of an arm and compared to the arm of the finder!

A further source of knowledge about the Saxons in the region is the burial ground found at Petersfinger. Although this falls within the parish of Clarendon, it was an important find and tells us much about the life led by people in southern Wiltshire in those far-off days. That the cemetery was found at all was serendipity, its presence being revealed by quarrying for chalk in May 1948. Although a number of graves were destroyed by mechanical diggers, once their presence was known a systematic excavation of the remainder revealed a large and important burial ground. In total some 63 graves were found. It is clear from the grave goods that many of the people buried here were of some importance.

The cemetery is located to the north of the Salisbury to Southampton railway line, and to the east of the track running from Milford Road across the eastern edge of Laverstock, on the western escarpment of Ashley Hill. No remains of a settlement have been found in the immediate vicinity although some have speculated that the cemetery may have belonged to a community across the river at Britford, dating from the early ninth century. Such a move to rising ground for interment, away from the waterlogged meadows of Britford would be consistent with other finds in the West Harnham area, where this pagan Saxon cemetery bears a similarly distant relationship to St George's Church.

The skeletons of the people buried at Petersfinger reveal a remarkable anthropological homogeneity, with longish faces and slightly pointed heads. They show that men were about five feet eight inches tall and women about five feet four inches. Most retained virtually all of their teeth, in good condition, suggesting a healthy lifestyle. Some graves contained warriors, evidenced by finds of sword, spear, shield and axe. The latter weapon was, at that time, associated almost exclusively with Frankish graves in England. A number of small button brooches (commonly found in Kentish Graves) and saucer brooches (from Chessel Down), both illustrated in Figure 4.2, have been found in female graves. These bear testimony to the non-

Figure 4.2

Brooches found

in female graves

in the Saxon

cemetery at

Petersfinger

provincial character of the community, as do many other ornamental finds.

Some finds come from as far away as the Midlands and Kent and some bear a resemblance to ornaments found in France. Early graves containing significant grave goods are positioned north-south, with poorer occupants being oriented east-west; later graves are the opposite. This suggests a change of fashion and provides evidence that the cemetery was in use for a long period, indicating a well established community. Thus, the region of central Wiltshire was one of mixed origins and this factor, coupled with evidence for long use of the cemetery, suggests a well developed community for whom trade, possibly linked with travel, was of significance.

Domesday: 1086 AD

The Domesday survey carried out after the Norman conquest was all-encompassing, recording details of property and lands throughout the kingdom. William the Conqueror sent out his commissioners to survey the kingdom which 20 years earlier he had won in battle and the result, initially known as *Liber Regis,* the 'King's Book', became the authoritative source of who owned what. Recourse to the book in subsequent years was a common means of resolving disputes and there was no appeal against it. Within less than a century, it had gained its nickname, Domesday, helped by quotation by the priesthood from Revelation 20:12, which stated: *'And I saw the dead, small and great, stand before God and the books were opened; and another book was opened, which is the book of life; and the dead were judged out of those things which were written in the books, according to their works'.*

At the time of Domesday, Alderbury was known as Alwarberie. (It is also spelt Alwaresberie in the original Domesday). There are entries under three headings of interest to our history; the lands of Hervey (and others), servants of the King, the lands of Waleran the Hunter and the lands of the Canons of Lisieux. The latter has caused some confusion over the years as the entry pertaining to the land held by Alward the Priest was interpreted by Colt-Hoare in his 'Modern History of South Wiltshire' as being land belonging to the Canons of Lisieux. Domesday, however, clearly states that this land was held by Alward 'from the King' as was land under the same entry held by Osbern the Priest. It is possible that Colt-Hoare had therefore made an inaccurate translation from Domesday, although Henry Penruddocke Wyndham's translation, published in 1788, reflects accurately the 'ownership' of the land at Alderbury. The land in Alderbury held by Edward is recorded as having belonged to Boda before 1066. The land held by Egenwulf from Waleran the Hunter was in Whaddon (then called Watedene); this was held by Bolla before 1066. Also in Whaddon, were lands held by two men-at-arms; this land was held by four thanes before 1066. It is recorded that these men could 'go where they would'; thanes held land from the king, in return for military service, ranking between a freeman and a nobleman.

5

THE HUNDRED, PARISH, AND MANORS OF ALDERBURY

The Hundred, Manors, and Parish of Alderbury were, for centuries, the vehicles for the administration of the public and religious life of the community. From early Saxon times southern England was divided for administrative purposes into shires, and they in turn were divided into hundreds which varied in size according to the nature of the land. It is thought that originally each was capable of supporting a hundred families.

At the time of Domesday (1086), Wiltshire comprised 40 hundreds. Although this number had been reduced to 29 by the end of the fourteenth century the shape and size of the Hundred of Alderbury – depicted at Figure 5.1 – remained little changed, apart from the loss of Plaitford Manor. The importance of the hundreds was later eroded by the gradual introduction of new judicial courts, regular police forces, comprehensive taxation procedures, and effective parliamentary representation.

Although responsible to the Crown, the Hundred of Alderbury was in private hands, annexed to the Manor of Winterbourne, from Saxon times until 1536. For almost all of this time the lordship of hundred and manor were in the keeping of the Earls of Salisbury. It then passed to Edward Seymour, brother of Jane Seymour, (the King's wife). Edward later became the Earl of Hertford and Duke of Somerset. In 1551 the Manor was disposed of but in 1662 the Hundred of Alderbury is seen to be still with the Seymour family. Soon afterwards ownership became fragmented as the importance of hundreds in the country's administration waned.

Within the hundreds lay the parishes and manors, both dating from Saxon times. The parishes were ecclesiastical divisions marking the areas of spiritual responsibility and catchment areas for tithes. The manors were the ancient feudal groupings of land and peasants under lords. Manors developed into political, social, and legal units, regulated in the main by a body of custom built up over the ages, and gradually acquiring the force of law within the particular manor.

The manor, as an administrative unit, lasted for hundreds of years before declining as a result of changes in land tenure and the balance between land and population, the free circulation of money, and the gradual centralisation of responsibility for taxation, justice, law and order.

Initially there may have been little correlation between the boundaries of manors and parishes. However, as increasing numbers of feudal lords exercised their right to build churches and nominate priests, the boundaries of manors and parishes increasingly came to coincide.

Hundred of Alderbury ~ Parishes and Selected Manors

Figure 5.1

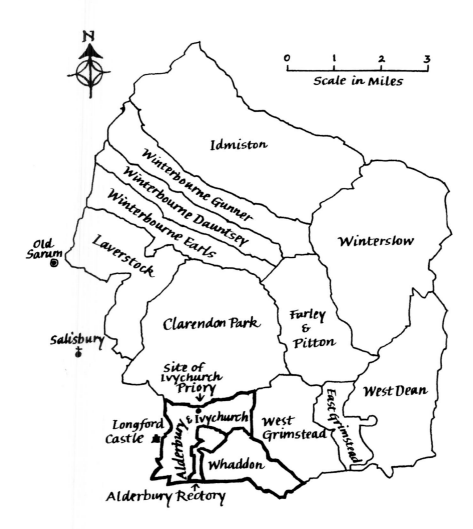

NOTE: Boundaries are approximate. Parish boundaries are mainly circa 1834. Boundaries of the manors of the Parish of Alderbury (heavily outlined) date from 1809.

Alderbury's parish boundaries would seem to have changed little throughout the centuries, and these boundaries have coincided with the external boundaries of its manors. At the time of Domesday there were two main manors in the parish, Alderbury, and Whaddon. They did not have common lordship. Subsequently, as described below, these manors were re-arranged.

Whaddon Manor

At Domesday, Whaddon Manor was held from the king by Waleran the Hunter, who had extensive holdings in Hampshire, Dorset and Wiltshire. He and his descendants held it until 1328 when it was given to Ivychurch Priory. During the period 1086-1328, Whaddon Manor was granted by Waleran and his successors to subordinate lords, first to Engeneulf and later – from 1268 – to Robert Walerand, his relatives the Plokenets (or Plugenots), and briefly, Robert de Bluntesdon. Some of these lords were men whose importance extended far beyond the local area.

Robert Walerand, a descendant of Waleran the Hunter, was a great favourite of Henry II. He was granted the governorship of numerous castles, including that of Salisbury in 1257. He was at various times Warden of the Cinque Ports, a King's Envoy and Negotiator, a Seneschal of Gascony, Warden of the Forest of Dean, and Steward of all the Forests South of the Trent. He was a judge, a Sheriff of Gloucester (1246-50) and Sheriff of Kent (1261-2). He took part in the Welsh wars, jointly held the Great Seal of England, and at the time of his death was one of four guardians of the country in the absence of the king in the Holy Land.

On his death in 1272 the lordship passed to Sir Alan de Plokenet, the son of Robert's stepsister, Alice. He too was a man of importance. Summoned to Parliament as a baron, he fought in the War of Gascony and in Wales, where he was the King's Steward and Constable of the Castle of Droselan. He had earlier been Governor of Dunster Castle, and was one of the Council for the Prince of Wales during the king's absence in Flanders. His son, also Baron Plokenet and Lord of the Manor of Whaddon, died in 1325.

Joan, sister of the 2nd Baron Plokenet, was the widow of Sir Henry de Bohun, the nephew of the Earl of Hereford. Sir Henry was killed by Robert the Bruce, in single combat, on the eve of the Battle of Bannockburn (1314). Joan de Bohun inherited from her brother the Manor of Whaddon, and amongst other manors, the Lordship and Castle of Kilpeck ten miles from Hereford. She is commemorated, as the Lady of Kilpeck, by an effigy and plaque in Hereford Cathedral.

Alderbury Manor

At Domesday, the Manor of Alderbury, including the church, was held by Alward the Priest, directly of the king. Sometime between 1100 and 1122

Alderbury church together with more than 100 acres of land and dependent chapels at Ivychurch, Farley, and Whaddon (all built subsequent to Domesday), were granted by Henry I to the Bishop of Salisbury. By this gift an additional manor was created within the parish, the Manor of Alderbury Rectory, with the Bishop as Lord of the Manor.

Soon after 1139 King Stephen founded the Priory of Ivychurch, which incorporated the existing chapel. It is likely that some land from the Alderbury Rectory Manor was transferred to Ivychurch at the same time. Thus a fourth manor was created within the parish of Alderbury, the Priory Manor of Ivychurch.

At the same time as Henry I's grant of part of the Alderbury Manor to the Bishop, or perhaps earlier, it would seem that the other part was granted to the Lord of the Manor of West Grimstead. West Grimstead, held directly of the king, had been in the hands of the forbears of the Grimstead family at the time of Domesday. Alderbury Manor and West Grimstead Manors, now held by their descendants, remained in their keeping until about 1380, when the manors passed to John Bettesthorne of Bisterne, near Ringwood. They subsequently passed, by marriage, to a junior branch of the Berkeley family. (The first Berkeley to be Lord of the Manor of West Grimstead was Sir John Berkeley a son of Thomas, 8th Baron of Berkeley, custodian of King Edward II who was murdered at Berkeley Castle.)

When Sir John's great grandson Sir William Berkeley was attainted by Richard III in 1483 the forfeited manors of West Grimstead and Alderbury reverted to the Crown. West Grimstead was returned to descendants of the Berkeley family in 1485 by the new King, Henry VII, and Alderbury was granted by the Crown to the Priory of Ivychurch – sometime between 1483 and 1534. The grant may well have been in 1486, the year after the Battle of Bosworth Field, when King Henry VII visited Salisbury and was received by the Corporation on Alderbury Common.

Although the Lords of the Manors of West Grimstead and Alderbury were not as powerful in other spheres as those of Whaddon, the legend of the slaying of a dragon by Sir Maurice Berkeley, the grandfather of Sir William Berkeley, mentioned above, shows one, at least, to have been equally colourful. Legend has it that shortly before his death in 1460, Sir Maurice Berkeley slew a dragon, which had its den at Burley Beacon, near Bisterne, where Sir Maurice had his family seat. A version of the legend is contained in the margin of a pedigree roll held at Berkeley Castle in Gloucester. It tells us that the children of Sir Maurice, and their descendants, bear for their crest a dragon standing before a burning beacon. The dragon is coloured green in a further manuscript at Berkeley. The beacon and dragon are both represented in carvings on the front of the present Bisterne House.

The tale is significant when it is realised that Sir Maurice Berkeley was Lord of the Manor of Alderbury at the time he performed his legendary feat, and that one of the Alderbury inns, dating from about the time of Sir Maurice, appears to have had no name other than 'The Green Dragon'.

Alderbury Rectory Manor

In 1190 the Dean and Chapter of Salisbury appropriated the Alderbury Rectory Manor to the support of the Treasurer of Salisbury Cathedral. Alderbury Parish passed from the jurisdiction of the Bishop to that of the Treasurer, who became Lord of the Manor, rector, and patron of the church, which had jurisdiction over Pitton and Farley. Having jurisdiction separate from the Bishop, and peculiar to itself, Alderbury Parish was classified within the established Church as a 'Peculiar'. As patron, the Treasurer held the advowson, that is, the right to nominate priests to the benefice. In 1800 the Rectory Manor, but not the patronage of the church, was leased to Jacob, the 2nd Earl of Radnor, who acquired the freehold, excluding the seven acres of Treasury Coppice, the following year. The history of the Rectory Manor between 1190 and 1800 is given in Chapter 6.

Ivychurch Manor

The Manor of Ivychurch Priory was founded between 1139-54, to provide for the spiritual needs of the local inhabitants, and of the royal household when visiting the adjacent Clarendon estates. The canons observed the rule of St. Augustine and held the priory site and other land directly of the king. The priory, sometimes referred to as 'Ederose', was sited on rising ground about three miles south-east of Salisbury, and a few hundred yards north of the site of the present-day inn, 'The Green Dragon', at Alderbury. Later

Figure 5.2

Remains of

Ivychurch

priors would have had an excellent view of the building of Salisbury Cathedral, which commenced in 1220.

In 1291 the manor possessed pockets of land at Laverstock, Shrewton, Salisbury, Barford St Martin, Winterslow and Grimstead as well as at Alderbury. There were numerous further additions, notably in 1328 and 1334 when the manor, church, and advowson of Whaddon, together with land there, were acquired. But the endowments of the priory were never of great value, and after an unfortunate period of spiritual and economic decline between 1349, (after the Black Death), and 1412, its finances were placed in the hands of trustees.

In 1534 the property possessed by the Priory was valued at £122. 18s. 6d. The Manors of Whaddon and Alderbury were listed as possessions. Two years later, in 1536, the Priory was dissolved by Henry VIII and the Manor passed to the Crown. There were then five priests and one novice. The mansion and outhouses were said to be in very good condition. A list of the priors from the time of its foundation until its dissolution is printed in the Victoria County History for Wiltshire.

Within a year of the Dissolution the Priory Manor was leased to Robert Seymour, the uncle of Jane Seymour, the king's late wife. It was subsequently acquired by the Seymour family and remained in their possession until 1551 when it was transferred by Edward Seymour, Duke of Somerset and Lord Protector of England, to John Salcot, Bishop of Salisbury. It remained the property of successive bishops of Salisbury until 1801 except for a break of 13 years during the Commonwealth.

From 1551 until 1647 the manor would appear to have been leased to the Earls of Pembroke, the priory buildings, covering about one fifth of an acre, being converted into a dwelling house by Henry, the 2nd earl (1534-1601). Amongst residents at the Ivychurch house during this period the two foremost names are Sir Philip Sidney, the poet, statesman, and soldier; and Sir George Penruddocke, the forbear of the Penruddockes of Compton Chamberlain. Sir Philip, whose sister Mary was the wife of the 2nd Earl of Pembroke, is believed to have written most of 'The Arcadia' at Ivychurch, around 1580. Sir George was an MP for Wiltshire and standard bearer to the Earl of Pembroke at the Battle of St.Quentin in 1557. It seems probable that he resided at Ivychurch between 1572-80.

In 1647 the manor was purchased by the Earl of Pembroke. In 1660 the Commonwealth ended and the purchase was rescinded. The manor was returned to the Bishop of Salisbury and leased in turn to various families. Between 1752 and 1757 the lease was held by Miss Emma Gilbert. Her father, John, was then Bishop of Salisbury, and lived at Ivychurch from 1754-57. The last lease was to the 1st Viscount Folkestone, in 1757. It remained with his family until the manor was purchased by his grandson the 2nd Earl of Radnor in 1801.

During the period 1801-88 it is known that one of the residents was Mr Hinxman a one-time Mayor of Salisbury, but from 1830 to 1862 the house was used as a school, run by the Sopp family.

In 1888, the building, which included much of the old priory, including the twelfth century cloisters, was demolished. A farmhouse – still standing – was built on the site of the north aisle and north transept of the original church. Built into the west wall are a number of sculptured fragments. They include a fourteenth century traceried panel, a number of capitals and corbels, and a moulded arch and recess. As late as 1956 the recess contained figures sculptured in high relief of St Peter and St Paul, each just under three feet high and dating from the 1160s. They have now been removed for safekeeping.

The only other parts of the priory/church complex remaining on site lie within a few yards of the farmhouse west wall, in their original positions (see Figure 5.2). They comprise a complete pillar, one arch support (part of an arcade), and parts of two arches. These were all part of the north aisle of the church.

There is but scanty information about the whereabouts of any surviving remnants: parts of stone capitals and columns form part of the fountain erected outside the Green Dragon at the beginning of this century; a carved fireplace is thought to be in the USA after having once been located in the Green Dragon; and there are wooden bosses in Salisbury Museum and at Pewsey Church, which also has some oak timbers which were at one time part of the Priory refectory.

Sculptured fragments from Ivychurch priory

Re-organisation of the Manors 1809

By 1801 all of the manors of the parish of Alderbury were in the hands of Jacob, the 2nd Earl of Radnor. They comprised Ivychurch Manor, which included the former manors of Alderbury and Whaddon, and the Alderbury Rectory Manor.

In 1809, Commissioners carried out a survey of common land and waste land in the parish, under the Enclosure Act of 1801, and an award was executed. The manors were re-organised into three manors, Alderbury Rectory, Alderbury and Ivychurch, and Whaddon. The revised boundaries (shown at Figure 1.2) were defined, and depicted on a map showing many of the award decisions. The 1809 map remains the definitive map of the manor boundaries, although their existence today has little significance.

The Earl of Radnor is the present Lord of the Manors.

The Whaddon – Alderbury Boundary Line

Since Domesday, when Alderbury and Whaddon were identified as separate manors, the residents have been jealous of their separate identities. But where today is the boundary between the two settlements? There is no simple answer. The published census returns (1841-91) provide only broad guidance, but this is consistent with the defined boundaries of the manors of the parish of Alderbury, which still have legal significance.

Alternative Boundary Lines between Alderbury and Whaddon

KEY
- - - - Northern boundary Whaddon Manor 1765
──── Northern boundary Whaddon Manor 1809
...... Alderbury / Whaddon boundary Parish map 1831

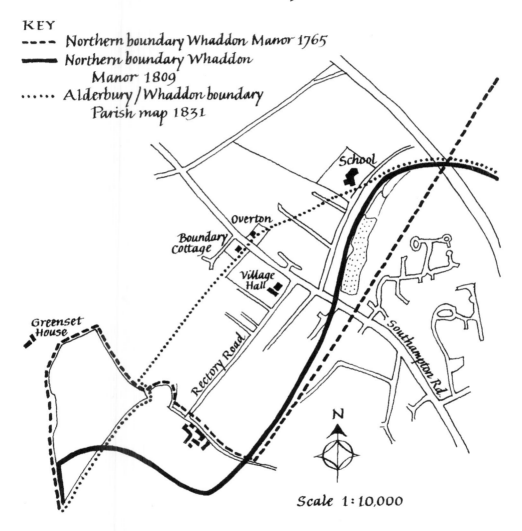

Scale 1:10,000

Figure 5.3

The first known map of Whaddon Manor is a sketch map dated 1765 prepared for estate purposes. Its boundaries are shown on the map at Figure 1.2.

In 1809 the boundaries of all of the manors in Alderbury Parish were re-defined, shown on the Enclosure Award map, and detailed in supporting documentation. The changes are also shown at Figure 1.2. The amended northern boundary of Whaddon Manor follows the proposed line of the ill-fated Alderbury Canal (see Chapter11). The other two parish manors depicted are those resulting from the various re-arrangements already discussed. The manor boundaries remain valid today.

The 1765 and 1809 boundary lines may be considered as possible present-day boundaries between Whaddon and Alderbury. There is a third possibility. Two parish maps of Alderbury dated 1831 and 1854, held at the County Record Office, show a line of demarcation marked 'Alderbury/Whaddon Boundary'. This line also appears on the Alderbury Tithe Map dated 1847. It differs from the manor boundary lines and is also depicted at Figure 1.2. The three different northern boundary lines are further shown at Figure 5.3 superimposed on a sketch map showing current street details.

The origin of the 1831 line of demarcation is not known. It may well have resulted from an attempt to re-define most of the northern Whaddon manor boundary by reference to known property boundaries instead of the route of a non-existent canal. The demarcation line has become important in recent times, having been used since 1970 as the dividing line between Alderbury/Whaddon when compiling electoral rolls. Before that date newly enfranchised voters living in the housing area north of the 1765 line and south of the 1831 line appear to have been placed at random on either the Alderbury or Whaddon electoral roll, and moved from one to the other from time to time.

All of the houses in this area have been built since 1765. Although the 1831 line to-day places them in Whaddon it is very probable that the 1765 manor boundary had existed for centuries prior to that date and the land on which these houses stand was in Alderbury during this time. If this were the case it cannot, today, be properly associated with the ancient history of Whaddon, the lordships of the Walerans and Walerands, the Plokenets, and the Lady of Kilpeck.

Thus it may be suggested that there is not a single Alderbury/Whaddon boundary, but two: the present-day electoral boundary division line, and the historical divide, either the 1765 or 1809 manor boundary. Perhaps the 1809 boundary should be ruled out: it replaced the more historic 1765 boundary and was based on the route of a canal which was not built.

6

HISTORY OF THE
ANGLICAN CHURCH IN ALDERBURY

About 634 Saxon England was converted to Christianity and there was possibly a place of worship near the site of the present church. Saxon remains were discovered when the nearby Tunnel Hill Road was constructed in the latter half of the nineteenth century and the yew tree that stands outside the church entrance may well have been associated with religious rites.

The early history of the Saxon church and its associated chapels and lands is inextricably linked with the history of the parish manors, and has been dealt with above. The present account is concerned with events from 1190 when the Alderbury benefice was established as a 'Peculiar' under the Treasurer of Salisbury Cathedral. At that time Ivychurch Priory had been in existence for over 40 years, and chapels at Whaddon, Pitton, and Farley for twice that period.

In 1341, Alderbury is mentioned as comprising a church and two chapels. It is probable that these chapels were those at Pitton and Farley (both built about 1100), for in 1649 a church survey recommended they be severed from Alderbury. This was not to come about until 1874.

By 1341, Whaddon chapel, which had had its own rectors (nominated by the Lord of the Manor of Whaddon and instituted by the Bishop of Salisbury), had been incorporated into the Manor of Ivychurch Priory. Worship continued at Whaddon for another 50 years and more, mass being said by the priors of Ivychurch. Between 1394 and 1536 the church at Whaddon fell into disuse, and Whaddon inhabitants worshipped at part of Ivychurch Priory set aside for that purpose.

In 1536 the monastery at Ivychurch was dissolved by the King but that part being used as a church, said to be in very good condition, escaped confiscation and continued to be used by parishioners. But there is no mention of it in a church survey dated 1548. Thereafter the Whaddon parishioners used Alderbury church, and the abandoned church at Whaddon gradually disappeared from sight. A note dated 1765 says 'There is reported to have been formerly a church at Whaddon, at Farmer Northeast's' and in 1815 the Vicar of Alderbury states 'vestiges remained until lately'. The exact site of the old church is not known although it is known that Farmer Northeast farmed Whaddon Farm.

By an Order in Council dated 1846 'Peculiars' were abolished. Alderbury ceased to be a 'Peculiar'. The Bishop re-assumed jurisdiction and became patron. A further Order in Council in 1874 separated the chapelries of Pitton and Farley from Alderbury.

42

Between these two dates, in 1858, a new church was built at Alderbury, on the site of the old one.

In 1963 Christopher Pooley was appointed Vicar of Alderbury: in 1964 he was, in addition, made Rector of West Grimstead. On 25 June 1971 it was confirmed that the parishes should be united as 'The Benefice of Alderbury and West Grimstead' and should comprise the Parish of Alderbury and the Parish of West Grimstead 'which shall continue distinct'. The combined benefice was styled 'Rectory', and in 1982 when the Rev. Canon WH Andrew became minister he was appointed as the first Rector of Alderbury and West Grimstead.

In 1985 members of St Mary's Church and Whaddon Methodist Church covenanted to share worship whilst remaining loyal to their own denominations. A copy of the document is displayed in St Mary's Church. The declaration was ratified and signed at a service held in the church on Sunday, 20 January 1985.

On 21 May 1991 the Privy Council approved a pastoral scheme for a new benefice named 'The Benefice of Alderbury (Team Ministry)' and the establishment of a team ministry. This united the benefices of Alderbury and West Grimstead, Farley and Pitton, West Dean with East Grimstead, and Whiteparish. The area was to comprise the parishes of Alderbury, West Grimstead, Farley with Pitton, West Dean with East Grimstead, and Whiteparish. The separate identities of the parishes were not affected. The team ministry was to consist of a rector and two vicars. The first rector would be the Rev. Geoffrey Rowston, Rector of Alderbury and West Grimstead. Subsequent rectors would be presented by a Patronage Board, chaired by the Bishop of Salisbury. Vicars, licensed by the Bishop, would be selected by the Bishop and the Rector jointly. The first two vicars would be the Rev. Philip Bosher, West Dean, and the Rev. Brian Skelding, Whiteparish.

Alderbury Rectory

For 500 years or more, until 1982, incumbent ministers at Alderbury were appointed as vicars. But the manor within which the vicarage lay was – and still is – called the Rectory Manor of Alderbury. There have been Rectors of Alderbury from the earliest formation of the manor until tithes ceased to be exacted, in the nineteenth century. These rectors, however, did not minister to the spiritual welfare of the parishioners of Alderbury. Indeed many were not ordained ministers, and some were women (centuries before the ordination of women in the established Church). In modern times this has led to some misunderstanding. Some clarification is needed.

The rectory is often regarded as the house occupied by the rector, the incumbent minister. However, in earlier times 'the rectory' referred, not to the house, but to the parish benefice, which included the church lands and buildings, the income from these lands, and the tithes of the whole parish. After the dissolution of the monasteries many rectories were sold or leased, with many or all of their rights, to lay persons (men or women) or groups of lay persons. They were known as Impropriate Rectors, or more commonly, Lay Rectors. In each case a vicar or curate was then appointed to minister to the spiritual needs of the parishioners. A vicar would be provided with a vicarage comprising accommodation, land, a proportion of the tithes, and sometimes a stipend. The Lay Rector would often have the right to nominate ministers. The common characteristic of all rectors was the right to receive the great tithes (corn, grain, hay, and wood) of the rectory. In modern times, following the abolition of tithes, only rectors holding office as ministers hold the title. Their appointment as parish priests with the title 'rector' merely reflects the histories of their particular benefices and they no longer have duties, responsibilities, and rights differing from those of vicars.

From 1190 the Treasurer of Salisbury Cathedral was both Rector and Lord of the Rectory Manor of Alderbury. It seems probable that until the Reformation successive Treasurers administered it and appointed and provided for ministers. From 1608 until 1801 (with a short gap during the Commonwealth), the manor and lordship were leased to lay rectors. The Treasurer retained and exercised the right to nominate vicars.

The extent of Alderbury Rectory is defined in a survey carried out in 1649. It included 86 acres of land, the rectory house (not the house where the vicar lived), tithes and payments in lieu of services. A further survey,

Figure 6.1

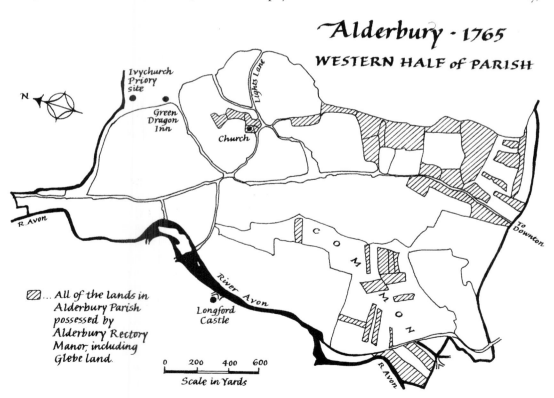

Alderbury · 1765

WESTERN HALF of PARISH

Ivychurch Priory site

Green Dragon Inn

Church

Lights Lane

R. Avon

N

C O M M O N

To Downton

River Avon

Longford Castle

R. Avon

⊘ ... All of the lands in Alderbury Parish possessed by Alderbury Rectory Manor, including Glebe land.

0   200   400   600

Scale in Yards

made in 1765, contains plans, and details of land plots, their names, type, acreage, ownership, and occupancy. It shows the location of the rectory house referred to above. Known today as Court House, it stands adjacent to the south and east parts of the graveyard. Already old in the seventeenth century its south face is thought to have been rebuilt in the early eighteenth century. The survey also indicates the existence of a vicarage house immediately to the south of the church. A map at Figure 6.1 based on the 1765 survey map, shows the extent of the rectory.

Lay Rectors of Alderbury

Date	Rector	Date	Rector
1608 - 1634	Richard Goldstone	1683 - 1722	Rev.GabrielThistlethwaite
1634 - 1640	Thomas Goldstone	1722 - 1740	Mrs Elizabeth Edmunds
1641 - 1645	Joanne Goldstone	1740 - 1758	Rev. Francis Edmunds
1645 - 1656	Jane and	1759 - 1770	Rev. Wright Hawes
	Eliz.Goldstone	1770 - 1774	Mrs E Longford and Mrs
1656 - 1660	Lay Rectorship in		M Purefoy
	abeyance (See text)	1774 - 1794	Tristram Huddlestone
1662 - 1677	Richard Goldstone		Jervoise
1677 - 1679	Francis Mercer	1794 - 1800	Rev. George HJP Jervoise
1679 - 1683	Sir Giles Hungerford	1800 (See text)	Successive Earls of Radnor

In 1809 the Enclosure Award abolished the rectorial tithes. (The small tithes, payable to the vicar, continued until 1865 when they were commuted.) As Alderbury Rectory Manor with its lordship and lands had been sold in 1801 the abolition of the great tithes saw the end of the rectory. The Church retained its small vicarage holdings and the manor continued under its new ownership with its name unchanged.

The list of rectors given above may be nearly complete, for only after the Reformation (sixteenth century) was the Rectory leased to Lay Rectors.

Richard Goldstone, the first recorded lay rector of Alderbury lived at Witherington Farm, just outside the Parish of Alderbury. His wife Margaret, née Ryves, died in 1616 and he died in 1634. Both were buried in the chancel of Alderbury church, in which there is a painted stone shield of their arms annotated 'Anno Domi 1612', and bearing their initials. The shield had been housed in the previous church, which was replaced in 1858. It had probably been affixed to the exterior of a house at one time.

The Rectory was subsequently held by members of Richard Goldstone's family until 1677 except for a short break during the Commonwealth, when the land, without the tithes, was sold by the state to Thomas Dove. The sale was subsequently rescinded and the land returned to the Cathedral Treasurer.

There is no evidence that the Goldstones occupied the Rectory House. It has been suggested that Goldstones lived in Alderbury House from early in the seventeenth century. The present Alderbury House, across the road from the church, was built in 1790 or 1791. There is evidence of an earlier house, in the same area in 1765. It was then owned by George Fort. Whether this house or another was that called Alderbury House is not known. Sir Giles Hungerford and all of the subsequent Lay Rectors up to 1800 were related by blood or marriage.

Although the ecclesiastical rectory ended in 1809 the Earl of Radnor's lordship of the Alderbury Rectory Manor remained unaffected. Perhaps for sentimental or historic reasons, he continued to be referred to as the Lay Rector or Impropriator of the Great Tithes until the 1850s.

Although the Parsonage or Rectory House went with the rectory lands many of the lay rectors elected to live elsewhere and the house was often sub-let and sub-divided. Occupants are known to have included John Bungay in 1765, Thomas Prewett and Henry Rumbold in 1835, and Stephen Prewett, Henry Beaumont, and Thomas Light in 1851. Incumbent vicars may also have been tenants of the Rectory House from time to time. At one time the Rectory House was in use as the village Poor House. This should not be confused with the Alderbury Union Workhouse that was at East Harnham.

Vicars and other incumbents of Alderbury and Whaddon

There were Saxon priests at Alderbury both before the Norman Conquest and possibly until 1110, when the church came under the jurisdiction of the Bishop of Salisbury. He, and later the Treasurer of the Cathedral, would then have been responsible for appointing priests. It may well be that for a period after its foundation, sometime after 1139, the monastery at Ivychurch was called upon to provide the local priests.

Early priests were not called vicars, a title introduced generally about the time of King John (1199-1216). The first recorded vicars of Alderbury appear in the list of bishops' appointments for 1403 and 1422. No explanation can be given as to why they should have been included in these listings when jurisdiction for Alderbury then rested with the Treasurer of the Cathedral.

There is no other mention of Alderbury in comprehensive listings of bishops' appointments covering the period 1297-1810. Unfortunately, records of appointments by Treasurers are incomplete, as is the listing of incumbent ministers, compiled from a variety of sources, portrayed in St Mary's Church. A copy is at Figure 6.2. Points of interest concerning some incumbents are given overleaf.

The Vicarage House

Where the early vicars of Alderbury lived is something of a mystery. It is known that there was once a Vicarage House on a site immediately south of the church, now part of the graveyard. In 1852 it was described as being

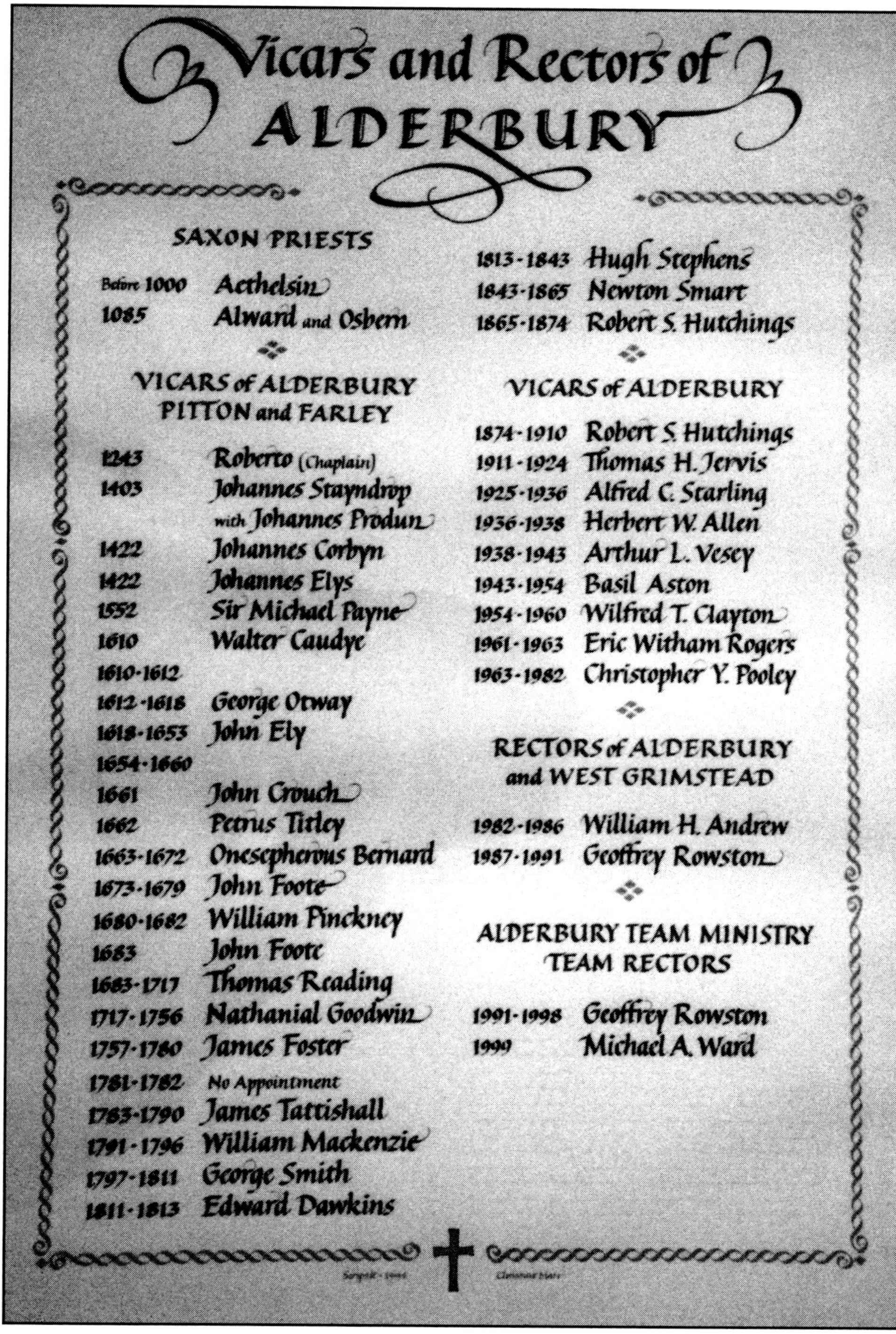

Vicars and Rectors of ALDERBURY

SAXON PRIESTS

Before 1000	Aethelsin
1085	Alward and Osbern

VICARS of ALDERBURY PITTON and FARLEY

1243	Roberto (Chaplain)
1403	Johannes Stayndrop with Johannes Produn
1422	Johannes Corbyn
1422	Johannes Elys
1552	Sir Michael Payne
1610	Walter Caudye
1610-1612	
1612-1618	George Otway
1618-1653	John Ely
1654-1660	
1661	John Crouch
1662	Petrus Titley
1663-1672	Onesepherous Bernard
1673-1679	John Foote
1680-1682	William Pinckney
1683	John Foote
1683-1717	Thomas Reading
1717-1756	Nathanial Goodwin
1757-1780	James Foster
1781-1782	No Appointment
1783-1790	James Tattishall
1791-1796	William Mackenzie
1797-1811	George Smith
1811-1813	Edward Dawkins

1813-1843	Hugh Stephens
1843-1865	Newton Smart
1865-1874	Robert S. Hutchings

VICARS of ALDERBURY

1874-1910	Robert S. Hutchings
1911-1924	Thomas H. Jervis
1925-1936	Alfred C. Starling
1936-1938	Herbert W. Allen
1938-1943	Arthur L. Vesey
1943-1954	Basil Aston
1954-1960	Wilfred T. Clayton
1961-1963	Eric Witham Rogers
1963-1982	Christopher Y. Pooley

RECTORS of ALDERBURY and WEST GRIMSTEAD

1982-1986	William H. Andrew
1987-1991	Geoffrey Rowston

ALDERBURY TEAM MINISTRY TEAM RECTORS

1991-1998	Geoffrey Rowston
1999	Michael A. Ward

Figure 6.2

Some interesting Vicars and other incumbents

1403-1422   **Johannes Stayndrop, Johannes Produm,** and **Johannes Corbyn** are the only incumbents at Alderbury included in Phillip's 'Institutions' which lists institutions (from the Bishops of Salisbury's Registers) between 1297-1810.

1612-1618   **George Otway's** cousin Humphrey was the father of Thomas Otway – the dramatist (1652-85).

1618-1650   **John Ely's** son James established the Ely Trust in 1692. John Ely may have continued as vicar for a number of years after 1650.

1661   **John Crouch.** The only mention refers to his indictment at Quarter Sessions for unspecified offences..

1673-1679   **John Foote.** After his ministry at Alderbury he was Rector of West Grimstead for 38 years.

1683-1717   **Thomas Reading.** After 34 years as Vicar of Alderbury he was Rector at West Grimstead for a further 27 years. He was Warden of Farley Almshouses from 1703-40.

1797-1811   **George Smith** was also appointed Rector of Manningford Abbot's (near Pewsey) in 1797 and Vicar of Urchfont (near Devizes) in 1802. From 1838 the simultaneous holding of two or more benefices was strictly controlled.

1843-1865   **Newton Smart** was responsible for instigating and building the new church in 1858, and, a year or two earlier, a new Vicarage House. He had been a curate at Alderbury 1830-2 and was Warden of Farley Almshouses 1833-55. He was Chaplain to the Archbishop of Canterbury 1836-68. Louis de Bernières, the author of 'Captain Corelli's Mandolin', a best-selling novel in 1997-8, is a direct descendant of Newton Smart by his second wife Frances de Bernière.

1865-1910   **Robert Sparke Hutchings** was born in Penang in 1819 in the last year of the reign of George III. His grand-daughter, whom he baptised at Alderbury in 1893, was still alive and active in 1988. He was Vicar of Alderbury, Pitton, and Farley until 1874 when Pitton and Farley became a separate parish. He then remained Vicar of Alderbury until his death, aged 90, in 1910.

'.... *a very old and dilapidated building now occupied by a labourer's family, quite unsuited for the purpose of a Vicarage....*' It was pulled down within a few years.

From time to time it would have been occupied by vicars, but at other times vicars lived elsewhere. Some held other appointments concurrently with their appointments at Alderbury, and may have chosen to reside in their vicinity, as did the two vicars who were also wardens at the Farley Almshouses. And it is more than likely that from time to time vicars resided at the Parsonage, or Rectory Manor House, as sub-tenants of Lay Rectors.

A new vicarage house, now known as Greenset House, was built about 450 yards SSE of the church and occupied by the vicar, Newton Smart, in 1855. The building was sold and a new vicarage house, now Woodlynne House, built in Lights Lane in 1937. From 1982 incumbents (now designated rectors) have resided in a rectory house, first at Twyneham Gardens, and since 1985, in The Copse. Both houses are located in modern developments in the populated part of Alderbury village.

The Parish Church

St Mary's Church, Alderbury dates from 1858, but from the time of the Norman Conquest, Alderbury church has been mentioned often enough to suggest that there has been a church at Alderbury continuously since that time. A little is known about the church that was there before the present one but nothing about earlier churches. It has been suggested, however, that the Saxon church must have been of an appreciable size as Alderbury was the mother church of an extensive 'forest' parish with a number of dependent chapels.

Figure 6.3 St Mary's Church, Alderbury, from a painting by John Buckler, 1805

The previous mediaeval church, demolished in 1857, was a plain roughcast building with perpendicular windows in the chancel, and a post-Restoration south porch. The building is described as having had a nave, possibly mediaeval, 45 feet by 20 feet 3 inches, and a chancel 26 feet by 15 feet six inches. There was also a belfry at the west end with a wooden turret. Outside the building stood the old yew tree, already referred to. A plan, by

Colt-Hoare, is incorporated into Figure 6.5. The overall length is seen to have been the same as that of the present church.

There is a watercolour painting of the old church, executed by John Buckler in 1805, in the library of the Wiltshire Archaeological and Natural History Society at Devizes. A faithful reproduction, presented in 1958 by the Dowager Countess of Radnor, hangs in the church. A drawing is reproduced at Figure 6.3. A painting, by W Shepherd, dated 1797, is also held at Devizes. It shows that at that time the turret was 50% higher than that shown on the Buckler painting.

In 1856 a faculty petition for the rebuilding of the church, to increase seating from 247 to 436, was approved. The specification, by SS Teulon, the architect, indicates that the new church was to be built on the existing foundations, extended as necessary. Stone and timber, if suitable, were to be re-used. Some nearby tombstones would need to be removed and remains re-interred.

The estimated cost of the new building was £2,500. Viscount Folkestone provided £500, there were grants from the Incorporated and Diocesan Church. The sum of £1,640, raised by private subscription, included a donation by Mr Fort of Alderbury House and £500 donated by Sir Frederick Hervey Bathurst in consideration of which 50 seats were set apart for the use of the people of Clarendon. The vicar, the Rev. Newton Smart, undertook to provide the balance of the sum required.

The church was completed in 1858 and consecrated by Bishop Kerr, the Bishop of Salisbury on 24 June. A recent drawing of the church is at Figure 6.4, and a plan at Figure 6.5 shows the layout of both the present church and the one it replaced.

A contemporary newspaper report contains a full account of the consecration ceremony and a description of the church which is briefly summarised below.

The church, built of flint with free-stone dressings and designed in the 'Decorated' style is elegant and well proportioned and is sited so as to command a singularly beautiful view over the Avon valley. The tower at the northwest is surmounted by a shingle spire, prominent and picturesque. The stonework of the south porch is framed with oak timber from the original church.

The interior of the church is imposing, peaceful, and pleasing. The roof is of open timber work, the seats are of stained wood, and the paving is of Staffordshire tiles. The arches of the nave and the archivolts of the doors and windows are ornamented with coloured brick arches of yellow, black, and red. The corbels which support the roof are beautifully carved with early floral designs. The pulpit is of Bath stone.

The numerous stained glass windows include one given by Mrs Smart, the wife of the vicar. It is inscribed to the memory of her father, Major-General HAC de Bernière, her mother, and her brother. Another, deserving of special mention, is in the south transept. It is probably by Hardman of Birmingham and is unique in that it has a green flying snake representing the devil.

Sketches of tiles etc in Alderbury Church

Figure 6.4
St Mary's
Church,
Alderbury,
1991

The balusters of the choir stalls are said to be early eighteenth century and probably came from the old church: the communion rails are made of wrought-iron panels composed from Scott's screen, removed from Salisbury Cathedral in 1959.

In 1911 there were several changes of note; the move of the organ from the rear of the church to the south of the chancel, the construction of an entry to the vestry from the chancel, the move of the font to the extreme west of the church, and the conversion of the space beneath the tower to a choir vestry. In recent years the north transept has been walled off from the main body of the church to form an additional vestry and the font placed near its doorway entrance.

When the new church was built many of the tombstones removed from the graveyard were used to pave the floor. One fragment reads:

Wife of John.....
Who died Oct y.....
Aged 116 (or 110) al.......
In age and weakness.....

51

The Church Choir

Mr H Stevens, vicar of Alderbury 1813-43, stated that 'The singing gallery without a Prewett is like plum pudding without suet'. Thus, he implied that there was, at that time, an established choir with George Prewett (the Clerk of the Parish Council) leading the gallery singers. Another member of the Prewett family, Stephen, was the leader of the village band which supplied music for the church, although there was, at some time, also a barrel organ. The large Prewett family sang or played for church services for many years.

At the consecration of the rebuilt church in 1858, it was several members of the choir of Salisbury Cathedral who sang, but by the end of the century, there was a thriving choir taught by Mr Freestone with Miss Hutchings, daughter of the vicar, playing the organ. The Alderbury parish magazines of 1901 refer to a choir supper, a choir concert, and carol singing by the choir at Christmas. There is a report on the Festival Service for All Saints Day on 3 November, which states that *'the orchestra assisted with great effort in the Psalms [and] beautiful All Saints Hymns, "The Saints of God" being especially well rendered by both choir and orchestra. Miss Hutchings presided at the organ and Mr Freestone conducted. The Magnificat and Nunc Dimittis were also very well sung by the choir'.*

The present organ was installed by Sweetland of Bath in 1889 and restored by Bishop and White in 1984. In 1911, the organ was moved from the rear of the church to its present position in the south of the chancel.

Mr John Carr, sometime headmaster of Alderbury School, was organist from 1945-74 and many school children sang in the church choir during that period. By 1969, Mr Carr was unfortunately rather deaf and had poor eyesight. Mary Dean 'had her children in the church choir join the Alderbury Singers for a carol service', implying that she had been taking choir practices.

In 1971, Mary Wharton became choir mistress. Starting with only six choristers the numbers grew steadily to 30, being greatly encouraged by the vicar, Christopher Pooley, who sang with them whenever he could. At first, only anthems for female voices were possible; nevertheless, the choir twice won the Church Choirs entry at the Devizes Festival, in 1976 and 1977. With a bass joining the choir and with Mr Pooley singing tenor, four-part music became possible from 1979. A special tribute should be paid to Miss Hazel Argar, who has sung with the choir for over 40 years and is still its mainstay.

When Canon Andrew became Rector in 1982, he decreed that all children should go to the Sunday School held in Whaddon, so the choir dwindled as the remaining choristers grew up and left the village, until only six adults were left. Even so, anthems were sung regularly and the choir joined in the Diocesan Church Choirs' Festival held in Salisbury Cathedral every summer, when it was possible to sing more complicated pieces.

Since 1972, the choir has sung special music on Good Friday and at the annual carol services, with fund-raising concerts for local efforts such as the swimming pool at the old school, the building of the new church school and the induction loop system for those hard of hearing.

The tradition of an annual social gathering continued. Mr Pooley took the choir for a picnic lunch each year and started the tradition of apples being given to the choir as they left the Harvest Festival Service. Later, Mr Carrick Smith (a member of the congregation) took the choir either to the pantomime or out to supper. More recently, there has been an annual supper at Mrs Wharton's house and the choir have received Christmas presents and Easter eggs. For many years, the Earl and Countess of Radnor have invited the choir to Longford Castle to sing carols around the tree on Christmas Eve and this has always been much enjoyed.

John Carr resigned as organist in 1974 and Philip Sibthorpe played for a year before being succeeded by Miss Alison Malcolm (now Mrs Hogg), who stayed until 1980. Ian Simpson played for the next year until Mrs Wharton succeeded at Easter 1981. Since Mary's death Graham Hunt has temporarily become organist and choirmaster.

On Advent Sunday 1998, the choirs of the seven parishes in the Alderbury Team Ministry joined together in St Mary's Church for a special Advent service. This was the first such venture, with 47 singers, Richard Godfrey at the organ and Mary Wharton conducting. It was so favourably received by the large congregation packed into the church that a repeat was planned for Whiteparish Church in the autumn of that year.

The Graveyard: St Mary's Church

Since 1606 details of burials have been entered in the Parish Register, but the locations of individual plots have not been recorded. Only one tombstone dated before the eighteenth century survives in the graveyard, which covers approximately one acre and surrounds the church. The location in the graveyard of many graves is not known. Surveys of graves have been made as follows:

1900 A Survey of all Tombstone Inscriptions. The survey is comprehensive and accurate but unfortunately there is no location map. The record is held at the Library of the Wiltshire Archaeological and Natural History Society at Devizes.

1960 Faculty Petition to Remove Headstones. Names, dates, and a plan are included, but there are a number of errors. (The removal of ten headstones only was authorised).

1985 Graveyard Plan and Listing. All plots recognisable as graves are plotted, and the names of those buried or commemorated are listed. Graves shown total 447, of which 428 are identified. 730 names are given. Information obtained from the 1900 and 1960 surveys was incorporated by amendment in July 1988. Documents are held in the church vestry and at the Wiltshire County Record Office.

A copy of the graveyard plan is at Figure 6.5. Individual plots are not shown with the exception of the oldest, dated 1641. The inscription reads.... *'Here lyeth Thomas Jones the elder who dyed on.....1641'*. No mention is made of a Thomas Jones in the burial register for that date.

The plan shows zones, each annotated to show the date of the earliest known grave lying within it. There was no recognisable change in the shape of the graveyard in the hundred years prior to 1858. It then comprised zones A-F, the area shown on the plan lying within the thick line. Zones H and K formerly comprised the vicar's house and garden. At the consecration of the church in 1858 the additions to the graveyard at zones G and H (and probably zone J) were also consecrated. Zone G was the gift of Viscount Folkestone, and zone H that of the vicar, following the demolition of the old vicarage house. Zone L and zone K (probably) were consecrated in May 1899, and zone M was added in 1930.

The digging of new graves in the church graveyard had ceased by 1985. Burials in vacant spaces in multiple graves and the interment of cremated remains continue. Other burials now take place in the municipal graveyard to the west of the church.

Figure 6.5

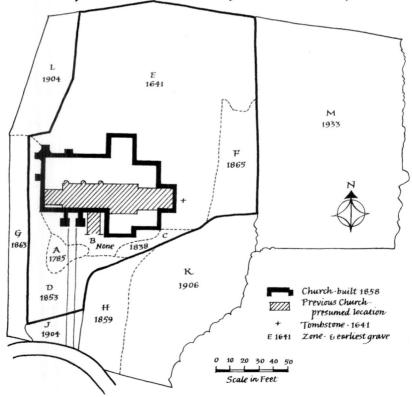

St Mary's Church & Graveyard · Alderbury · 1985

7

NON-CONFORMISTS
AND ROMAN CATHOLICS

Quakers

The story of non-conformity in Alderbury and Whaddon begins with the Society of Friends, or Quakers, to give them their more popular title. George Fox founded the original society in the Midlands in 1648 during the religious upheaval of the Civil War.

Despite, or maybe because of, the penal statutes passed by Parliament following the Restoration, the 1662 Act of Uniformity, the 1664 Conventicle Act and the 1665 Five Mile Act, Quakerism spread throughout the country. Wiltshire was no exception.

Quite when the Alderbury society was founded is not known but it must have been after 1669 as the Episcopal Returns in that year state that there had been no non-conformists in Alderbury or Pitton for the past three years although a small group of Anabaptists was reported in Farley. (Farley and Pitton at that time were part of the parish of Alderbury).

Alderbury's Quakers were first mentioned in 1677 when Richard Hilliard was imprisoned by the Bishop of Salisbury's court for not attending worship in the parish church. He must have been in and out of prison as he appears in the lists of prisoners for several succeeding years. In 1683 Richard was presented to the court 'for keeping unlawful conventicles and assemblies in his house'. Richard and his wife Mary, with their sons Richard and Philip subsequently emigrated to America where they are noted for the part they took in founding the state of Pennsylvania.

Alderbury's Quaker meetings clearly drew members from a large area of south Wiltshire, as in 1681 two Warminster residents, William Forrest and Jone Whatley, were married at Alderbury: and until the Salisbury society was founded some time before 1697, a considerable number of Salisbury residents, including several of the more prosperous citizens, came to the meetings at Alderbury.

Its importance is underlined by the fact that out of 22 Quaker burial grounds in Wiltshire the only two in the south of the county were at Fovant and Alderbury. The site of the Alderbury burial ground, which is marked on an early nineteenth century map, can be located today. Halfway up the old road from the Three Crowns is a field gate from where a raised causeway can be seen crossing the field to another gate leading on to the bypass. On the other side of the bypass is another gate with a field track running alongside a hedge (this track is shown as Quakers' Drove on the map referred to above). The Quaker burial ground is shown on the tithe map of 1848 as being at the far end of this track, on the left-hand side. The field was called 'Quakers' Ten Acres'.

By 1690 Alderbury's Quakers were recorded as meeting in the house of Giles Spicer and in that same year Thomas Elcock 'of Waddin near Sarum' was buried. Like Richard Hilliard, Thomas had appeared at the Quarter Sessions in 1683 and 1684, presented by the parish constable for not attending church.

An indication of the relative wealth of a number of the Alderbury Quakers may possibly be determined from the fines imposed on them in 1686 for being at a meeting in Alderbury. Richard Hilliard was fined £20, a considerable sum at that time; also fined were George Harris £20, Robert Hilliard £10, John Milliege £10, Giles Spicer £10, Robert Shergold £9. 15s. 0d., Thomas Elcock £5. 5s. 0d., Roger Wheeler £1. 5s. 0d., Philip Pine 5s. 0d. and Rowland Williams 5s. 0d. It is known that Rowland Williams' occupation was a weaver and Thomas Elcock had been described as a yeoman but the occupations of the others were not stated.

From the end of the century the history of Quakers in Wiltshire was one of gradual decline; quite when the Alderbury society failed is not known but by 1717 the Salisbury society was the only one remaining in south Wiltshire.

Primitive and Wesleyan Methodists

Alderbury had a very early connection with the Wesley family through a pupil of John Wesley (Westley Hall), who married Wesley's sister Martha. In 1736 Hall came to Fisherton Anger as a curate and began freelance preaching in the district establishing a meeting in the coach house at the Green Dragon at Alderbury.

In 1746 Hall broke with the Wesleys and the cause of Methodism in the Salisbury area suffered a very great set-back. John Wesley visited Salisbury a number of times in the following years and he wrote 'I met a little company, gathered up out of the wreck... and exhorted them to go on in the Bible way...' At that time the group was meeting at Quidhampton but by 1750 it had recovered sufficiently for the first chapel to be opened in Salisbury.

Alderbury's Methodists must have travelled to Salisbury to worship until 1802 when 'the dwelling house of John Cook, Methodist' was registered as a Dissenters' Meeting House. By 1824 there were fourteen members at Alderbury. Henry Cook was their leader with Joseph and Martha Pearce, Daniel Bell, Joseph and Elizabeth Rowden, John and Ann Fry, Thomas and Sarah Haines, and Mary White.

From 1829 onwards the circuit records begin to show a number of the brethren from Alderbury being accepted as local preachers around the circuit, among them Mark Phillips, Job Sutton, Henry Dowty and Thomas Fry. The last named had a brief trial in 1844 but the report on his preaching was not favourable and he himself decided 'that he was not called to the work'. Henry Dowty subsequently emigrated to Willunga in South Australia where he became a Wesleyan Methodist preacher.

The Alderbury chapel, built in 1825, had seating for 150 people and from the 1851 religious census it is apparent that numbers had grown to the point where the attendance was 146 at the afternoon service and 162 at the evening service (this out of a population of 742 for the whole of Alderbury and Whaddon). The chapel, shown below, stood on land known as Chapel Row on the south side of the Southampton Road end of Folly Lane. There were several small cottages adjacent. In the 1970s the chapel and cottages were pulled down and the present small housing estate of Old Chapel Close was built on the site.

Meanwhile, at Whaddon, a Methodist Dissenters' Meeting House had been registered with the Justices in 1807 with the names of Jonathan Southwell, John Smith, Susannah Hayter and Rebecca Williams mentioned.

In the Methodist Church at large, the Primitive Methodists had broken away from mainstream Methodism in 1813 and they laid great emphasis on open-air preaching and praying. Quite when the Whaddon Methodists joined the Primitive Methodist Church is not known at present but by 1847 they were meeting together in a house in Whaddon, holding both morning and evening services. The house was probably that of Mr J Marshall, who was at that time a preacher in the Salisbury Circuit.

Figure 7.1

The Wesleyan

Methodist

Chapel,

Folly Lane

On the death of his father in 1852, George Dowty (1818-1910) moved back from Downton to Rose Cottage (now Jasmine Cottage) on the Green in Alderbury where he had been born. He opened his house for the purpose of holding religious meetings; he had been a Primitive Methodist preacher since 1843. He was eventually to become the Whaddon society's first Steward when they opened their chapel in 1884.

Methodism flourished in both Alderbury and Whaddon and it is interesting that the Anglican vicar, the Rev. RS Hutchings wrote in 1909, in answer to the Diocesan Visitation Enquiries, that out of a total population of 650 the probable number of dissenters was about 300. He described them as Wesleyan and Congregational and said their numbers were stationary. The Rev. Thomas H Simms, writing in 1915, did get the names right as Wesleyan and Primitive Methodists. However, he stated that their probable number was about 150 and that membership was stationary. In view of the national figures it is probable that this was wishful thinking on his part and the Rev. Hutchings' figures were a better estimate.

Certainly in 1912 a new Sunday schoolroom had been added to the Wesleyan Chapel in Alderbury with the usual foundation stones laid by prominent people and, with a nice touch, one course of white bricks being laid by 60 local children. About 100 people then sat down to tea in a large marquee. At a meeting in the evening Gypsy Smith, the famous evangelist, addressed a congregation of several hundred outside the marquee.

That schoolroom was pressed into daily service during the early part of World War II when some evacuees arrived, although this continued for only five months. It was also used at that time by the Coal Club, the Smallholdings Association, the British Legion, the Women's Institute and Wiltshire County Council's medical and dental clinics.

Nationally, the various strands of Methodism came together again in 1932 when the Wesleyan, Primitive, and United Methodist Churches combined into the one Methodist Church we know today. However, the Alderbury Church was in one of the Salisbury circuits while Whaddon Church was part of the Woodfalls Circuit. In 1949 the various circuits combined to form the present Salisbury Circuit stretching from Amesbury in the north to Fordingbridge in the south.

It is recorded that in 1949 there were only fifteen active members in the Alderbury Church. Eric Lockyer became the Steward in 1945 and combined that appointment with the posts of Secretary, Treasurer and Caretaker. In 1970 he had to resign his posts due to ill-health and as no one could be found to take over his various duties the decision was taken to close the chapel and dispose of the property.

Meanwhile the Whaddon Church had continued to flourish with members of the Dowty, Peck, Clarke and Newman families taking a prominent part in its service. When Tom Dowty senior died in 1950 he was Secretary, Choirmaster and Chapel Steward. At that time William Clarke was Treasurer and Chapel Steward with Mesdames Clarke, Russell and Crook and Mr C Newman as organists.

Figure 7.2
The Roman
Catholic Chapel
of the Holy
Family,
formerly the
Primitive
Methodist
Chapel,
Whaddon

By 1985 Ecumenicism had grown to such an extent that a Covenant of Partnership was signed by Methodists and Anglicans in the village and on those months where there was a fifth Sunday, they held a joint service.

This must have helped when, due to a declining membership and a number of key members having left the village, the Whaddon Church found itself unable to continue. Details are not known as the last minute book of the Whaddon Church Council cannot be found. What is known is that the building was sold to the Roman Catholics. From the account book of that period we know that half of the available funds went to the West Grimstead Methodist Church and half to purchase books for the Alderbury and West Grimstead Church of England Primary School.

Roman Catholicism in Alderbury and Whaddon

There is a recorded case in the seventeenth century of a prosecution of a Catholic called 'Greene of Alderbury and Brigmerston' for not attending church. Apart from this, history tells us nothing about any Catholics living in Alderbury and Whaddon but they would undoubtedly have attended mass in Salisbury.

The first recorded mass in Alderbury was said in 1955 at the home of the Thesiger family at Hillside in Clarendon Road. In 1956 Cedric Thesiger bought second-hand a large wooden hut, presumably army surplus, and arranged for it to be erected on land adjoining Hillside which is now occupied by five new houses on the corner of Clarendon Road and Southampton Road. There were problems from the outset: it soon emerged that he had bought not one hut but, from the varying colours on the sections and the twelve different holes in the roof for chimney stacks, a collection of sections from several huts. All the metal brackets and floor bearers had gone and most of the main posts were rotten at the feet and had to have new feet scarfed on to them. The new chapel was eventually completed in 1958.

By 1987, when the building was being prepared for painting, warnings were received not to attempt to change the window frames lest the walls fall down! Fortunately, at that time the possibility emerged of selling the site for housing and purchasing the Whaddon Methodist Chapel. While that building was being refurbished the Catholic congregation was invited to share the Anglican church and hold an early Sunday morning mass. The refurbished chapel was occupied in 1990 and sharing continues as the Anglicans still hold a Sunday School in a room at the Whaddon chapel.

Figure 7.3

Former Catholic

Chapel

at Clarendon

crossroads

8

THE INFLUENCE OF
MAJOR HISTORICAL EVENTS

Plague and Pestilence

Through the ages, history rarely remembers the details of minor trials and tribulations relating to the public health, no matter how significant they may have been to the rural population concerned. Rather, it is to the major epidemics that historians must turn in order to develop a picture of bygone ailments. True, much has changed in the last 50 years, due primarily to the introduction of antibiotic treatments for diseases which would otherwise have high mortality rates. However, other factors such as the introduction of hospitals and sanatoria in the eighteenth century and vast improvements in sanitation during the latter half of the Victorian age have made major contributions.

For an impression of the local effects of these great events in history, we must turn to the records for Salisbury, which include specific mention of Alderbury, adding detail to our chronicle of village life.

The earliest epidemics recorded in the local history of Alderbury relate to the plague. That this is so is due mainly to the presence of Ivychurch Priory. The earliest record of its effect on Alderbury is to be found in the Calendar of Patent Rolls, which tells us that in 1341, the community at Ivychurch was severely affected by the Black Death. Only one out of fourteen clergy survived; the prior and twelve canons succumbed. The survivor, James de Groundwell, informed Edward III and in the absence of anyone to contest an election, the King made de Groundwell the prior of Ivychurch. It is probable that many others who would have worked at the priory also perished but history does not record their passing.

Smallpox, known colloquially as 'the pox', was endemic in England in times gone by. This acute, highly contagious viral disease caused severe aches, fever and vomiting and often left pitted scars or pock marks on the skin of its victims. It was a major killer until the development of a vaccine by Edward Jenner (1749-1823). His discovery, in 1796, that inoculation with cowpox gave immunity to smallpox was a great medical breakthrough. Salisbury endured several major outbreaks of smallpox, some severe, before effective vaccination was available, suffering terribly in 1723, when 1,244 persons contracted smallpox and 165 died. Further serious outbreaks occurred in 1752 and 1766. Jenner's method of vaccination was to arrive shortly after 1796, with vaccination becoming compulsory in 1853. Wiltshire was divided into 63 vaccination districts, managed through seventeen Unions. One of these was the Alderbury Union, which is described in more detail in Chapter 12.

Royalist or Roundhead?

Did our forebears in Alderbury favour King or Parliament? It is probable that like most of southern Wiltshire they had Royalist leanings. However, a number would have been conscripted and most would have become weary of the depredations of both sides and eventually joined the 'Clubmen' movement.

No towns in south Wiltshire were fortified. Both armies passed through it at various times. Both sides claimed the right to exact taxes and both armies lived off the land, demanding to be fed. South Wiltshire was relatively unscathed as no major battles were fought, with only skirmishes at Salisbury. Both Wardour and Longford Castles had Royalist garrisons, the former being famous for Lady Arundell's defence, holding out for five days in 1643 with only 25 retainers against a Parliamentary force of nearly 1,300.

Longford Castle was garrisoned by the Royalists in October 1644, with Sir Bartholomew Pell in command. In the spring of that year the King had issued a Commission of Impressment requiring the constable of each hundred to provide a number of able-bodied men to fight in the Royalist armies. However, Colonel Pell is recorded as complaining that the catchment area allocated to him for impressment was so small *'that I am not able to get near the number of men assigned to me'*. Undoubtedly men from Alderbury and Whaddon were conscripted.

Figure 8.1

Longford

Castle

under siege

In the spring of 1645 the countrymen decided that they could stand no more and 'peace-keeping associations' of Clubmen bent on protecting their homes and communities from destruction emerged spontaneously, particularly in the western counties, calling on both sides to settle their dispute in more peaceful ways. In the weeks following their inception the Clubmen grew bolder and more insistent, clashing indiscriminately with Royalist and Parliamentary patrols. On 13 June 1645 the leaders of the Clubmen met the commanders of both the Royalist garrison at Longford and the newly established Parliamentary garrison at Faulston House near Bishopstone in the Chalke valley. Their purpose was to arrange a treaty between the two sides until the result was known of a petition the previous month from the Wiltshire Clubmen to Parliament. To ensure the two garrisons' compliance the Clubmen offered to pay both sides £50 weekly while the arrangement held.

Early in August Cromwell bloodily dispersed the Wiltshire and Dorset Clubmen at Hambledon Hill near Blandford and in October decided that Longford Castle should be taken. Lord Coleraine the owner of the castle, although a close friend of the King and a generous contributor to the Royalist coffers, had moved into his steward's house in Britford with his large family, leaving Colonel Pell to adapt the castle to the needs of defence. Rose trees and ancient vines at the bases of the three drum towers were savagely pulled up and the gardens devastated to make room for outworks and earthen banks. Trees in the park were felled. Cromwell's forces arrived on 16 October 1645 and took up position near what is now Home Farm, using the high ground. Cromwell soon sited a battery on Picked Mead, the field between Home Farm and the river, and sent the usual demand for surrender.

On 18 October, castle and garrison were surrendered with hardly a shot fired in anger. One shot, however, had barely missed Cromwell. Fired from a window in the castle it killed an officer at his side. The two men had been deciding how best to storm the castle. Colonel Ludlow took up occupation of the castle with the prime purpose of protecting the Parliamentary Commissioners who sat in almost daily session at nearby Faulston House deciding the fines to be imposed on the Wiltshire Royalists for their part in the Civil War. Robert Long of Whaddon was one of those fined. As for Longford Castle the building was not deliberately damaged but the inhabitants of Alderbury Hundred were required to level the earthworks and other defences around the castle.

The Swing Riots

In the 1820s Wiltshire's labourers were worse off than those of any other county, a whole family having to subsist on 7s. 0d. a week. When William Cobbett in his travels across England came to Wiltshire in 1826 he made his way down the Avon Valley and he wrote:

'In taking my leave of this beautiful vale I have to express my deep shame as an

Englishman, at beholding the extreme general poverty of those who cause this Vale to produce such quantities of food and raiment. This is, I verily believe it, the worst used labouring people upon the face of the earth. Dogs and hogs and horses are treated with more civility; and as to food and lodging, how gladly would the labourers change with them!'

Four years later the labourers of sixteen counties across southern England took part in a series of uprisings in protest over the low wages, poor living conditions and the introduction of threshing machines. The troubles started in Kent in August 1830 and spread north and west and by December most counties south of a line from Norfolk to Worcestershire had been involved. The disturbances varied from place to place. In many places threatening letters were sent, many signed by the mythical 'Captain Swing', stacks and barns were set on fire and mobs of rioters made demands for higher wages. Machinery of all sorts was destroyed, with threshing machines being a particular target, since these were seen by the farm labourers as taking away their winter employment. There had been riots among agricultural workers before but none on so large a scale. Although there were rumours that foreigners were involved, inciting the labourers to an English Revolution, similar to those in Europe, in fact the whole thing was on a local level with leaders, or 'Captains', being chosen from the community. Bands of men from one village travelled around the villages in their area gathering men, destroying machines and sometimes demanding money from farmers. News of what was happening passed rapidly from village to village and the idea spread.

By November 1830 the troubles had reached the Salisbury area. On market day, Tuesday 23 November, a large mob of rioters was coming along the London Road, having previously attacked farms at Newton Toney and Idmiston. The magistrates in Salisbury called out the Wiltshire Yeomanry and at Bishopdown fifty mounted troopers dispersed a mob of over four hundred with only trivial injuries and without drawing their swords. Good leadership avoided the wholly unnecessary bloodshed which was to occur just two days later at Tisbury. Twenty two prisoners were taken. The next day news reached Salisbury that a mob was gathering at Alderbury having made its way from Whiteparish by way of West Grimstead. Mr Fort, of Alderbury House, and Lord Radnor, the two principal local landowners, went out to meet the mob, hoping to persuade them to disperse peaceably. They also sent a request for the Yeomanry who, when they arrived, found a large mob gathered in the village. They had been destroying machines in the area and had stopped at Alderbury to collect their forces before marching on Salisbury, hoping to join up with the other group from the north. They had been to the house of Henry Rumbold, a farmer at Alderbury, and demanded money, being given four half crowns. They also demanded money from Thomas Wolferston. When the Yeomanry arrived, the leaders of the mob were in the Green Dragon Inn trying to decide what to do, having heard of the defeat at Bishopdown the previous day. The Yeomanry quietly surrounded the Inn and took twelve prisoners, allowing the rest to disperse to their homes, which they did without any further disturbance. The prisoners were bound, loaded into a wagon, and driven under escort to the County Gaol at Salisbury.

By this time the government, who had previously allowed rural magistrates to deal with the rioters, considered that the magistrates in Kent had dealt too leniently with the problem, allowing it to spread. A new Home Secretary, Lord Melbourne, decided to set up a Special Commission to deal with those in the worst affected counties, which included Wiltshire. By December 1830 over 1,400 men and women had been rounded up and were awaiting trial, after which 19 were hanged, over 600 sent to prison and 480 transported to Australia. A third of the convictions were from Wiltshire and Hampshire with Wiltshire having the greater number. Among those charged were: 'Abraham Jacob, (otherwise known as Abraham Lucas), charged with having feloniously endeavoured to obtain money from Thomas Wolferston at Alderbury by threats and menaces; Samuel Hatcher, William Cook, Thomas Light, and William Rogers junior, all of Alderbury, charged with riotous conduct, breaking threshing machines, and extorting money by threats and menaces, at the above place; Henry Herrington, William Luffman and Thomas Gange, charged with having riotously assembled and broken a threshing machine at West Grimstead.' Of these, only Abraham Jacobs and Samuel Hatcher were acquitted. The others were found guilty of machine breaking and were sentenced to be transported for seven years.

Many of the 480 transported to Australia were given a free pardon in 1836. The majority stayed in Australia having found living conditions far better than they had ever enjoyed in England. Thomas Light, however, who had been born in West Grimstead and worked as a labourer, had four children there and a wife, Martha, who kept the village school. He returned to England from Tasmania in 1838. In the 1841 census he is shown as living at Alderbury with his wife and one of his sons and working as an agricultural labourer. In the 1851 census for Alderbury he is described as a farmer of seven acres.

World War I

The outbreak of World War I in August 1914 began a conflict that was to bring to each side appalling injuries, great devastation and the loss of millions of lives.

A wave of patriotism and recruitment swept Britain and there was a large exodus of young men from their work to join Lord Kitchener's 'new army of volunteers'. On the home front the people of Alderbury and Whaddon, as in every part of the nation, supported the war effort as best they could. Many joined the Red Cross Voluntary Aid Detachment, volunteering to be on call day or night, meeting trainloads of wounded servicemen, driving ambulances, helping at hospitals or guarding railway bridges, gas works, water works and public buildings. Alderbury had its own Red Cross unit in the village under the direction of Ralph Macan, Lord Radnor's agent, of Alward House. Longford Castle housed a Red Cross hospital for the wounded. Women took over the jobs of those men called to war duty; there were as many as 50 'land girls' working on farms in the district. Those skilled at sewing and knitting sent off parcels of clothing and comforts to prisoners of war, refugee camps and the many theatres of war. Some Belgian refugees, it is said, were lodged in Alderbury for a while.

Contemporary editions of the Salisbury Journal reveal some interesting local information. In November 1914 it was reported that a fortunate survivor of the war at sea was the Hon. Edward Pleydell-Bouverie, the 15 year old son of the Earl and Countess of Radnor. He was a midshipman aboard the cruiser HMS Hogue, which was sunk by enemy submarines in the North Sea. He spent three-and-a-half hours in the water before being rescued and taken to Holland. An item of December 1915 tells of the parcels sent by the Alderbury Scouts to local servicemen on active service in France, Flanders, the North Sea, the Dardanelles, Serbia, and Egypt. Each parcel contained a cooker and refill, a tin of 50 cigarettes, chocolate, six khaki handkerchiefs, a pencil and Christmas cards plus a pair of mittens, the gift of Mrs Ralph Macan. On 4 August 1916 there is an account of a crowded service held at Alderbury Parish Church which was followed by an open-air public meeting at which the following resolution was passed: *'That on the second anniversary of the declaration of a righteous war, this meeting of the citizens of Alderbury records its inflexible determination to continue to a victorious end the struggle in maintenance of those ideals of liberty and justice which are the common and sacred cause of the Allies'*. Was this just a patriotic gesture – or a morale-boosting response, perhaps to some bad news of local casualties?

With naval warfare restricting imports from abroad, food shortages were widely predicted and the parish council minutes of 1917 contain a request from the War Agricultural Committee that steps be taken to increase the quantity of food grown in the area. A sub-committee of councillors inspected all the cottage gardens and allotments in the parish. Only two, one in each of Alderbury and Whaddon, were found to be unproductive.

Victory came at last in 1918, and the armistice was signed at the 11th hour of the 11th day in the 11th month, the moment subsequently marked each year on Remembrance Day by a nation-wide silence. In Alderbury and Whaddon, 126 men served their country in World War I. Of those, 26 did not survive. Many of those returning were terribly mutilated in mind and body and many more were unable to find any peacetime employment. To help these struggling comrades and their families, voluntary support groups were formed leading, in 1920, to the formation of the British Legion. The Alderbury branch was started the following year. Money is raised by an annual 'Poppy Appeal' as each Remembrance Day approaches: the survival of the poppy, despite the complete devastation on the battlefields of Flanders and Picardy, being taken as a symbol of hope, reassurance and remembrance.

work, on evenings and at week-ends. Attendance became difficult during hay-making and harvest time, as local people helped out on the farms in Alderbury and the surrounding areas.

By July, the LDV had been renamed 'The Home Guard'. Now considered a valuable home defence force, its members were issued with uniforms and equipment. Alderbury and Whaddon had a fine Home Guard unit, the Alderbury Company 7th Wilts. Battalion. An early commanding officer was Major General Sir Henry Everett KCMG, CB of Alderbury, who retired in 1942. At this time, well before the construction of the modern bypass, the road through Alderbury and Whaddon was the main route to Southampton and Portsmouth. This, together with as many as eight railway bridges and the railway line itself, had to be protected. Defences included tank traps, laid to one side of bridges, to stop enemy tanks crossing. These comprised concrete blocks with a hole in the centre, sunk across the road at intervals. Stakes could be put into the holes to impede access. Large concrete blocks to each side of the road gave some protection for local defences. There was also a deep ditch alongside the railway line.

ARP badge

Exercises for the new force took place in any available space, including the field behind the Post Office in Old Road. Also used were the one-time gravel pit, the timber yard (now 'Silver Wood'), Ashley Hill, and land near Petersfinger. It is reputed that training also took place with a group of commandos, in which the Home Guard had to prevent capture of the railway bridge at Whaddon. This exercise took place on a dark night, when the resourcefulness of the Home Guards proved very effective. Heavy material was collected, sewn together to make a curtain and slung across the road underneath the bridge. The 'enemy' was driven back by the Home Guard manning old flame throwers filled with water. 'Enemy' uniforms were covered in rust from the water. On some nights, women volunteers provided refreshments at Mr Tozer's Farm Cottage (at Matrons College Farm) used as a Home Guard depot. General Montgomery, who frequently visited the area, believed strongly in the Home Guard. Treating them as front line troops, he ensured they trained to adapt to any form of fighting.

As the air war intensified, home defences became increasingly important. It was necessary to be vigilant at all times, noting and reporting any parachutists from planes which had been shot down, whether British or German. The Air Raid Precautions (ARP) Wardens were also tasked with such reporting. No street lights were permitted, nor were road signs. No lights were to be showing from windows or open doors. Vehicles and bicycles were only allowed very dim lights, and none during air raids. One got used to being guided along the roads by looking at the silhouettes of houses and trees, against the night sky.

During 1941-42, the numbers of the Home Guard varied; young men were conscripted into the forces and others had to retire at the age of 65. In 1942, compulsory enrolment to the Home Guard was introduced in some areas. This required men to attend drills and musters in order to maintain the Unit's efficiency. Generally, there were 48 hours of training per month and non-attendance could lead to prosecution in a civil court.

There is a story amongst local folk which tells that sometime during the war, the Home Guard captured a German parachutist at Ashley Hill. The crashed plane, a Junkers JU-88, was not found. The airman is believed to have visited since the war, but it is said that there was no record of the missing plane. In December 1944, the Government decided that there was no longer a threat of a German invasion and the Home Guard was disbanded, but they were allowed to keep their boots and uniform – just in case!

The Unfortunate Accident and The Home Guard Hero

Figure 8.2

William Foster

GC MC DCM

William Foster was born at sea on 12 December 1880. As soon as he was old enough, he joined the Royal Fusiliers, serving in the Boer War before transferring to the 2nd Imperial Light Horse. After being engaged in several actions he was badly wounded and sent home, eventually being discharged as medically unfit in October 1902. He eventually rejoined his old regiment, the Royal Fusiliers. When the First World War broke out he was serving as a Company Sergeant Major with the 4th Battalion. He saw service at Mons and later in the Ypres Salient, where he was again wounded. In January 1915 he was mentioned in despatches and in June, by then a Warrant Officer, Foster was awarded the Distinguished Conduct Medal. At the School of Musketry, Hythe, he served as an instructor, proving to be a magnificent shot. He was later commissioned and served with the 3rd Battalion, winning the Military Cross in September 1916. Foster then transferred to the Army Service Corps. In 1918, he served with a British Military Mission, remaining with them for some time after the war. Now a Captain, Foster returned to London on leaving the army and moved to Wiltshire, where he lived near Alderbury.

By the time World War II broke out Foster, now aged 61 years, was a veteran soldier. He became a Lieutenant in the Alderbury Home Guard soon after its formation. Whilst instructing a group of recruits on the techniques of grenade throwing from a slit trench on Ashley Hill, Clarendon, one man threw a live grenade which failed to go over the parapet. It stayed briefly on the top, then to everyone's horror, rolled back and lay at the men's feet. Swift action by Foster, who threw himself on the grenade, saved the men, but sadly he was killed when it exploded. For his brave and selfless action, he was posthumously awarded the George Cross, announced in the London Gazette on 27 November 1942. The decoration was presented to his widow at Buckingham Palace, by King George VI.

At a subsequent memorial service in St Mary's Church, Alderbury in January 1947, a mural tablet was unveiled and dedicated to Foster's memory by Lt Gen. John Crocker, General Officer Commanding in Chief, Southern Command. The stone tablet is surmounted by a replica in silver of a George Cross surrounded by a laurel wreath. Underneath in gold lettering is the following inscription:

72

In memory of
Lieut. William Foster G.C.
Home Guard who at Ashley Hill
on the 13th September 1942 threw himself
on a live bomb whereby he lost
his own life but saved about 30
men who were standing nearby
from death or serious injury

Greater Love hath no man than this that a man
lay down his own life for his friends S. John xv:13

The George Cross

The tablet was provided by the Alderbury Company of the Home Guard, and other friends. Prayers dedicating the tablet were said by the Rev. B Aston DSO. Among the congregation were family members, the Home Guard, and Maj. Gen. Sir Henry Everett. Foster's grave is in Alderbury churchyard.

A Welcome Home Party, 1947

At the end of the war in 1945, a Welcome Home Fund was formed for the ex-service men and women of Alderbury, Whaddon and Clarendon. The Fund was run by the parish council, assisted by Sir Henry Everett (Hon. Treasurer), Colonel D Haskard, the Rev. B Aston, Mrs Stevens, Mr F Whitcher and Mr Musselwhite. At a meeting on 9 May 1947, there were 133 illuminated addresses framed, and enough money had been collected for each person to be given £2.

These gifts were presented to all those present at the Welcome Home Party held on 19 May 1947. After a short speech by the Chairman of the Committee, Mr AV Eyres, in which he referred to the 14 servicemen who gave their lives in the war, a one-minute silence was observed. Major General Sir Henry Everett then said a few words of welcome, after which a supper and drinks were served. Entertainment was provided by Mr Douglas Horner, with his clever conjuring, and 'The Dialogue of the Wiltshire Lad'. The Entertainment Sub-committee, which had raised most of the funds, comprised Mr and Mrs Busby, Mrs W Newell, Mrs Simpson and Mr Unwin. The Hon. Secretary was Mr FR Simpson.

The party was held in the hut of the HQ Army Cadet Force (Alderbury), which was situated in the sand pit by St Mary's Hall Whaddon. The hut was said to have been the old NAAFI hut, transferred from the field (now tennis courts) off Old Road. A photograph of the party showing about 54 ex-service men and women, was published in the Salisbury and Winchester Journal on 23 May 1947. A number of these people have recently been identified and in some cases they, (or their families), are still living in the area.

The servicemen who lost their lives during both world wars are remembered by their engraved names on the War Memorial situated on the village green by Old Road. There is also a list of names, with service rank, above the small organ in the south transept in St Mary's Church.

In addition, the name of G Turner appears on the War Memorial (but not on the roll in the church) and Lt W Foster of the Home Guard is recorded on a separate plaque, as described above.

1939 IN HONOUR AND REMEMBRANCE 1945

FW Carter, Lce-Sergt. Royal Engineers	AWT Hatcher, Pte. 2nd Queens Royal Regt.	JW Snook, Pilot Officer Royal Air Force
MV Christie Miller, Lieut. Coldstream Guards	JWC Kidd, Sergt. Pilot Royal Air Force	N Wathen, Sergt. Royal Corps of Signals
EG Grout, Pte. Royal Army Service Corps	RC McLeud, Lieut. Scots Guards	WC Witt, Guardsman Coldstream Guards
S Gumbleton, Sub. Lieut. Royal Navy	S Mitchell, Pte. Infantry	J Woodrow, Pte. Suffolk Reg

Wartime Memories

Many Alderbury residents can recall the years of the last war. Some of their recollections are retold here, painting a tableau of what life in the village was like during those times of conflict. The following recollection is told by Vera James.

'At the outbreak of World War II, my Dad, George James, was tenant farmer at Belmont Farm, Southampton Road, Clarendon. Myself and two brothers and a sister had been born in the farm house. The first three years of the war were spent at Belmont, after which we moved up to the Alderbury village, Dad taking over Hole Farm from my grandfather.

Alderbury, at that time, seemed to be full of army personnel and also evacuees, children from Portsmouth. Anyone who had any space at all in their homes had army personnel or evacuees compulsorily billeted with them. At Belmont, we had three men from the 5th Tank Corps living in our quite small front room. There was an army camp of Nissen huts set up in the woods between Alward House and Old Shute Road, on the Lower Alderbury Road. Alward House was requisitioned by the forces.

Saturday night dances, whist drives and other social events were held in the WI hut

74

along the old back road in Alderbury. There was a tank trap erected in the area behind the then Post Office and members of the Home Guard held their practice sessions there.

At Belmont, I remember watching very frequent convoys of troops, tanks and armoured vehicles travelling along what was then the main road to Southampton, on their way to cross the Channel. Night after night, waves of German planes flew over en route to blitz one or another big town. At the age of ten years, I remember being afraid of that continuous drone and of spending many evenings on a mattress under the table in the living room, which was considered to be a safe place! The Anderson shelter in the garden at Belmont was used whenever the sirens sounded. An ominous orange glow could be seen from Alderbury, filling the sky on the nights of the Southampton blitz.

I believe there were some bombs dropped on Alderbury, one of which fell in the wood below Ivychurch, besides Hole Farm. Safety at Hole Farm meant "down to the cellar"from a stairway leading from the kitchen, and blackout in the front and middle rooms was effected by drawing up the original built-in wooden shutters from the window sills. Living on a farm must have been a tremendous help when it came to eking out the food rations for a family of six. We had milk, eggs, vegetables and fruit from the garden. Our Jersey cow, from amongst a mixed herd, provided milk from which Mum made butter; eggs were preserved in water glass preservative fluid; delicious rabbit pies and stews and a chicken every now and then supplemented the meat ration. Every farmer was allowed to kill one pig a year for their own family's consumption. The local butcher from Whaddon, Mr Newell, came to slaughter the pig at Hole Farm. It was the usual custom for farmers to share a pig between them, twice a year. I remember salted joints hanging from hooks in the cellar – not much of the animal went to waste.

It was a national requirement during the war for potatoes to be grown on a proportion of the farm land. Groups of senior children were bussed out to the farms to help with the potato picking.

There was no real supplement for clothes rationing; Mum used to knit balaclava hoods for us as well as for the troops. Disused parachutes, made from tough silk material, could be bought without ration coupons and these were made into slips and night-dresses, etc. At the end of my school life, my navy blue gymslip was cut down and became a skirt for the office! Clothes were darned and mended for continuous use.

As children, we loved to watch Mr Riches at work in his smithy, at the junction of Old Road and the road leading to the Green Dragon, shoeing horses and twisting great pieces of iron in the roaring fire. The Post Office was at the side of the cottage in Old Road [now known as Ye Old Post Office Cottage], and the village shop was at the end of the row of houses in High Street, approachable directly by steps [now overgrown] from the main road. There was a big walnut tree on the Green and nuts from it were a special treat after a windy night.

Several of the fields at Hole Farm were full of cowslips in late spring and mushrooms in autumn. Wild daffodils filled the woods below Ivychurch. A large thatched tithe barn stood in the field on the left, on the road going down to Hole Farm, and a granary stood on staddle stones at the entrance to the farm buildings. A natural spring from the side of the roadway fed a pond in the field in front of the house. A landmark of the farm, which could be seen from miles around, was the seven or eight trees which stood on the high hump, in the field by the main road to Alderbury. I believe several of the trees were at one time struck by lightning and I remember the group with dead trees still standing, with just three or four live trees amongst them.'

War memorial

on The Green

9
THE GROWTH OF THE VILLAGES

Settlements

The Saxons appear to be the earliest people to settle at Alderbury, and evidence suggests that there may have been two separate sites. In 972 the settlement was referred to as Aethelwarbyrig – a place-name meaning 'the fortified place of Aethelware'. This almost certainly would have been a hill-top site, and although its whereabouts is not known it may have been where a number of earthworks have been found at the northern end of the village, as described in Chapter 2. This hilltop site may have been settled several centuries previously.

In 1086, at the time of the Domesday survey, at Alwarberie, as it was then known, there was a Saxon church and some form of village existed. The site would have been pleasant and sunny, above the frequently flooding river, but close to the common meadows where cattle needed daily attention. There was a water supply in the nearby hollow and a withybed for thatch. The road, from Sarum to Downton and the port at Christchurch, passed by at the foot of the slope: a relatively busy route offering some social contact and trade. But despite these advantages the village did not continue to develop in this part of the parish.

It is possible that the church, at the centre of religious life of the very wide area of Alderbury Hundred, actually had very little local significance and the usual pattern of a village centred on a parish church and served by one priest was slow to develop here. Perhaps the position of Alderbury Common and Treasury Common restricted building, although a few dwellings are identified on eighteenth century maps uphill from the church and along the lower side of Folly Lane.

For whatever reasons, the main focus shifted to the hilltop, around the crossroads joining Silver Street, Folly Lane and Clarendon Road to the road from Salisbury to Southampton. By the Middle Ages Southampton had become a very important wool exporting port, and as Salisbury was a wool collecting centre, this road would have been very busy. Here on the hilltop were the inn and the smithy.

From the crossroads, cottages ranged down from the upper end of Silver Street, a short walk to the Longford Estate where many of the villagers worked. By the nineteenth century this hilltop site was quite well developed, with a shop, post office and Methodist chapel.

It is difficult to see any past focus of settlement in Whaddon. Through the centuries it was always a sparsely populated area. In 1428, a Poll Tax review of 'poor parishes', that is those with fewer than ten households –

specifically mentions Whaddon in Alderbury. To the end of the nineteenth century maps show Whaddon as an area of a few dispersed farms and cottages. The site of Whaddon church is not accurately known, but it may at one time have caused more clustering of cottages around Castle Lane and Bungay Lane. The Southampton Road seems to have had little influence, apart from a smithy located on the corner where the southern end of Castle Lane meets the road.

The censuses from 1851-91 do not help in detailing growth of the settlements as the enumerator, Edwin Prewett, was very reticent in identifying actual names of lanes and cottages, recording 'near the chapel', or 'near Lights Lane'. He seems to have had particular problems with Whaddon, where he notes 'places called by some Frogham, Whaddon Lane and Spider's Island'. This uncertainty no doubt accounts for the variation in the number of households recorded in subsequent censuses, as illustrated below.

	1871	1881	1891
No. of households in Whaddon Lane	13	3	9
No. of households in Spider's Island	3	15	1 3

Many more households than buildings were recorded in Whaddon than any maps of the time show. Allowing for more than one family under one roof, there are still curious discrepancies. For instance, in 1851, a total of 13 households was registered as being in Frogham; in 1891 there were still three in Frogham and two were now recorded as being at Frog's Bottom. No map, whether contemporary or present day, has been seen to give any indication of the whereabouts of Frogham or, for that matter, Whaddon Lane.

Some changes were slowly taking place at the beginning of this century. Alderbury Common was now in the ownership of the Earl of Radnor, and some parcels of land along the Clarendon Road had already been sold as smallholdings. The record of the sale of 11 plots shown on p81 is taken from a document dated 1907.

The coming of the railway in 1847 had little immediate impact on both settlements, as neither Alderbury Junction nor Whaddon boasted a station. Had one been built at Whaddon, sand and brick clay may have been exploited on a commercial scale. As it happened, the only change was a new lane, Junction Road, leading from Southampton Road to Alderbury Junction, where a few buildings appeared and that would seem to be all.

Alderbury and Whaddon remained physically separate until the changes that came after World War I. Then, in a short period before World War II, 99 private dwellings were built. Infilling and linear developments of bungalows and chalet bungalows along the main road began to link the two villages, and to change the face of Whaddon for all time. A council development at Spider's Island initially added 43 houses.

Two Centuries of Settlement Growth

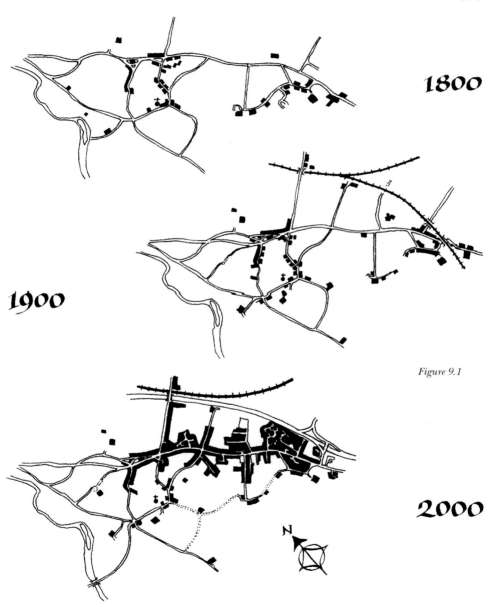

1800

1900

2000

Figure 9.1

The Conservation Area in Alderbury

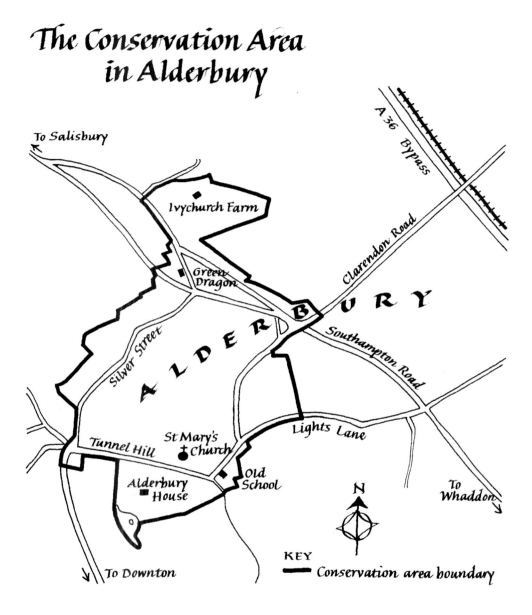

Figure 9.2

**Conveyance of Smallholdings at Alderbury [total of 14 acres]:
vendor – the Right Honourable Jacob Earl of Radnor**

Charles Tucker	James Dean	Edward Thorne
Platelayer	Carpenter	Brickmaker
No. 11 of 14	No. 8 of 14	No. 5 of 14
£20. 12s. 6d	£25. 0s. 0d	£27. 0s. 0d
Thomas Northeast	George Dean	Edward Glass
Postmaster	Carpenter	Publican
No. 4 of 14	No. 9 of 14	Nos 1, 2, & 3 of 14
£27. 10s. 0d	£25. 0s. 0d	£82. 0s. 0d
Owen Noyce	Mark Nowell	*Witnessed by*
Gardener	Chimney Sweep	*Thomas Dowty*
No. 10 of 14	Nos 6 & 7 of 14	*Builder of Whaddon,*
£25. 0s. 0d	£25. 0s. 0d	*Alderbury.*

The piecemeal development of Alderbury and Whaddon over some fifty years left many sites suitable for infilling, and paved the way for Wiltshire County Council to state, in 1961, that the villages were 'suitable for expansion without adversely affecting the character of the area of the settlement itself'. The Development Plan for Alderbury and Whaddon (1961) gave approval for building on 11 such infilling sites, providing 70 houses. A further 12 sites were recommended, with 320 dwellings. The subsequent residential building completed the physical link between the two villages.

By the time of the Structure Plan of 1991, all the above potential infilling and off-road sites had been developed, and in the past ten years further residential sites have continued to take land, leaving only one broad area of 'acceptable' potential development – that between existing built-up areas and the by-pass. So far, efforts to develop this have been resisted, as the number of houses it could contain would of necessity lead to other facilities being required which would no doubt adversely affect the character of Alderbury and Whaddon as they are today.

The completion of the by-pass in 1978 made the villages more desirable places in which to live. The style of modern housing layout, with one access road leading to cul-de-sacs, together with the many existing trees, effectively hides the extent of most of the new housing from the main road, so that the overall impression to the passer-by is of a long, pleasantly wooded and well tended village. The older part of the village has been protected by its status as a conservation area, shown in Figure 9.2. And so it keeps its secret – the hidden origins of Silver Street, Old Road, Folly Lane – and the church.

Peopling the Past

Population details for a parish, even one as significant as Alderbury, are particularly difficult to obtain for mediaeval times.

Conveyance records are one of the primary sources of information for this period and Alderbury is mentioned in both the thirteenth and fourteenth century records of Feet of Fines. But these references are very brief and only refer to 'four acres of meadow' (1281) and 'one messuage and one virgate of land' (1325) as attracting the attentions of the taxman at the time of Edward I and Edward II.

Poll tax records are generally a more useful source from which to gauge population size and the 1377 Poll Tax lists Alderbury as having 95 tax payers and Whaddon, in the parish of Alderbury, as 16. A century later, in 1428, following a review of 'poor parishes', Whaddon would not have been liable for tax at all, by then having fewer than ten households.

Passing references to the people of Alderbury are found in such official documents as the minutes of Quarter Sessions. These provide such snippets as '1586 Epiphany Richard Tutt of Alderbury, yeoman, pleads not guilty to an indictment for the repair of the Queen's highway' but they do little to give a picture of the people of Alderbury at that time.

Sources of population information often improve in the sixteenth century after Thomas Cromwell's decree, in 1563, that all parish churches should register every marriage, baptism, and burial performed – the beginnings of civil registration of marriages, births and deaths as we know it today. Unfortunately Alderbury's parish registers have not survived for the late sixteenth century, so we have records only from the early seventeenth century onwards, and these are not consecutive or complete. The numbers of baptisms, marriages and burials recorded in the first year of certain decades taken at random are shown below.

Baptisms	Marriages	Burials
1611 - 3	1611 - 3	1611 - 12
1641 - 7	1641 - 6	1641 - 6
1651 - No entry	1651 - No entry	1651 - No entry
1691 - 11	1691 - No entry	1691 - Not available
1711 - 10	1711 - 2	1711 - No entry
1741 - 9	1741 - 3	1741 - No entry

Remembering that the accuracy of recording cannot be taken for granted, there seem to be rather few entries, suggesting a small population base.

Wills and inventories add the greatest details to the picture of village life, not only in indicating relative wealth but in giving contents of rooms and possessions. In the sixteenth century, the wills and inventories of two blacksmiths make interesting reading.

Extracts from the will of John Denis, blacksmith, dated 1669, are given below.

'to my fonne John the fume of ten pounds to be paid when hee fhall be one and twenty years of Age

...to my fonne John the best of my Silver Spoons to be delivered at one and twenty years of Age

to my fonne Richard the fume of Ten pounds to be paid when hee fhall be one and twenty years of Age

to my fonne Richard the other of my Silver Spoons

to my brother Charles my little Boars ...'

All the rest of his *'goods movable and nonmovable'* he leaves to his wife Mary. The inventory includes, room by room, the following:

	£.	s.	d.
Dwelling houfe and shoppe	12.	0s.	0d.
in the hall...pewter	3.	5s.	0d.
one iron pott and other iron goods	1.	0s.	0d.
in the chamber ...two Bedds and all the other goods	7.	4s.	0d.
two silver spoons	0.	10s.	0d.
in the buttery ... Cheefes and Barrels	3.	13s.	0d
in the shopp... workinge twols and all other goods	19.	16s.	9d
one grindinge Stone and trough	1.	0s.	0d.
one hogg	1.	0s.	0d.
wood	0.	18s.	0d.

His total estate was worth £52.16s.9d., in contrast to that of another contemporary blacksmith, John Harris, whose estate was valued at over £94, excluding his house and shop. Thus the following inventory gives a picture of the interior fittings of a rather more affluent household.

Extracts from the inventory of John Harris, blacksmith (1696), reveal the following:

	£.	s.	d.
all his warring Aparrell	2.	0s.	0d.
all his brass and putter	4.	0s.	0d
in the hall...1 table, 4 stools, 1 settell, 5 chares and 1 Baron Raike	1.	0s.	0d.
...hand jion .tonngs and spitte	0.	10s.	0d.
in the buttery...the Barrells and tubbs	0.	15s.	0d.
in the new chamber ...2 beedsteds, 2 cord mats, 2 coffers and chest	0.	17s.	0d.
... 2 pillows and Bolster and other Bedden	1.	10s.	0d.
in the other chamber...2 bedsteds, 1 fether beed, 2 bolsters, 4 pillows,..	4.	0s.	0d.
...2 rouggs, 1 stool, 2 blankets, curtains	1.	15s.	0d.
all the towles in the shoppe for smithering	8.	0s.	0d.
one pigg	0.	15s.	0d.
the chees in the house	0.	8s.	0d.
fome ould Lumber goods	0.	15s.	0d.

The will of Thomas Moody, (1729), a butcher, makes over fifteen separate bequests of money to members of his family together with a bequest of £2. 0s. 0d. to the poor of the parish. In total, his bequests of money total nearly £1,000, including the £26 specifically bequeathed to ensure that his wife, children and son's widow have mourning clothes for his funeral! Apart from this considerable amount of money, other items meriting a specific mention are his household linen and his leasehold and freehold land in the village. The latter includes lands at Archers Meadow, Alderbury Common Meadow and Trepders Living. He was indeed a rich man.

A further will, that of Elizabeth Nash (1738) described as a 'widow and victualler', gives insight into personality rather than relative wealth. All bequests relate to valued possessions

'...to my Son John my Wedding Ring (the Posie), our Large Bible and a Common Prayer Book, our Damask Table Cloth and Two Damask Napkins and all his Fathers Wearing Apparel...to my daughter Elizabeth three Rings, the one being plain Gold, the other two with Stones, one Large Common Prayer Book and the Smallest Bible, one Damask Table Cloth mark'd with my name and two Damask Napkins, and also all my Wearing Apparell both Linen and Woollen... that my daughter Elizabeth shall have and receive the sum of Ten Pounds over and above the one half part of moeity of my aforesaid effects when sold and turned into money... and all other moiety... to my son John'.

And so to the nineteenth century, when population figures are available for the parish of Alderbury based on the development of annual censuses taken every ten years.

Though primitive at first, the census process was gradually refined and is an invaluable source of population data. For the first time it enables comparisons to be made on a ten-yearly basis. From 1851, relationship to the head of household, exact age, employment and place of birth were entered for each individual, giving a comprehensive view of the people of the parish.

The table below gives the total population figures for Alderbury taken from the Victoria County History of the Counties of England.

Total population for Alderbury									
1801	1811	1821	1831	1841	1851	1861	1871	1881	1891
430	448	588	690	741	742	697	658	667	678

In the early part of the century, low wages and unemployment made conditions in rural Wiltshire particularly severe. Some labourers migrated to the towns and some overseas – not always voluntarily! A further loss of young men and women can be seen in the following extract from a population structure.

Structure of population					
	1851	1861	1871	1881	1891
Men/women 15-29 years	181	79	151	143	132
Men/women 30-45 years	124	51	86	97	116

Hunger, malnutrition, and overcrowding in cottages still threatened to make some villages into rural slums, and to ease the situation Earl Bruce, later to become the Marquess of Ailesbury, organised the Wiltshire Emigration Society whereby, in 1850, certain applicants, if 'the sort of person required by the colonists' were given free passage to Australia. All had to find their own way to Chippenham for their free rail journey to Plymouth. Most of the applicants came from the northern area of the county, but there were a few from Downton, Pitton, Winterslow, Clarendon and Clarendon Park – and Alderbury.

Those from Alderbury, sailing from Plymouth to Adelaide, were: William (40) and Kezia (38) Pearce and four children who sailed on the 'Marion' on 18 March 1851; Ambrose Phillips (21) single, sailed on the 'Marion' on 18 March 1851; Thomas (27) and Sarah (29) Putcher [Butcher], sailed on the 'Thetis' on 27 May 1851; Henry (39) and Mary Jane (33) Vickery and son, sailed on the 'Thetis' on 27 May 1851.

The journey took at least fourteen weeks. All arrived safely despite the fact that on 29 July the 'Marion' ran aground and was wrecked off the coast of South Australia, with loss of everything except lives.

Those emigrating through the Wiltshire Emigration Society were too small in number to affect the local population figures and there must have been many who went overseas by other means. Two entries in subsequent censuses show returned emigrants. In 1871 Newton Bungay (35) a grocer, and his wife Susannah, (32) both born in Alderbury, had three children aged ten, five and three, all born in New South Wales. Their one-year-old child was born in Alderbury. In 1881, Fred Lewis (47) a gold labourer, born in Alderbury, and his wife Thirza, born in Clarendon, had three children living at home aged 17, 13, and 11, all born in Victoria, Australia.

While young men and their families must have had many qualms and shown great courage and fortitude in emigrating to unknown lands across the ocean, there was another category of employees who were often far removed from their home parish; girls and women in service who were 'living in'. Their first employment seems to have been local, but any subsequent improvement took them away, sometimes quite considerable distances, probably because they were recommended to new posts by their mistresses, or moved with the families they worked for. Through the years of the nineteenth century censuses, over 80% of those in service in Alderbury were some distance from the parishes of their birth;

Northumberland, Sussex, Bedfordshire, Cornwall, Dorset and Ireland. Many of them were still in their teens, and they must have missed growing up with their brothers and sisters.

Not all population movement was outward. In the mid nineteenth century many thousands came to this country from Ireland, driven out by the potato famine. In 1861 three families of Irish descent were living in Alderbury. Some of them subsequently moved on, but one family and the son of another stayed for at least ten years.

The occupations given throughout the years of censuses from 1841 to 1891 show without any doubt that Alderbury and Whaddon were agricultural settlements, relying quite heavily on the Clarendon and Longford estates for livelihood. By far the greater majority of men were employed as agricultural and farm labourers – as many as 109 in 1851. There were also 40 general labourers. By 1891 the total number of all labourers had fallen to 75. Machinery had largely taken the place of manual labour.

In contrast to the great numbers of labourers, farmers do not figure to any great extent. At any one time there were some three dairymen, at Shute End and Lower Road, close to the meadows; three farmers, all located in Whaddon; and one or two bailiffs. With one exception in one census, the farms are not named.

Many young men, as apprentices and journeymen, acquired the crafts and skills necessary to maintain the villages and the estates, with carpenters, blacksmiths, bricklayers, and gardeners well represented. Shoemakers, tailors, bakers, and beer-sellers provided items that people would in earlier times have made for themselves, while the women (mainly unmarried or widowed) were laundresses, dressmakers and milliners. Very few of the married women were employed, most of them probably being very well occupied at home managing their large families.

Clearly some craftsmen passed their skills on to their sons but few of the sons continued the tradition. An exception was the Prewett family, master carpenters and journeymen carpenters throughout the century. Similarly the Fry family provided generations of bricklayers – and also two Methodist local preachers in Charles and Thomas!

From 1841 Alderbury always boasted a postman and a policeman. The coming of the railway meant that from the 1861 census, there were always some plate-layers and railway labourers shown; 1881 saw the addition of signalmen, a timekeeper and a porter. By this time there were twelve railway workers living in the parish, though not necessarily working locally.

Despite the local sources of gravel, sand and clay, industry is not well represented. In 1841 an 'excavator' living in Silver Street may have extracted the local gravel. By 1881 there were four brick-makers, one living 'near the chapel' and one living in Clarendon Road, both probably working in the Clarendon brickworks, while the two young brick-makers lodging at The Three Crowns were most likely to have been working in the brickworks at West Grimstead.

Amongst the expected occupations there are some unusual ones – what exactly did a drowner, a boot closer, a match faggot maker, and a bird keeper do?

At any one time there were some ten householders in the parish who were of independent means; fund holders, annuitants and one landowner. Apart from those serving the church and the school, there were very few professional people, with two surveyors, a solicitor, and a Royal Navy captain being the only representatives throughout the six censuses. There was no doctor. Two 'white collar' workers appear, but it is clear that very few of the Alderbury residents had occupations that would have taken them out of the village to work. These examples together emphasise the role of the village as a rural community functioning between the two large estates.

There must have been some unemployment, but it would seem to be covered by entries such as 'servant out of place'. There were very few such entries, the majority being teenage girls. Almost everyone over the age of twelve gave an occupation and some of those employed were only nine years old.

A few, on reaching a good age admitted to retirement, or gave their occupation as 'formerly...' but most continued to give their working employment whatever their years. An interesting group of ten 'pensioners' appeared, five in the 1841 and 1851 censuses, one in 1871, and a further four in 1881. All are men aged between 44 and 47. From the detail in some of the entries, they are retired soldiers, marines, and sailors. What campaigns did they enlist for? Although they were 'sons of the parish', after they returned to Alderbury they were all in lodgings. With two exceptions, none stayed beyond ten years.

The two exceptions tell different stories. Charles Lucas, born in Alderbury about 1829, was the eldest son of James Lucas, an agricultural labourer. Twelve years old at the 1841 census, he does not appear again until 1871 when, with his wife Ophelia, he is living in Whaddon – a Greenwich pensioner. His children were born in Gosport, Portsea, Alverstoke and Southsea. In 1881 he is entered as a naval pensioner and in 1891, when he was 62, he was a dairy farmer in Whaddon! Meanwhile all his brothers and their families were either labourers or carters – so there was a local lad 'made good'!

Herbert Hartford (Harford) was born in 1836, the third child of Thomas, an agricultural labourer. By 1851 he had left home, and his mother was a widow. She did not marry again but became a charwoman and then a laundress. When Herbert had returned as a naval pensioner by 1881 she lived with him, one hopes, in relative comfort.

It did not seem to be unusual in Alderbury to live to the allotted three score years and ten. There were usually fifteen or so septuagenarians at any one time – twenty nine in 1891. And there were always twice as many men as women! The same was true of the few reaching eighty years. In 1851 Martha Pearce, a schoolmistress born in Farley, apparently reached 94 years of age, but the record for longevity in the nineteenth century goes to Mary Jones, a farmer's widow born in Middlesex, who died in 1872 aged 95. (The twentieth century record goes to EA Herbert who died in early 1990 aged 102.)

Under the 'hundred year rule' such details as those above are not yet released for the 20th century, but population totals are available.

Twentieth century population for Alderbury										
1901	1911	1921	1931	1941	1951	1961	1971	1981	1991	1996*
650	649	731	735	-	997	1038	1120	1235	1859	2077
*the latest year for which figures are available										

From these figures it can be seen that the early decades merely maintained the population totals of the previous century, but after the watershed of World War I there was a steady increase as the concept of a place for retirement took hold, and improved public transport allowed people to live in Alderbury while working elsewhere. Throughout the south of England a movement began to return to the countryside to live, though not to work. This trend increased phenomenally after World War II, when car ownership gradually became more commonplace. Here, one could live in Alderbury and work in any of the four major towns and cities within easy reach, or commute even further afield. Planning decisions, the completion of the by-pass, a new school and improved sewerage services together gave great impetus to residential development. Thus the population of Alderbury doubled in fifty years, and in this year 2000 will undoubtedly see further increases.

10

ROAD-NAMES AND BUILDINGS

What's in a name?

Like all villages we have our share of unusual road names. The origins of some are obvious, some are unknown, some are argued about, some are old and some are new. *Clarendon Road* is among the obvious, it leads to Clarendon House. *School Hill* falls into this category, the road where the old school still stands. *Spelts Lane*, or *Old Vicarage Lane* as it is now known, by the old school, led to Spelts Copse and a former vicarage, now known as Greenset House. *Old Road* was the original main road from Salisbury, which wound its way up from Shute End Road before the new turnpike road took the more direct route.

According to the Oxford University Press 'Place Names of Wiltshire', *Shute End* is derived from the Old English 'sceat', a corner, being a projecting corner of the parish. It has been suggested that *Silver Street* comes from 'silva' or 'sylva' the Latin word for a wood. We do not know why *Folly Lane* is so called, but some believe it may be derived from the Norman French 'folie', meaning foliage.

The origins of *Lights Lane* are a cause for argument. There are those who think it comes from the Mediaeval English 'liche', a body, being the route taken by those carrying bodies to the church for burial, although at that time there were virtually no houses in that part of the village. Others would argue that it took its name from the Light family which has been in the area for hundreds of years.

Junction Road led to the railway's Alderbury Junction. *Tunnel Hill,* on the other hand, is associated with the canal tunnel which led from the lake in the grounds of Alderbury House and under the road. There are a number of older residents who can remember a culvert or tunnel under the road, emerging by the line of trees in the field below the church. The south side of *Canal Lane* backs on to the vestiges of that canal, the ill-fated Salisbury and Southampton Canal which has been written about elsewhere in this book.

Some of the modern roads have names commemorating the history of the area: *Waleran Close* named after the huntsman to whom William the Conqueror gave the manor of Whaddon: and *Eyres Drive* named after Giles Eyre who built the folly known affectionately to all villagers as 'The Pepperbox'. This is actually in Whiteparish but being such a landmark its name has, at various times, been adopted by a number of Alderbury organisations. It also gives its name to *Pepperbox Rise.*

Windwhistle Way off Avon Drive took its name from Windwhistle Farm which once stood there. *Windmill Close* similarly gets its name from the

The Pepperbox

89

windmill which once stood on the high ground in that locality. It has been said that *Spider's Island* took its name from a symbol for that windmill which, on the 1809 map, resembled a spider.

Some roads are named after local residents such as *Bungay's Lane,* where the Bungay family lived, off Castle Lane. Similarly, *Whitcher's Meadow,* a modern road off Clarendon Road, is on land which belonged to the Whitcher family until recently.

Castle Hill was so named in 1790 according to documents in the Longford Estate records. As the highest point in the hamlet of Whaddon it is likely that in Norman times there could have been an earthen motte there. It may have been the site of Whaddon church referred to elsewhere. *Castle Lane* was the earliest recorded name of the road here but during the nineteenth century it appears to have been called Whaddon Lane, before reverting to its original name.

Frogham is a name which has gone out of use and relates to an area rather than a road. It was in use in the nineteenth century censuses and appears in a number of property deeds; it appears to cover the area of Castle Lane and the few houses to the north. *The Barracks* was also a name in use in that area and members of the history research group would dearly like to hear from anyone who can throw any light on this.

Buildings

We now turn to look at some of the older properties in Alderbury and Whaddon and a few from adjoining parishes that have close associations or are of particular interest. Old documents and maps held at the County Record Office indicate a number of early dwellings in the village and many of the properties investigated have in fact been built on the sites of former dwellings. For ease of recognition when strolling through the village, houses are here grouped together in small clusters. The houses mentioned are included for various reasons; some are listed buildings, some have details given in the County Record Office, some are of anecdotal interest as related by village residents and others have historical connections. As it has not been possible to include all the old houses in this publication it is hoped that the following information will spur on the house detectives amongst readers.

The first group to be considered is to be found on or around the village green in the conservation area.

The earliest documentation at the Wiltshire County Records Office of *The Forge* and *Forge Cottage* consists of an indenture dated 1699 for a smith's shop, house and garden to Thomas Stringer and Edwin Clare, naming the previous occupant as Langly. In that year Thomas Stringer was Lord of the Manor of Ivychurch and there is an attractive plaque commemorating him in the church. A further indenture dated 4 August 1807 from Lord Radnor to Elizabeth Tutt, her daughter Elizabeth, and Stephen Bungay her son is signed by Elizabeth, possibly indicating an educated woman. Also mentioned is the former blacksmith George Tutt (her husband) and before him John Harris. Between 1828 and 1857 the freehold was leased to the Dowty family at a rent of five shillings per year. The present forge was built in 1909 around the old one whilst it continued working and subsequently there has been enlargement in 1998. Gates for Longford Estate lodges were made at the forge, those for **Alderbury Lodge** in 1929 and the remainder after World War II.

The **Green Dragon Inn** situated on the old toll road is listed as a fifteenth century hall house with sixteenth century cross wing. It is a plastered timber-framed building under a tiled roof with brick stacks. A late gothic carved stone fireplace from Ivychurch used to stand in the hall but this was moved to America c.1930. No evidence of its resting place has yet been discovered. Several village stories are associated with the Inn, the main one being that Charles Dickens stayed there and featured it in his novel Martin Chuzzlewit. Many people believe that an underground sealed passageway in the Inn led to either Ivychurch or Longford.

Lake House is listed as a mid nineteenth century detached house of English bond brick under a Welsh slate hipped roof. The estate house is documented on 5 May 1809 as sold to Mr Nathaniel Lane and inherited by his son Charles Lane Lake in 1842. **Fountain View** is a twentieth century double-fronted house. Mr Northeast relates that it was built in 1927 by his grandfather, the retired postmaster. The land was purchased from Mr Penny the well known Salisbury horse dealer, who kept his horses in Alderbury. The present house is on the site of the old stables. **Jasmine**

Figure 10.1

Ye Old Post

Office Cottage,

c.1920

right, Tom

Northeast's

father, mother,

plus Mary and

Gladys

Cottage is a former Estate cottage known as ***Rose Cottage.*** The present owners believe that the original part of the house is over 200 years old and may have been a residence for the estate river keepers. The inner lining of the roof still has its original hazel branch construction.

Ye Old Post Office Cottage is another double-fronted, thatched cottage which was renovated around 1950, when cob walls were discovered. It served as the village Post Office until 1956, when these facilities were moved to Whaddon. Two village families ran the post office during this century, the Northeast family until the 1920s and then the Maidment family. The last recorded postmaster was Algernon Maidment. The postmaster was also the Air Raid Precautions warden during World War II. *Cherry Tree Cottage* is listed as eighteenth century and is a good example of an Estate cottage. It was formerly thatched but when bought by Mr Howe in 1937, it had a slate roof. A map dated c.1820 shows a windmill in the field behind the cottage but there are no visible remains of this nowadays.

We now move to Silver Street, one of the older areas of the village. The house called ***Old Timbers*** is listed as being a late seventeenth century detached Estate cottage. It comprises square panelled timber framing with straight bracing and herringbone brick infill to the upper storey, under a half-hipped thatched roof. It was renovated around 1962 by the Longford Estate, from two formerly derelict cottages of which no records remain. The present owner, Mr Cochrane, found remains of old brickwork when digging in fence posts and reports the presence of an old brick culvert running parallel with Silver Street and situated in the woods.

Number ***28 Silver Street*** is listed as dating to the eighteenth century, an Estate cottage with direct step access to the road. It comprises Flemish bond

Figure 10.2

View looking

down Silver

Street, c.1986

SILVER STREET
1986

92

brick with a weather-boarded extension under a hipped thatched roof. A local story concerns the village washerwoman who supposedly lived here and indeed, a Mrs A England, laundress of Silver Street is recorded in Kelly's Directories from 1925-40. Apparently the Longford Estate agent who lived at Alward House was offended by the view across the fields of lines of washing and planted the stand of trees between his home and Silver Street to improve his visual amenity. *Rookwood* is a detached house comprising three former estate cottages. The owners have indicated that a well in the house is dated c.1500. *Wisteria Cottage* is a nineteenth century cottage, formerly occupied by a local builder. *Rose Cottage* is listed as being a late seventeenth century detached Estate cottage renovated in around 1950. It comprises a square panelled timber frame with straight bracing, on a brick plinth, under a hipped thatched roof. It was occupied for many generations by the England family who farmed the surrounding land.

There are a number of interesting old buildings in the area around the church. *Holly Tree Cottage* in Folly Lane has been renovated and extended, utilising the windows from the previously adjacent Wesleyan Chapel demolished in the 1970s. *Totterdown Cottage* in Folly Lane is a part-thatched former Estate cottage dating back to the late eighteenth century. It was the former home of the 'Carrier', who operated until the bus service started in 1921. Mr Hibberd ran his own service to Salisbury on market days leaving Alderbury at ten am and returning at four pm. The service started in the late 1800s and the return fare was 3d. per adult and 1d. per child. It was later the home of Mrs Rumbold, the Countess of Radnor's maid. Tom Rumbold, the carpenter of Folly Lane is listed in 1925 in 'The Salisbury Directory'. *Yew Tree Cottage,* at 8 Folly Lane is listed as a mid nineteenth century, well-designed example of an Estate cottage but the current owner believes that the presence of wattle and daub walls in the central core indicates an older, eighteenth century building. It is made of a Flemish bond brick under a Welsh slate hipped roof. It has a central, castellated porch with hood. Before the National Health Service came into being, it was the home of the village nurse, who was allowed to live there rent-free by the Longford Estate. Formerly known as *Ivy Cottage*, it has been privately owned since 1976 when it was substantially renovated. At one time it may have housed one of the Longford Castle cooks, as legend records a cook setting fire to the chimney. *Woodlynne House*, in Lights Lane, is a double-fronted twentieth century house built as a vicarage but has been privately owned since 1983. Numbers *5*, *6*, and *7, School Hill* are listed as seventeenth century Estate cottages with 1950s renovations. The houses are comprised of squared panelled timber frames with brick infilling under thatched hipped roofs with brick stacks. Numbers 5 and 6 are a pair, with herringbone brickwork to the upper storey. *Greenset House* is a substantial red brick house with patterned burnt headers under a clay tile roof, with mainly stone mullioned windows. Formerly known as The Vicarage, it was built c.1855. Canon Hutchings, who once lived here, is believed to have had an observatory in the garden at one time.

Near to the church is ***Alderbury House,*** a late eighteenth century country house built for George Yalden Fort Esquire in 1791 on or near the site of an earlier one. The main house is of ashlar with an attached brick wing under a Welsh slate hipped roof. Stone from the demolished belfry of Salisbury Cathedral was purchased by the contractor, Henry Ford of Wilton, for use in the building. The house stands in landscaped parkland and includes a lake which was constructed as part of the ill-fated Salisbury to Southampton Canal. The house has been attributed to James Wyatt, the architect responsible for the restoration of Salisbury Cathedral, but recent research by a team of American architects links the house to the London firm of Sir Robert Taylor and Samuel Pepys Cockerell. Between 1788-91 their chief draughtsman was Benjamin Latrobe, who later became America's first professional architect. Drawings of Alderbury House exist among his papers. Professor Snadon and his associates are currently writing a book on Benjamin Latrobe for publication in 2001 or 2002 when further information will be available. The house may have been used during World War II for military purposes but no documentary evidence exists.

Alderbury House Lodge is listed as being of importance due to its connection with Alderbury House. It is a mid nineteenth century cottage of Flemish bond brick under a half-hipped, tiled roof with brick stack. Several courses of eighteenth century brickwork along the base of the west and north walls suggest evidence of earlier building on the site.

Court House, a brick and timber-framed building, situated about 50 metres to the east of the church, has an interesting history. There has been at least one earlier house on the site and a sixteenth century rear wing is incorporated into the present building which dates from the early and late periods of the eighteenth century. A parish survey of 1814 indicates that it was the village poor house at that time. In the 1851 census the house is referred to as 'The Parsonage' and accommodated three families. It

Figure 10.3

Alderbury

House

94

remained sub-divided until well into the twentieth century when it was sold into private ownership. In 1973 it was advertised for sale in the magazine 'Country Life' as a 'Queen Anne Country House'.

Figure 10.4

Court House

The Old School House building was described in the English Heritage survey of 1982 as a brick and timbered mediaeval hall-house of the late fifteenth century. The interior was originally open to the roof and floored over in the seventeenth century. An estate survey of 1765 indicates that the site was then owned by George Fort and contained a farmhouse, lands, yards, barns and gardens in the occupation of George Gray. Early in the nineteenth century Lord Radnor acquired the site and the list of successive leaseholders includes the names Windsor, Lawrence, Tanner and Bungay. Lord Radnor founded the school there in 1838. It was sold as a private dwelling in 1993 .

Figure 10.5

High Street,

from the cross-

roads, as it looks

today

95

The building at the far end of High Street is first recorded as being **The Old Goose Inn,** after which it became the village store and a butcher's shop. It finally become the Cooperative Wholesale Society store until its closure in the late 1960s, at which time it was converted into private dwellings. An interesting photograph of the shop is shown below.

Figure 10.6

High Street,

c.1885

On Clarendon Road, there is a small house set into the bank on the north side. Now called **Long Close,** this was built by John Belstone, a bricklayer born in Alderbury in 1793. Belstone was a ratepayer, had three children, married twice and lived in the house for over 40 years. The plaque on the front of the house bearing the inscription 'JB 1830' is a reproduction although the original one is not lost. It is built into a wall at the rear. Mostly rebuilt now, the layout of the original house has been retained.

There are also many interesting buildings in Whaddon. **Castle Hill House**, known at **Mount Pleasant Farm** until 1920, is an early nineteenth century detached house. A tablet with the date 1826 is recorded by the Royal Commission for Historic Monuments. **The Old Cottage** in Castle Lane is a detached early eighteenth century former Estate cottage with deeds indicating private ownership from 1914. An eighteenth century barn, at the rear of the property, which is large enough to house a horse and cart leads the owner to believe that the cottage may have been occupied by a carter or similar substantial person. Fragments from Ivychurch are built into the cottage. **Canal House,** on Southampton Road, was built in 1870 on the site of a former dwelling which was purchased together with all the surrounding land on which the more modern houses now stand, for £50. From the beginning of the century it appears to have been the home of one of the village milkmen. The construction of the **Old Police Station** was commissioned by the Wiltshire Constabulary as the area Police Station and the home of the Police Sergeant. Constables from the surrounding villages were required to attend meetings here every Friday morning. It was decommissioned in about 1982. A village story describes the last policeman to live here as being seven feet tall and as someone who had a hook on the ceiling of the Green Dragon to hang his tankard on so nobody else could reach it! Similar tales refer to the 'giant' as being a soldier! **The Three Crowns** at Whaddon is a mid-eighteenth century to nineteenth century inn, traditionally believed to be on the site of a hostelry visited by three Kings, Edward III, David of Scotland and John of France. The tale relates that this visit occurred when the latter two were being held prisoner at Clarendon after the Battle of Poitiers in 1356. No documentary evidence to support this has yet been discovered.

Figure 10.7

Plaque at

Long Close

One of the better documented buildings in Whaddon is **Matrons College Farmhouse,** known in the last century as **Charity Farm.** This eighteenth century farmhouse constructed of brick, with stone and flint bands, is probably a rebuild of an earlier building of which there is now no evidence

Figure 10.8

The Three Crowns

Whaddon, 1995

extant. Endowed by the Bishop of Salisbury to fund Matrons College in the Cathedral Close, this provided dwellings for widows of clergy. It became a private residence in the 1980s. The land is now owned and farmed by **Alderbury Farm,** the owners of which tell that it was once a training farm for monks from Winchester. A second farm building, **Tottens Farm** (believed to have been opposite The Three Crowns), is also one which is no longer a working farm. Parts of these farm buildings date back approximately 350 years according to the present owners and the barns of the former farm were used as staging points for the coaches on the Salisbury to Southampton route. Changes of horses could be obtained there and space was available for coachmen to sleep in the top of the barns.

Figure 10.9

Matrons

College Farm

MATRONS COLLEGE FARM

Turning our attention to Shute End, we find a number of interesting houses and cottages. The property known as **Avon Turn** was, until recently, the home of the Dowager Countess of Radnor. **Ferry Cottage** is situated by the turn of the River Avon and was the home of the Hazel family, who for many years ran the Alderbury to Britford ferry. The Women's Institute history of Alderbury records *'old Mrs Hazel recalled taking Charles Dickens across in the ferry'.*

St Marie's Grange was designed by and built for the Victorian architect Pugin and presents a splendid vision of Gothic domestic architecture. Constructed for himself and his new bride he wrote, *'it is the only modern building that is compleat in every part in the antient style'.* Extracts from Pugin's diary indicate some interesting snippets; *'26 January 1835 masonry work began; 29 January contract signed; 15 September began sleeping at the house'.* The plot of land slopes sharply down to the river and the house had to be built near to the upper edge of the plot near to the road in order that Pugin could exploit the views to Salisbury Cathedral and Longford Castle. The distinctive house took its Gothic design from the French style, with steep roofs, turret and tower, but it was to prove rather impractical. The house was small, in spite of its grand pretensions; the original design was lacking a staircase (except for that in the tower) and it had no entrance hall. Pugin and his family lived in the house for only a year, moving after his wife developed ill health and it was sold in 1841. The new owner took immediate steps to improve the house, both adding to the accommodation and altering the internal layout. Most importantly, a spacious entrance hall was created and a staircase added.

Figure 10.10

The Ferry at

Shute End

There are a number of major houses in the area of particular note; although some fall just outside the parish boundary, they are of such significance to warrant a mention in this volume. Many have been documented in their own right and the interested reader will be able to seek further information from other sources. Perhaps the best known of these properties is *Longford Castle*, situated at the 'long ford' on the River Avon between Alderbury and Britford. The castle was commissioned by Sir Thomas Gorges c.1578, for his new Swedish wife Helena Snakenburg, a lady from the Swedish Royal Court who was formerly a Maid of Honour to Elizabeth I. She persuaded Sir Thomas to demolish the earlier house built by the Cervington family and replace it in 1578 with a building based on the castle at Uranienberg. The cost was nearly the end of Sir Thomas as huge piles had to be driven into the marsh but serendipity took a hand when, at the time of the Spanish Armada whilst he was Governor of Hurst Castle, Helena acquired the rights to a wreck from Queen Elizabeth I. This proved to be laden with silver bars and the project to construct Longford Castle became secure. It was completed in its original form in 1591.

The castle was built with a triangular central courtyard and circular towers at each corner. It was garrisoned for the King in the Civil War. During World War I it was used as a hospital for British officers. A letter from Lord Montgomery of Alamein ('Monty') in the castle archives confirms that he occupied Longford Castle as his headquarters during World War II; security procedures prevented detailed records from being kept. The castle is the family home of the Earls of Radnor. Nearby *Alward House* is the home of Viscount Folkestone, the heir to the Earl of Radnor.

The Trafalgar Park estate was acquired by Sir Peter Vandeput in 1725, for whom *Trafalgar House* was built by John James in 1733. There were additions in 1766 by John Wood the younger and Nicholas Revett. The property replaced an earlier house by the river, **Standlynch Manor**, which Vandeput demolished. The park and house were renamed Trafalgar when they were given by the Treasury in 1814 to the heirs of Viscount Admiral Nelson in gratitude for his services to the nation. The south wing was gutted by fire in the 1860s and rebuilt by William Butterfield. The 4th Earl Nelson died without issue in 1947 and the Trafalgar Estates Act 1947 ended the pension, allowing the sale of house and land. It was sold to the Duke of Leeds in 1948, after which a serious outbreak of dry rot in the north-east wing rendered the section uninhabitable, a state in which it remains to this day, although the rot has been successfully arrested. In the mid 1990s, most of the estate's 3,500 acres of park land was sold, and today the house is owned and run privately by the Trafalgar Park Trust. It is now used as a business centre and arts venue, and has been used as a film set.

In the neighbouring parish of Clarendon is another example of a large and ancient estate. This has an eighteenth century country house, which is presently unoccupied. The extensive estate contains the ruins of **Clarendon Palace**, a mediaeval hunting lodge and pleasure palace, whose last recorded royal visitor was Elizabeth I in 1574. The palace was documented as unfit for use so she dined in the ranger's lodge. Today, the estate belongs to the Christie-Miller family.

There are currently four working farms associated with the parish of Alderbury. **Hole Farm,** which is actually just inside the parish of Clarendon, is based on cattle. Neighbouring **Ivychurch Farm** is an arable farm concentrating mainly on corn, with some beef cattle. Attached to the farm are the ruins of **Ivychurch Priory,** created by the Norman kings to administer to the spiritual needs of the royal court when in residence at Clarendon Palace. **Rectory Farm** acquired its name after the 1809 Enclosure Award and indicates an association with Alderbury Rectory Manor. It has a listed eighteenth century barn which is currently used as a cow shed. The fourth farm, **Alderbury Farm,** is a working arable farm with some sheep and horses. It has been farmed by the same family for over 50 years.

Figure 10.11

The Fountain

Alderbury and Whaddon also have a number of village features, many of which are well known in the area. Perhaps the best known of these within the parish boundary is **The Fountain,** standing on the village green and dating from the early twentieth century. This incorporates several of the double shafts of Ivychurch Cloisters with their capitals, including a kind of merlon design.

100

The Fountain was 'opened' in 1903 to commemorate the Coronation of Edward VII and in recognition of the piped water supply which was paid for by the Earl of Radnor. Prior to the arrival of piped water, villagers had to carry water from the local springs. The Fountain has a trough at the bottom for dogs and one higher up for horses and fastened to either side were mugs on chains.

The *village war memorial* is also on the village green. It was erected in 1922, on land donated by the Earl of Radnor. The lime, oak and beech trees surrounding it were given by Lady Everett. The memorial itself comprises a concrete column with inscribed names on a stepped plinth.

There are a number of surviving early milestones in the village, an example of which is to be found at the junction of Clarendon Road with Southampton Road. This marker, dating from the nineteenth century, comprises a cast iron three sided pillar with shields on two sides, bearing the inscriptions 'TO SARUM 3 MILES' and 'TO SOUTHTON 19 MILES'.

A similar marker, most of which had rusted away by the end of 1997, was situated at Shute End to the east of the main road. There is a milestone in Whaddon, near to the Post Office stores, bearing the words 'SARUM 4½' and 'SOUTHTON 18'. An interesting parish boundary post is situated on the west side of Shute End Road. This is a Grade II early nineteenth century cast iron panelled supporting post in T-form. It bears the raised lettered inscription 'ALDERBURY – LAVERSTOCK'.

Figure 10.12

The milepost at Clarendon cross-roads and the milestone at Whaddon post office

Perhaps one of the best known village features in the area is the folly known as the *'Pepperbox'*. This was built 1606 by Gyles Eyre, a local landowner whose family tombs are to be found in St Thomas's Church in Salisbury. Situated on the chalk ridge overlooking the Avon valley, it may originally have been used as a lookout allowing ladies to follow the progress of the local hunt. Local residents report its being used in World War II as a lookout post by the Home Guard. Legend records that in the nineteenth century it was a notorious hide-out for highwaymen awaiting the coaches toiling up the adjacent hill.

Figure 10.13

The boundary post at Shute End

There are a number of other features, perhaps now insignificant in themselves, but reminders of their importance in days gone by. At the corner of Folly Lane is a water pump, the only one remaining after the removal of others by the Water Board. Running from the top of Clarendon Road to Shute End was a deer leap, traces of which can still be seen alongside Old Road. In parts, this is 12 feet wide; it was originally dug to retain the deer within Clarendon Park. On Shute End Road, there is a Victorian post box, the oldest in the village. This is painted in the traditional 'pillar box' red, made of cast iron and set in a free-standing brick plinth. It bears the embossed letters 'VR'.

Brick-making in Alderbury and Whaddon

Figure 10.14

The Victorian

post box, Shute

End Road

During the 1960s a substantial study was carried out by the newly formed Salisbury and South Wilts. Industrial Archaeology Society which resulted in the publication entitled 'Brick-making in the Parish of Alderbury, Wilts. with particular reference to the Whaddon Brick-works'.

The particular nature of the substructure and soils of the area (see Chapter 3) are proved from maps and ancient records to have been exploited for bricks, tiles and pottery since the thirteenth century. The local hand-made bricks and tiles are still visible as part of the structure of many village properties.

The Whaddon brick-works was founded about 1904, on land leased from Matrons College Farm, by the Hand family who owned it until its closure in 1976. The site is now covered by the bypass, the entrance being on the eastern side of the Southampton road just past the former railway bridge. In 1925 Walter Tanner is listed as the manager with at least nine other employees. The family tradition continued with Ralph Tanner who was the brick-maker in 1962. He lived in Castle Lane and is remembered by older residents in the area who visited the works and helped out at busy times on a voluntary basis.

The society visited the site in 1966 and noted that it consisted of one kiln which was 30 feet long and 15 feet wide and fired from 16 fireplaces, clay pits, and various machinery. The manufacturing methods and types of tools in use were virtually unchanged from those of the eighteenth century. In the 1960s the kiln was fired twice a year and coal had replaced wood as fuel.

In addition to standard bricks specials were also made for use in fireplaces and bay windows. It was estimated that with an assistant Ralph Tanner could make two bricks in less than a minute. Before the purchase of a lorry in the 1920s bricks were taken twice a day by horse and cart to Salisbury: each load was approximately 350 bricks.

Figure 10.15

Brickmaking at

Whaddon, 1969

11

TRANSPORT AND COMMUNICATION

Pre-Roman, Roman, Saxon and Mediaeval Roads

The earliest roads were the ridgeways, created by prehistoric travellers who used the driest paths. These paths also avoided cultivated land on the valley floors and lower slopes. In fine weather, the 'summerways' between valley and ridge provided an alternative. The ridgeways belonged to no-one and everyone and received no maintenance. As well as these long distance paths there were routes which led from village to village within a local area. There was an intersection of ridgeways close to Alderbury.

There is no evidence of a Roman road through Alderbury and Whaddon. Much of what is known of early roads comes from information in Saxon Charters. The earliest date on which a road in this area is recorded in a charter is 972. In 1286, reference is made to this charter, granted by King Edgar, which describes a route from Alderbury to Amesbury, via Petersfinger, Milford and Old Sarum. The Saxon word for a through road was 'herepath' from which comes our word highway. They referred to a Roman road as a 'stræt' or street, meaning a made road as compared with an unmade ridgeway, and a local road as a 'weg' or way.

Figure 11.1

Kissing-gate

near Greenset

House, Old

Vicarage Lane

The presence in this area of two places with 'ford' in their names tells us that there were probably several cross-valley routes passing through the area. Britford or Brytfordingea as it was in 670 and Longford or Langeford in 1086, were the foci of routes from villages on both sides of the River Avon. Although Milford (or Meleford) is outside the parish, the crossing of the River Bourne here is relative to our story as the road referred to in the 972 charter crossed the river at this point.

In the fifteenth century, when Salisbury was exporting wool through Southampton and one third of all the traffic leaving Southampton was bound for Salisbury, the road most likely to have been used was the one through Romsey and Whiteparish entering Salisbury at St Martin's Church. The exact route through this parish is not clear; Ogilby's map in 1675 showed a route from Pepperbox similar to that of the original turnpike.

103

Early Tracks and Roads

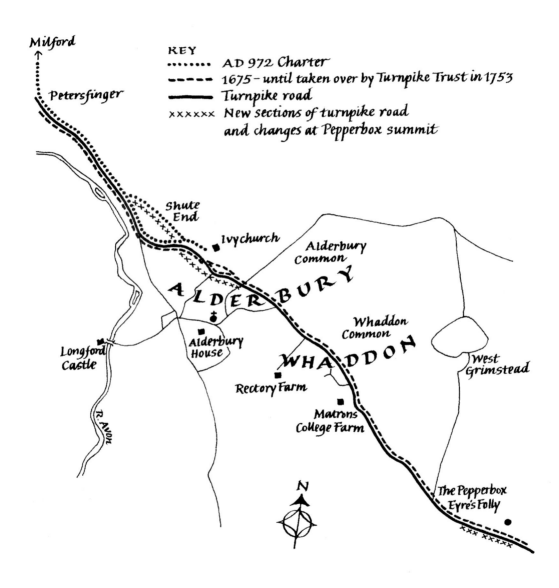

Figure 11.2

Later Transport Developments

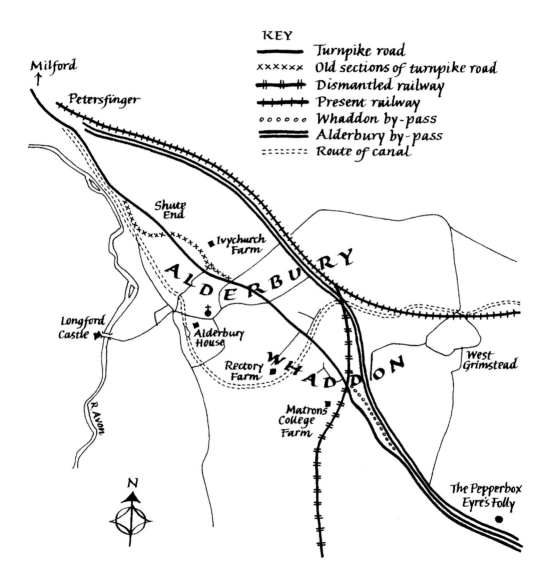

KEY

————	Turnpike road
××××××	Old sections of turnpike road
╫╫╫╫	Dismantled railway
┼┼┼┼	Present railway
∘∘∘∘∘∘	Whaddon by-pass
══════	Alderbury by-pass
┄┄┄┄┄	Route of canal

Figure 11.3

Coaching and Turnpike Roads

In 1753 an Act of Parliament allowed a Turnpike Trust to operate through Salisbury. One of the two routes to be run by the Sarum and Eling Trust was Salisbury to Southampton. It passed along St Ann Street to Tollgate Road, behind St Martin's church to the Southampton Road and through the tollgate at Petersfinger, following what is now Marshmead Close, Clarendon, continuing to what is now the junction between Shute End Road and Southampton Road. After about 500 yards on the Shute End Road the turnpike turned sharply up hill to pass close to Ivychurch Farm and in front of the Green Dragon Inn. From there it continued on what is now Old Road to the cross-roads of Clarendon Road, Folly Lane, and Southampton Road, where the three mile marker can still be seen. It then followed the Southampton Road line to the four and a half mile marker near the Post Office and continued, to pass in front of the Three Crowns public house a short distance to the west of the A36 which has the same line. After crossing the Whiteparish hill the turnpike then continued to Landford, with two alternative routes from there.

The Trust kept its roads in excellent condition with frequent applications of gravel and flints to keep the surface good in spite of erosion by frost and daily use; in dry weather water was sprayed on the roads to keep the dust down. The road was considered one of the best in the country.

Two major changes were made to the road within the Alderbury parish boundaries. In April 1834 a proposal was made to reduce the Whiteparish hill (Pepperbox) by 20 chains (a quarter of a mile) in length and 20 feet in height. The Earl of Radnor and Thomas Bolton Esq. agreed to allow a temporary road over their land while the work proceeded. The work was completed by May 1835.

The second change was the realignment of the Alderbury Hill section, first referred to in the Trust minutes of 17 January 1838. In July 1840 it was recommended that improvements should begin at the two mile marker (of which remnants still exist in the hedge across the road from St Marie's Grange) and terminate near the Green Dragon Inn at Alderbury. The land required from Lord Radnor was just over two and a half acres which he agreed to sell for £178. 3s. 1d. In addition he required £54. 19s. 10d. to compensate his tenants Mr Lewis, James Bungey and Letitia Bungey for loss of gardens and fruit trees. Sir Frederick Bathhurst of Clarendon agreed to accept £80 per acre although he considered £100 per acre would not be too much in view of the severance of his estate. Two and a quarter acres were purchased from him and additionally, £44. 3s. 0d. was paid to him for timber to be cut down.

In November 1841, the surveyor reported that the first part of the new line had been opened in late October and the Green Dragon section was now being built, as was the part at the plantation near the Old Goose Inn. On 17 November 1842 all work was complete, the steps to the Old Goose Inn were made and before Christmas the parish road leading from Alderbury to Grimstead was also finished.

The new line cut out the steep curved section from Shute End Road to the three mile marker and replaced it with the smooth mile-long hill from St Marie's Grange to the cross-roads, which is in use today. It was stated that some of the expense of the new line, which was £2,596. 13s. 2d., could be eased by the sale of gravel from the old road site. Although several bore holes were dug, coarse gravel was not found and on 20 June 1844, it was agreed that the old road could be put into repair and the responsibility of the Trustees should cease.

Use of the original turnpike through Alderbury had increased yearly until 1839 when 40 stagecoaches a week in each direction were passing through the Petersfinger tollgate. Stagecoach and private hire together accounted for 40,000 passengers annually. Many types of passengers and freight passed through the tollgate en route to Romsey, Winchester, Southampton, Gosport, the Isle of Wight or the Channel Islands in a wide variety of vehicles. All had to pay a toll except for the Royal Mail Coaches. These must have been a magnificent sight as they approached the tollgate with post-horn blowing to announce their arrival so that the gate could be opened to allow them to proceed without delay. The maroon, scarlet and gold coaches, made to the Royal Mail specification by coach builders and operated by contractors, were the preferred means of travel on 26 routes by 1793. The guard, wearing a Post Office-supplied uniform of scarlet coat and black hat, with a brace of pistols to defend the mail, and a timepiece with which to log the journey, must have seemed as important as any ship's captain. The mail coaches carried four passengers inside and four outside, the horses were changed every seven to ten miles and galloping was forbidden. Matched horses meant a more comfortable ride for travellers with less likelihood of the coach turning over. The reputation they held for dependability and good timekeeping was demonstrated by the fact that in some places people set their clocks and watches by the arrivals and departures of the Royal Mail Coach.

However, by 1842, when the realignment was completed, the stage-coaches passing through Petersfinger had dropped to 37 per week in each direction and after the introduction of the railway from Southampton in 1847 they ceased. Kelly's Directory of 1850 shows no coach departures from Salisbury to Southampton but describes the location of the railway station and states that omnibuses from the local hotels met trains.

Although the railway put an end to the long distance coach-borne and freight traffic, the road saw an increase in use by local carriers. The figures for 1865 show that each week 33 carriers were taking local people, their goods and produce, back and forth to Salisbury from the local villages. Most journeys took place on Tuesday or Saturday and each carrier had his favourite inn from which to start and finish the journey. In the Post Office Directory of 1867 more than a dozen names of carriers are shown as serving the local routes from three Milford Street inns; The Goat, The William IV, and The Catherine Wheel. The Saracen's Head in Blue Boar Row and The Roebuck in Butcher Row also served as starting places for return travel. Of those used by Alderbury bound travellers only the Coach and Horses in Winchester Street is still in business under the same name. Letters arrived at the Post Office in Old Road each morning at seven o'clock brought by Mr Parsons, and mail was sent out at six o'clock each evening. The name of Samuel Hibberd is shown in the 1895 Kelly's Directory as the only carrier based in Alderbury.

Railways

Several rail routes to Salisbury were considered between 1837 and 1844 when a branch from the London to Southampton main line was authorised. It was to run from Bishopstoke (Eastleigh) to Milford through Alderbury and was owned by the London and South Western Railway. An industrial estate off Tollgate road is on the site of the Milford terminus.

When opened in 1847, first to freight, then to passengers, the branch ran close to the route of the old Salisbury to Southampton Canal from Alderbury to the River Test, then on to Romsey and Eastleigh. The first 22 wagons to enter Salisbury station carried coal for the needy. The train was described in the Salisbury and Winchester Journal as 'an engine scampering along dragging after it twenty or thirty wagons'. At this time, trains to London ran from Salisbury, past Alderbury and via Eastleigh to Nine Elms. Down trains from London to Salisbury ran five times per day and up trains four times daily. As well as the London trains there were also six trains per day to and from Gosport, making 21 passenger trains alone passing through Alderbury.

There was never a station at Alderbury, either on the main line or the branch line, although there was a small 'halt' on the main line for railway employees and their families to board trains for Salisbury. However an Alderbury resident had the distinction of being the first passenger. The line had been constructed from Romsey as far as Alderbury and the railway's chief engineer, accompanied by the contractors, boarded an inspection train at Romsey for Alderbury where the official party adjourned to Phillip's Hotel for lunch (this hotel has not been identified at the present time but does not appear to have been either the Green Dragon or the Three Crowns as both held those names prior to 1846). Mr. Buckell, a Salisbury dental surgeon who lived in Alderbury, had been treating some patients in Romsey and managed to get a ride on this train.

The Salisbury Journal also records that for the return journey some Alderbury residents begged an 'experimental trip' as far as Grimstead. Reluctantly this was agreed to but to their dismay the train did not stop at Grimstead, continuing to Romsey where the unfortunates were left to plod the eight miles back to Alderbury, the victims of what the Journal later described as a 'droll practical joke'.

In 1857 a new and more direct route from London to Salisbury also terminated at Milford. When in 1859 The Salisbury and Yeovil line arrived at Fisherton Street Station a tunnel built to connect the stations on each side of the city allowed Milford to be abandoned as a passenger terminus and Fisherton to be used by all. However it continued to be used as a goods yard until closed in August 1967.

In 1866 Salisbury and Dorset Junction Company opened a branch line from Alderbury to West Moors. This joined the Castleman Line, named after a Wimborne solicitor who promoted it, and dubbed the 'corkscrew'. The Alderbury to West Moors link made it possible for passengers to travel from London to Dorchester and Weymouth via Salisbury, cutting out Southampton. Furthermore, it was expected that imported goods from Poole would be transferred inland; people from the hinterland south of Salisbury with their produce would use it to reach the market, and watering places on the south coast would become accessible to more people. There were four trains each day but only third class carriages were available between Wimborne and Salisbury. Was this some comment on those who used the line?

The branch was closed on 4 May 1964, at the time when Dr Beeching was closing many rural lines. The alignment of the junction had been altered in 1943 and the junction was removed altogether in August 1970. The signal box to the south-east of the junction was closed four months later. The abandoned line to West Moors crossed part of the old canal near the village school in Firs Road, crossed the road by a bridge near the present post office, then ran between Matrons College Farm and The Three Crowns on its way to Downton. It can be seen as a white chalk scar when looking west from Witherington Down. The route used today to reach Southampton by train from Salisbury is the same as that which brought the first trains to Salisbury in 1847.

Figure 11.4

Alderbury

Junction

River Transport and the Canal

From early in the 17th century there was interest in making the River Avon navigable for commercial use from Salisbury to the sea at Christchurch. John Taylor, with others, rowed from Christchurch to Salisbury to prove it could be done. The Mayor in 1627, John Ivie, supported the scheme and later, so did Bishop Seth Ward. Work started in 1675 and in spite of financial difficulties which slowed progress, 25-ton barges are known to have reached Harnham bridge by 1684. Despite severe floods in 1690, the Avon Navigation was in use until 1715. Shallow draught sailing barges took two days to travel from Christchurch to Salisbury. By late 1744 two unsuccessful attempts had been made to re-establish links with the sea.

Yet another attempt was made, starting in May 1795, when an Act of Parliament was passed allowing the Southampton to Salisbury Navigation Company to build a canal from the eastern side of Southampton to the Andover Canal at Redbridge, and from Kimbridge on the same canal to Salisbury, following a route through Alderbury.

Although open and carrying toll-paying freight from west of Southampton Tunnel (Marlands) to Alderbury Common by March 1803, the money raised was running out and a decision had been taken in November 1802 to build a temporary wooden railway to join the end of the canal at Alderbury Common to the Turnpike road (now Southampton Road) for transportation of cargo. Completion of the canal to Salisbury was still intended at this time but meanwhile, work was to start immediately on the small wooden railway. It was estimated to cost £61. 11s. 11d. for the 629 yard length. Neither the exact route of this railway nor evidence of its existence are certain. What is known is that in June 1804 George Jones the surveyor sued for unpaid wages and threatened to sell off the railway. There would have been ample time between November 1802 (when work began) and June 1804 for it to have been built and used. The Historical Transport Map of Wiltshire refers to an 'Alderbury Wharf to Turnpike' narrow gauge railway from 1803-8.

Difficulty in raising money from shareholders, coupled with construction problems with the tunnel at Southampton recurred throughout the period from 1795 to 1808, when the final meeting was held and the Alderbury arm of the canal abandoned. There is no evidence to uphold the belief that unexpected sand in the Alderbury area caused the failure of the venture.

The Salisbury arm mostly reverted to nature and can still be seen today in some places as a line of bushes or trees where it was not ploughed out. The reservoir in Clarendon Park which was to supply the summit still contains water, as does the summit itself. This section, alongside Firs Road, is the best known remnant within the parish boundary. The remainder is dry. The line of the working is shown on an 1811 map as reaching Petersfinger via the west side of the turnpike road; passing Rectory Farm, before turning north to Silver Street and along the east side of Witherington Road to Old Road. It then crosses to the west and runs close to the site of St Marie's Grange. Some physical remains can be seen easily from the summit to Silver Street and near St Marie's Grange. The route of the canal is shown on the transport map on page 105.

Public Transport of Today

The Highways Act of 1862 made possible the formation of thirteen highway districts from the three hundred parishes formerly responsible for road maintenance in Wiltshire. The 1878 Highway Act aimed to equalise the cost of road maintenance as turnpike trusts were wound up and costs which had been borne by them fell on the county. At that time, main roads were downgraded but that was not the case with any in this parish.

Road users were reporting problems in the early 1900s. In November 1909, Mrs Staples wrote to Wiltshire County Council to complain of the state of the road at Dog Kennel Farm. *'Her gardener's wife had had to wade knee deep through water to get home from Salisbury'* she said. A similar complaint came from Clarendon Parish Council the next spring and by 1911 agreement had been reached with the landowner to cut a drain to ease flooding from Brick Kiln Lane. A grant of £438 was made to Salisbury Rural District Council to pay for it. This is near the site which still floods today.

In January 1912, a 400 yard stretch of road in Alderbury was to be spray tarred at a cost of £20, in the same month the first request to the Roads and Bridges Committee for a 'danger sign' to be erected near the railway bridge at Whaddon was received. Later that year, a footpath from Whaddon to Light's Lane, along the Southampton Road, was requested by Salisbury Rural District Council, but this was deferred and it was still awaiting consent in 1914. The fact that the railway bridge at Whaddon was one of a handful of places county-wide chosen as a site for a traffic census in August 1914 may give an indication of its place in the increasingly busy road system.

In early 1921 Wilts and Dorset buses were serving Alderbury and Whaddon daily on the Salisbury to Southampton route, while carriers Hatchet and Vincent still provided local transport on several days a week. By 1923 Kelly's Directory shows that motorists and cyclists were being served by MJ Enright, proprietor of the garage. Those who did not own motor cars could hire one from him. The Three Crowns 'Hotel', (proprietor WJ Dyer), was providing accommodation for the motorist and claimed that 'omelettes were their speciality'. At Bridge Garage, Whaddon, Edwin Austin Parsons advertised his motor engineering services from 1927.

After the Road Improvements Act 1925 the county surveyor considered that the A36 Whaddon to Salisbury Road should be amongst those dealt with in the first year. However when the Trunk Road Act of 1936 was introduced the A36 was not one of the first to be included. By 1948 a sub-committee of the Roads and Bridges Committee was shown an alternative route for the A36 trunk road from Bath to Southampton which by-passed Alderbury and Whaddon. The by-pass was to start at the junction of a proposed London to Penzance motor-road at Dog Kennel Farm,

Petersfinger, following the line of the railway to Alderbury junction and rejoin the then existing trunk road in the vicinity of the electricity sub-station south of Whaddon.

In September 1951 a letter from the Ministry of Transport South Western Division in Exeter, to the Clerk of Wiltshire County Council, requested that they include a list of trunk roads in their development plan. Among others on the list was a Whaddon by-pass on the north-eastern side of the Three Crowns.

At the same time a correspondence was in progress between the Clerk to the Parish Council, FR Simpson, and the Wiltshire County Council Clerk requesting a 30 mph limit from the Three Crowns to the Green Dragon. This followed an accident on 21 November 1947 involving four cars and a pedestrian, an Alderbury woman who died eight days later from her injuries. A request for a speed limit had already been made in 1937; the new request was refused in 1948 because 850 yards of restriction already extended from south of the Three Crowns and 1,600 yards could not be granted. The scattered nature of the development, provision for light pedestrian traffic and a comparatively low accident record were also cited as reasons for the refusal. However, the correspondence was continued in 1950 by CF Moody, Clerk to the Parish Council, and supported by Mrs Edith Sargent on behalf of the Women's Institute.

The decade from 1968 saw several changes to the roads in the villages. The railway bridge near the post office was removed in that year and the road was straightened. The following year, Spider's Island roads were adopted in two stages, then during 1970-71 the railway bridge on the Whaddon to Grimstead road was demolished and Firs road, Rectory Road and Waleran Close were adopted. The Copse (stage one) and Old Chapel Close were next in 1978-79.

Meanwhile, greater changes were taking place. An Alderbury by-pass had been investigated in 1969 with a view to removing the constant stream of heavy traffic along Southampton Road, and restoring the peace and quiet of earlier times. The parish council had feared a road-widening scheme through the middle of the village, so the plan came as some relief. A public meeting helped the planners to decide on the best route for the bypass, using the line of the old railway track.

The by-pass was duly completed in 1978 and Southampton Road became C336. Where the new road crossed the summit of the old canal cutting there was some in-filling done, and councillors pressed for the rest of the canal to be filled, for safety reasons. However, the heritage and environment lobbies won the argument and the canal was left as it stands today.

When a traffic report was made in 1995 it showed that of 914 employed residents of the parish, 77% drove to work, 8% were car passengers, 4% travelled by bus and the remainder went by rail, bike or on foot. As the millennium begins, Alderbury and Whaddon are still served by Wilts and Dorset Bus Co. with about thirty buses a day and three a day on Sundays.

12

LOCAL GOVERNMENT AND PUBLIC UTILITIES

The Vestry Committee

The vestry's origin was the calling together of parishioners to discuss church business. It was basically an ecclesiastical organisation. With the suppression of the monasteries in 1547 and the lack of any consistent method of helping the poor, some parishes appointed Collectors of the Parish Alms. The first Poor Law Act of Elizabeth in 1563 made this compulsory and in 1597-98 this post was combined with Overseer of the Poor. Each year two persons were appointed Overseers to levy a poor rate and to supervise its distribution. Virtually no records of this exist for Alderbury but a number of houses in the parish have been used at various times for housing the poor and needy.

Another parish officer selected by the vestry was the parish constable. Originally the constable was an officer elected by the Court Leet, along with the offices of ale taster, hayward, pinder and other minor officials. Successive acts of parliament in the sixteenth and seventeenth centuries promoted the parish as an area for secular administration, superseding the manorial courts which fell into decay, except in respect of their right to regulate the transfer and inheritance of estates.

The Surveyor of Highways was an office set up under the 1555 Highways Act, to which parishioners were selected by the vestry. Like other secular offices the appointments were actually made by the Justices of the Peace for the County. These posts, usually held for one year, were unpaid and as they were somewhat onerous many tried to avoid them. The surveyor was required to survey the parish highways three times a year and to organise the statute labour. Each able-bodied householder or tenant was legally required to give four days labour a year; in 1691 this was increased to six days.

The vestry had always been able to levy a church rate and it was a logical step for it to impose a rate for social purposes. However in the late eighteenth century changing economic and social conditions within the country put a great strain on local poor law administration. This led to a waning of the powers of the vestry.

The cost of poor relief rose dramatically in the period 1784 to 1813, more than tripling. Eventually in 1834 the Poor Law Amendment Act changed the system and parishes were grouped into Poor Law Unions each having a shared central workhouse. Similarly, the 1835 Highways Act provided for the unification of parishes into highway districts and allowed the payment of district surveyors. In 1888 main roads, including those established by the turnpike trusts, became the responsibility of the newly-formed county councils. Meanwhile, in 1839, the County Police Act enabled counties to set up their own police forces and Wiltshire was the first to do so.

In 1894 the Local Government Act established parish councils and the secular functions of the vestries were transferred to them. Unfortunately, there are virtually no vestry records surviving for Alderbury to give any idea of the workings of the social, as distinct from the ecclesiastical, functions of the vestry.

Poor Relief and the Alderbury Union Workhouse

The problem of the poor has exercised the minds of parliaments since Tudor times. The early poor laws made each parish responsible for providing enough funds and work for its own 'impotent poor'. Parish overseers administered the system and were empowered to collect poor rates from property owners. They were permitted to send 'sturdy beggars' back to their own native parishes. However, by the nineteenth century, social and economic factors aggravated by high food prices, riots and ever-increasing costs to ratepayers, made radical reform inevitable. In 1834 the old poor laws were swept away and the new Poor Law Amendment Act came into force resulting in the national network of large union workhouses referred to above. Each union workhouse was administered by a board of guardians which engaged a paid staff to run it. The rules were regulated by a commission in London to ensure uniformity, economy and discipline. Conditions inside 'the house' as it was called, were based on the principle of 'less eligibility', that is, they were worse than those faced by the most lowly paid worker outside.

Thus, a harsh regime was put into place for almost the whole of the next century. It was designed to deter all but the truly desperate and to encourage thrift and resolution in the search for work, however badly-paid. In hindsight, to those used to the cushion of twentieth century social security, the Union Workhouse system was a black mark in English history. To those condemned to live there, it was a humiliating, spirit-destroying experience, though for many, a life-saving one.

The Alderbury Union was one of 600 unions created by Act of 1834. It consisted of the parishes of Alderbury (with Pitton and Farley), East and West Grimstead, Winterslow, Clarendon, Downton, Whiteparish, Landford, Standlynch, Nunton and Bodenham, Odstock, Homington, Coombe Bissett, Stoney Stratford, West Harnham, Milford, Britford, Fisherton Anger, Stratford-sub-Castle, Laverstock (with Ford) and The Close in Sarum.

A meeting of The Board of Guardians took place at the Three Crowns Inn in November 1835. The agenda was:

'to take into consideration the present Poor House accommodation... also to select

114

and mature a plan for a Union Workhouse'. It was reported that: *'There are two houses, one at Alderbury and the other belonging to The Close at Salisbury. Also some cottages about a mile from Downton in that parish which are occupied by these parishes respectively and are inhabited by paupers put in by the respective parishes rent free. That of Alderbury affords accommodation for eight or ten families – the cottages at Downton for about the same number and that in the Close for three or four. But in neither of these cases is there any master or mistress or any sort of regulation or discipline. In each case they are used as separate tenements by the persons inhabiting them but without paying rent'.*

Two small workhouses at Whiteparish and Downton had been found to be unsuitable for extension into the type of large institution envisaged by the Act. It was necessary to close these and all poorhouses. In Alderbury, the rectory house, next to the church (now named Court House), was the poorhouse for a short time. The location of the cottages at Downton, mentioned in the report, remains a mystery. Pairs or rows of cottages were leased by parishes from time to time for poorhouse accommodation and it is claimed that Ladies' Cottages, in Castle Lane, Whaddon, were once used in this way. Sadly, the overseers' registers of poor relief are missing but details of applications for outdoor relief were recorded in the Alderbury Union minute books. It is safe to assume that the reasons for needing help remained much the same as in previous generations. The plight of the needy makes sad reading – young widows with large families and insufficient earnings to feed them; smallpox and fever sufferers too ill to work; absconding husbands leaving wives and children to fend for themselves; children needing leg-irons; funeral expenses and so on.

It is intriguing to learn that sites at Whaddon and Clarendon were the favoured locations for the new union workhouse. A sub-committee reported:

'that after the best consideration they could... only find two places at all suitable – the one at the western extremity of Sir Frederick Bathurst's property on the knoll and a little to the west of Peter's Finger gate... (sic) the other site is at Whaddon on the Common on the north side of the turnpike road and, either on the west or east side of the Grimstead Road... the land on the west side of this land belongs to the Widows' College and is of very little value...on the other side the land belongs to Lord Radnor and partly to the estate of Mr Whitchurch...'.

At a later date both of these recommendations were rejected: Whaddon was too far from the city and the Petersfinger site was exposed to the fog and draughts of the water meadows. Eventually, the Board settled on two acres of land on the hill at East Harnham, in the parish of Britford, as the most suitable site. It was

'...free from trees and with no buildings within a quarter of a mile... and free from dampness'.

The new workhouse was finished by the end of 1836 and could accommodate up to 200 paupers. It was maintained by the rate payers of

115

the union. At that time, Alderbury had 26 rate payers, including, at the bottom of the scale, John Belstone, who owned a small house on Clarendon Road, which still exists.

The workhouse population was intentionally isolated from the rest of society. Inmates were not allowed outside without permission of the master. There was strict segregation of men and women, even married couples. Mothers were parted from their children as soon as they started in the workhouse school. Beggars or tramps were accommodated nightly in separate outbuildings and were given food in return for performing menial tasks.

Workhouse clothes were worn. A press advertisement of 1840 inviting tenders for the supply of clothes and cloths for the workhouse gives some clues as to the uniform:

'men's hats. Boys' caps... stout fustian trousers lined... men, women, girls' and boys' knit worsted hose... white and green round frocks for men and boys... women and girls' stays... chambry drabbet... light blue handkerchiefs & dark blue check ditto... dark striped linsey... house flannel... unbleached calico... stout hessian... stout blue print... fustians... drab cloths for men's coats... twilled calico... white canvas for linings... unbleached brown holland... linen check for women's aprons'.

The workhouse infirmary became a refuge for the infirm and chronically ill. At first treatment was largely ineffective, but later the medical profession campaigned for, and obtained, better quality medicines and resources. Unmarried pregnant women without any means of support came into the workhouse infirmary for their confinements. Many babies grew up in the workhouse knowing no other home until they were apprenticed and 'boarded-out'. The Board took great pains to see that each apprentice was brought up as one of the family. The regulations demanded that they should: 'learn lessons of industry, frugality and self-discipline and be brought up in the fear of God'.

Diet in the workhouse, though sufficient, was deliberately monotonous and unappetising. The day-to-day running of the workhouse was the responsibility of the master and matron. The first master was dismissed from his post in 1842 because of irregular actions regarding a legacy received by an elderly widowed inmate – and also for defrauding the Union of the expense of maintaining the widow when she was able to be independent!

The 1851 census indicates that seven Alderbury-born parishioners resided in the workhouse: a 71 year-old farm labourer, a 42 year-old widower with two sons aged 15 and 12, a mother aged 42 and her son of 14, and a 14 year-old boy.

In 1867 the Salisbury and Alderbury Unions were amalgamated. It was decided to build a new and bigger workhouse to accommodate 400 people, between the Blandford and Odstock turnpike roads. It was completed in 1879. In 1880 the name was officially changed to the Salisbury Union Workhouse. From the late 1890s life became easier for inmates as

*"fustian":
thick twilled
cotton cloth
with short
nap, usually
dyed dark
colours*

*"linsey":
coarse wool
on cotton
warp*

*"holland":
linen*

*"chambry":
strong cotton
fabric with
coloured
warp and
white filling*

*"drabbet":
drab twilled
linen used for
smock frocks*

Alderbury Union.
DIETARY
OF THE
UNION WORKHOUSE.

ORDER OF THE POOR-LAW COMMISSIONERS,
Dated the 16th day of April, 1841.

		BREAKFAST.		DINNER.						SUPPER.		
		Bread.	Gruel.	Cooked Meat.	Potatoes or other Vegetables.	Soup.	Meat Pudding.	Suet Pudding.	Bread.	Bread.	Cheese or Butter.	
		Oz.	Pints.	Oz.	lb.	Pints.	Oz.	Oz.	Oz.	Oz.	Oz.	Oz.
Sunday,	Men -	6	1½	—	—	2	—	—	8	6	2	1
	Women	5	1½	—	—	1½	—	—	5	5	2	1
Monday,	Men -	6	1½	—	1	—	—	12	—	6	2	1
	Women	5	1½	—	1	—	—	10	—	5	2	1
Tuesday,	Men -	6	1½	—	—	2	—	—	8	6	2	1
	Women	5	1½	—	—	1½	—	—	5	5	2	1
Wednesday,	Men -	6	1½	6	1	—	—	—	—	6	2	1
	Women	5	1½	5	1	—	—	—	—	5	2	1
Thursday,	Men -	6	1½	—	1	—	—	12	—	6	2	1
	Women	5	1½	—	1	—	—	10	—	5	2	1
Friday,	Men -	6	1½	—	—	2	—	—	8	6	2	1
	Women	5	1½	—	—	1½	—	—	5	5	2	1
Saturday,	Men -	6	1½	—	1	—	12	—	—	6	2	1
	Women	5	1½	—	1	—	10	—	—	5	2	1

The Guardians of the Poor of the said Union are empowered to allow to each old Person, of the age of sixty years and upwards, resident in the Workhouse, one ounce of Tea, seven ounces of Butter, and eight ounces of Sugar per week, in lieu of Gruel, for Breakfast.

Children, under the age of nine years, resident in the said Workhouse, to be fed, dieted, and maintained with such food, and in such manner, as the said Guardians shall direct; and Children, above the age of nine years, and under the age of sixteen years, to be allowed the same quantities as are prescribed in the above Table for Women.

The sick Paupers, resident in the said Workhouse, to be fed, dieted, and maintained in such manner as the Medical Officer of the said Union shall direct, who may also order (in writing) such diet for any individual Pauper as he shall deem necessary; and the Master of the Workhouse is to report such direction to the Board of Guardians, who shall sanction, alter, or disallow the same at their discretion.

J. MEARS, PRINTER, POULTRY-CROSS, SALISBURY.

Figure 12.1 Dietary of the Alderbury Union Workhouse, 1841

administrative changes and the nation's attitude towards the poor became more sympathetic. Entertainment, visits, newspapers, books, better food, tobacco and little luxuries were allowed. In the twentieth century, national insurance schemes and old age pensions were introduced leading to a comprehensive system replacing poor relief. The union workhouse system was abolished in 1930.

Mutual Benefit Societies and Medical Insurance

The bleak prospect of the union workhouse caused prudent people to save what they could for a 'rainy day'. Insuring with a Friendly Society was popular among the working class, especially during Victorian and Edwardian times. Apart from the comfort of a measure of security, these societies provided their members with some colour and excitement in life with each society having distinctive regalia, band-led parades and feasts. In reality, only the skilled craftsmen could afford the subscriptions.

In 1838 a 'Benevolent or Self-supporting Medical Institution and Benefit Club for Salisbury and the Neighbourhood' was formed with the Earl of Radnor as patron, the Bishop of Salisbury as president, and a host of wealthy trustees including George Fort of Alderbury House. Subscribers to a 'free fund' contributed a small weekly amount which provided for medicines and the attendance of a surgeon in case of sickness or accident. Each farthing of an annual subscription entitled a member to one shilling a week when disabled from work. The accounts of 1840 indicate that 161 people from Alderbury were insured by the Benefit Club.

The foundation in 1766 of the Salisbury Infirmary for the relief of the sick and lame poor gave needy people the possibility of being treated there, free of charge, on the recommendation of a doctor or benefactor. After World War I the infirmary required more funds than the hospital could raise through voluntary contributions. An old subscription list of the Salisbury Infirmary League of 1903 was reconstituted to enlist financial aid from wage-earners, especially in the country districts. Voluntary helpers collected small weekly sums from members in villages and workplaces, that is, one penny for those earning less than £1 a week; twopence for individuals over 21, fourpence for a family and twopence for the children of an unwaged widower or widow. (It must be remembered that a working man earned between £1 and £2 a week.) If a member became an inpatient in any hospital in the country, the League paid 10s. 6d. per week maintenance to that hospital. Alderbury resident,Major-General Sir Henry Everett of Avon Turn, served on the League's committee and older residents still recall some of the collectors: Miss Ethel England who rode her bicycle between stops along the Lower Road, AT Freeman (headmaster of the school) and Mrs Gumbleton, remembered as 'the lady in black'. The League was discontinued in 1948 when the National Health Service (NHS) was formed and treatment was free to all.

Another local charity, formed after World War I, was the Alderbury and

District Nurses' Association, organised by a group of local ladies supported from 'the Castle'. A nurse, who was also a trained midwife, was engaged to tend many of the medical needs in the community, and in the early days, doing her rounds by bicycle. The 'nurse's house', as it was known, was an estate cottage on Folly Lane (Yew Tree Cottage). The service was free to all villagers although contributions were welcomed. The Association was dissolved at the end of 1948 at the start of the NHS, although a district nurse lived in that same house for several years afterwards.

The Ely Trust

John Ely was born in Alderbury in August 1638, one of the seven children of John Ely, Vicar of Alderbury. In his will (1692) he left £100 to buy land, the annual rent from which was to be spent to help poor boys of the village to get started as apprentices in trade. Land purchased at Whaddon brought in an annual income of £5. The trust was administered by the Vicar of Alderbury, the churchwardens and the overseers until 1894, when the newly-formed Parish Council took over the administration and appointed trustees. The terms of the trust were subsequently altered to include 'advancement'. One payment, in the early 1980s, was to Nigel Northeast, an excellent young cabinet maker and member of a family whose name appears regularly in the annals of Alderbury. In 1992 the trust's funds stood at £230. In 1996 all of the funds were passed to a new charity, 'Alderbury Relief in Need'.

The Thistlethwaite Trust

In 1708 The Rev. Gabriel Thistlethwaite, Rector of Winterslow and Lay Rector of Alderbury, placed 10 acres of land (near Treasurers Dean Wood) in trust. The beneficiaries of the £10 annual income were the Rector of Winterslow (£2. 10s. 0d.), the Rector of Huish (£2. 10s. 0d.), and the poor of the Parish of Alderbury who received the balance. There were increases in the income over the years. The Alderbury recipients, usually elderly widows or households with large families, received their gifts from the Rector, a trustee, at Easter. Two other trustees were appointed by the parish council after its formation. Like the Ely Trust it was absorbed into the new charity 'Alderbury Relief in Need' in 1996.

The Parish Council

The Local Government Act of 1894 established parish councils, the lowest rung of local government, marking the end of church control of parish affairs. Each parish was granted powers to elect a council to administer minor matters within its boundaries. It was responsible to the next higher authority, in Alderbury's case, the Salisbury and Wilton Rural District Council (RDC).

The first council meeting was on 31 December 1894 and the elected councillors were the Rev. RS Hutchings (chairman), S Parsons (vice-chairman), E Prewett, W Hickman, G Dowty, R England, H Hatcher, J Dowty and J Newport (Clerk).

The new council first obtained the parish map from 'Squire' Fort to ascertain the boundaries of the parish and the rights of way. A major concern was the inadequate water supply that came from various springs and dip wells. The councillors engaged a water engineer to survey the possibilities for improvements but the cost involved was too high for the parish to bear. A further problem was that of the poor state of the footpaths and roadways, so gravel was purchased for the worst places.

Many celebrations were arranged by the Parish Council in subsequent years. In 1897 there were celebrations to mark Queen Victoria's Golden Jubilee. The village band was engaged to lead a procession to St Mary's Church for a thanksgiving service and then to the cricket field where a meat tea was provided for all parishioners. The meal included two free pints of beer for each man with minerals, ginger beer, and tea for ladies and children. Sports events followed and in the evening there was a torchlight procession and a firework display. There were 674 people in attendance and the total cost, raised by voluntary subscription, was £41. 0s. 3d. Similar celebrations were arranged for the coronation of Edward VII in 1902 in the grounds of Alderbury House and for the coronation of George V in 1911, in the field at Alward House – but no beer was allowed on these occasions!

In 1902, when the new Earl of Radnor made provision for an abundant supply of water within reach of all the houses, the council, in appreciation of his generosity, made plans to erect a commemorative drinking fountain at The Green. The Earl offered some of the stonework from Ivychurch Priory and suggested as architect, Mr Gambier Parry. The cost of £93. 18s. 6d. was raised by voluntary subscription and the fountain was officially 'opened' in November 1903.

From 1906 onwards, the council was alerted to the new dangers presented by the speed of motor vehicles. In some places the high banks on either side of the road made it almost impossible for pedestrians to escape the traffic, especially when 'baffled by headlamps' at night. The County Council, which was responsible for highways, resisted the repeated appeals for improvements at dangerous corners. It was not until the early 1930s that banks were cut back, pavements constructed along the main road, and corners widened and rounded near blind spots.

In 1929, the council secured ownership of the recreation ground from the Longford Estate, in exchange for the gravel pit near Pope's Bottom. Its use, in perpetuity, was to be only for games and recreations with no dwelling houses, businesses or manufacturing premises. The wooden shelter at Silver Street bus stop came from the grounds of Alward House in 1942, and was purchased from the Earl of Radnor.

In 1965, the RDC fulfilled a promise made before World War II – the erection of street name plates. By this time, there were houses on some

120

unnamed lanes. The residents of the cul-de-sac parallel to Rectory Road, chose the name 'South Way', and those who lived in the 'Lights Lane Loop', preferred the name 'Oak Drive'.

For over a century, successive parish councillors have given generously and freely of their time. Their efforts have largely gone unheralded, but due tribute is paid here for their worthwhile work on behalf of the residents.

Figure 12.2

Alderbury

Band, in front

of the The

Fountain,

c.1902

A C Maidment

third from left,

H Maidment

eighth fom left

Community Policing

For centuries unpaid parish, or petty constables were responsible for keeping law and order in rural areas. They were largely ineffective in the face of increasing crime and unrest. In the winter of 1838, theft and sheep-stealing were so common around Alderbury that Lord Radnor and his neighbours formed a small private police force to patrol the area.

Wiltshire did not have a paid professional police force until the end of 1839. It was the first county authorised by Parliament to form its own constabulary. Since then its motto has been 'The Oldest and the Best'. Before that, in 1829, Sir Robert Peel had founded the Metropolitan Police Force in London (nick-named 'bobbies' or 'peelers'). The Salisbury City Police Force was formed in 1836 and remained independent until 1944.

Wiltshire Constabulary started by recruiting 200 constables, about one for every 1,200 inhabitants, organised into 'divisions' and led by the Chief

121

Constable and eight superintendents, four of them mounted. The constables lodged and worked in the community and at 17s. 6d. a week, were quite well paid. However, the hours were long and arduous and the discipline exacting. There was a rapid turnover of personnel in the early years; in fact the first Alderbury constable served for only one year in 1840-41. Always on call and with long, late night foot patrols, they would arrange to meet with their colleagues from adjoining districts to exchange news and messages. They were provided with uniform, an oil lamp, a staff, handcuffs and a book of instructions. The familiar helmet was not adopted until 1879. Policemen had to be able to read and write to make reports but training was not available until 1855. Later in the century, the invention of the bicycle proved a boon enabling them to cover their areas much more quickly.

Figure 12.3

Victorian

policeman

In 1930 a county police station with living accommodation for the sergeant's family was built in Whaddon, next to St Mary's Hall, on Southampton Road. In 1938 a police house in Firs Road was rented by the county from the local builder, Eyres and Son of Silver Street. The Southampton Road station controlled Alderbury, Whaddon, Clarendon and Petersfinger: the policeman from Firs Road covered West Dean, West and East Grimstead and Farley. The buildings are now in private ownership. The present police station is on Grimstead Road and is open during limited hours.

Older residents recollect some of the local 'bobbies' with affection. George Hatcher remembers Sergeant Webb of Old Road, who retired to do security work at Longford Castle. Tom Dowty recalls Sergeant Titt, who never reported the boys but kept them in good order – with the edge of his cape... 'worse than a stick!'

Water Supplies

Until 1902 there was no reliable supply of water except from springs and dip wells. The water engineer engaged by the Parish Council advised sinking a well at Ivychurch, pumping water into a closed reservoir, with distribution through cast iron mains to points of supply around the area, with eight pillar fountains at convenient sites. The cost involved was beyond the finances of the parish council and nothing further was done. It was therefore a great relief to all when, in 1902, the Earl of Radnor decided to build a reservoir at Ivychurch. The Ordnance Survey Map shows an area designated as 'Pump House Plantation'. For a time the problem was eased. However, early in the 1950s, the Longford Estate decided not to undertake to supply water to Whaddon when a new estate of houses was planned. Instead, in 1952, the Rural District Council arranged for West Hants Water Company to supply piped water from a reservoir at Standlynch. After a public enquiry in 1954, it was agreed that the whole problem would be solved if the Longford mains were taken over by the RDC and piped water supplied to the rest of Alderbury. But this did not happen until 1956 when, as a consequence of a protest about the lack of water facilities from the residents of Folly Lane, High Street and the old Chapel area, the RDC obtained ministerial sanction to go ahead with the work. An old water standpipe still exists at the corner of High Street, probably left there by an oversight.

Information from the records of Wessex Water, the current suppliers, show that substantial mains were laid in 1960 to install sufficient distribution pipe-work to the established properties along Southampton Road, to the south-west of Alderbury and through to Whaddon. Further development took place in 1990 and the infrastructure was extended again in 1994 to developments to the north side of Southampton Road between Alderbury and Whaddon. In 1997 much of the spine water main was re-laid in modern plastic material with a larger diameter.

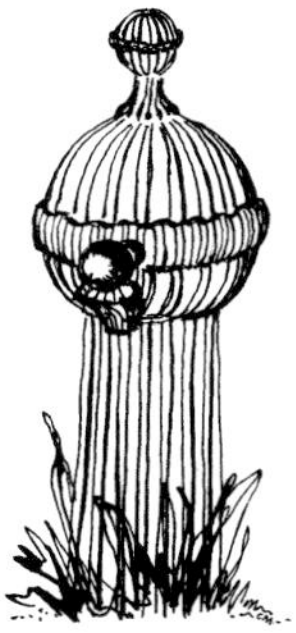

Sewage Services

The days before mains sewerage came to rural areas are recalled by Frank Moody.

'Sanitation was primitive – the "loo" was down the garden, assuming there was a garden, if not it was in the shed. A sentry box about three feet square with a platform seat about two feet high. The "classy" ones had a lower seat alongside for a child. There were many variations but all with the basic elements. A heap of soil and/or ashes was standing to cover the deposits against flies – the bugbear of all sanitation and hygiene.

An improvement to the system was a four gallon oval bucket that could be carried away under the cover of darkness and the contents consigned to the compost heap. In city and suburban areas "night soil" as it was called was collected through the night on horse-drawn vehicles and taken away and deposited on farmers' fields (by invitation). Those were the days before chemical fertilisers.'

In 1950 the Parish Council complained to the Director of Education that Alderbury School still had bucket lavatories. The Director promised that they would be cleaned out twice a week instead of once.

The provision of public sewers in this area was undertaken by the RDC but not completed until 1964. The scheme provided several kilometres of sewers with four pumping stations and connection to the Salisbury Sewage Treatment Works opened at Petersfinger in 1965.

Electricity, Gas and Street Lighting

Frank Moody writes:

'Soon after the 1914-18 war ended "Cats Whisker" wireless sets were introduced. They were so-called because the tuning contact was a single strand of electric flex wire just a few inches long inside a glass dome and operated by a tiny handle outside. The other end was jiggled against a small lump of crystal seeking a live contact. The operator was probably the only person who could hear anything and headphones were

Figure 12.4

Water pump at the corner of High Street

essential. Reception improved by leaps and bounds and it was soon possible to buy a one, two or three valve set…'.

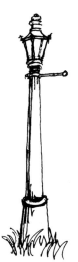

Homes had electrical power from about 1933 but at first they could be wired up only for lighting until Alderbury and Whaddon were connected to the National Grid. In 1934 the Parish Council was keen to have five electric street lights erected at the bus stops along the main road but an estimate for their installation and maintenance seemed high. The Salisbury Gas Company gave the assurance that a gas main would be laid to the village and it was decided instead to have gas lights. During World War II however, the lights fell into disuse and they were not reinstated after the war due to the expense. In more recent years, new housing developments have included street lighting and in 1997 some lights were again erected along the main road.

December 1957 saw the last supplies from the Salisbury Gas Company. After that it was supplied by British Gas from Southampton. Manufactured gas was superseded by natural gas from the North Sea in the 1970s.

12.5 Gas lamp

Telephones

Although Lord Radnor had a telephone at some time between 1897 and 1904, telephony did not generally become available in Alderbury until 23 July 1920, when a Call Office was opened by the Post Office. This would have been a telephone or kiosk, located in or near to the Old Post Office in Old Road and connected to the manual switchboard at Salisbury.

As use of the telephone grew, a Central Battery Signalling Number Two Exchange was installed, again it is believed, in the Old Post Office. This exchange comprised a manual switchboard, with an operator. It came into service on 31 March 1928, with 21 exchange lines and 24 telephone sets connected.

Between 1 April 1946 and June 1947, a Unit Automatic Exchange, known as a UAX13 replaced the manual switchboard. The exchange had, by then, a total of 81 lines with 102 telephone sets connected. It was possible for one telephone line to be shared by two subscribers on this type of exchange. This UAX equipment was modular in construction and had the ability to be extended with the addition of further units as demand for telephones grew. By now, telephones had dials and Alderbury telephone numbers became three digits long. This was the first time subscribers could dial other local and adjacent exchange numbers without the assistance of an operator. The equipment was powered from the mains, with a lead-acid battery as a backup against mains electricity failures. The exchange building was a purpose-built 'B1' brick type, located within the old timber store area off Southampton Road, where Silver Wood is now situated. The land was leased from the Longford Estate. Sometime between 1 April 1951 and 31 March 1952, the facility for subscribers to dial '999' directly was added and the exchange had grown to 115 lines, with 141 telephone sets connected. Access to the 'speaking clock' was added between 1 April 1957 and 31 March 1958 and by that year, the size of the exchange had grown to 144 lines and 182 subscribers.

The ability to direct-dial national calls was added between 1 April 1967 and 31 March 1968 when Subscriber Trunk Dialling (STD), was introduced. Prior to that all such calls were made via the Salisbury manual board. Exchange size had steadily increased to 255 exchange lines and 366 telephones.

The forecast demand for telephones in Alderbury indicated that the UAX building would be full by the end of the 1970s. As part of British Telecom's modernisation plan, it was decided to move the exchange from the leased site to a newly purchased freehold site off Junction Road. A new 'SW' type building was erected on this site and on 12 December 1978, a new Plessey non-director electronic exchange known as a TXE2 was brought into service. With this new exchange, Alderbury became a satellite of Salisbury, with telephone numbers becoming six-digit Salisbury numbers. At that time, there were 497 exchange lines and 631 telephones. This exchange had a backup stand-by generator installed within a separate engine house to supply power should the mains supply fail. A backup battery took the exchange load until the engine came up to speed.

International Subscriber Trunk Dialling was possible from 31 March 1982, by which time there were 620 exchange lines with 800 telephones connected. The TXE2 exchange equipment was replaced with a System X digital exchange during July 1989. This offered the 900 subscribers at that time the facilities and benefits of a modern digital network. These included faster, quieter connections, more facilities and, later, itemised billing. The shared service facility was not supported by digital exchanges so customers with shared lines had to be converted to exclusive working. This required the provision of some additional local cables and ducts between the exchange and the premises of some customers. The much smaller size of the digital equipment made it possible to install the new exchange within the existing building without the need for an extension. The working size of the exchange in 1999 stood at 1,300 customers.

13

EDUCATION

The Path to Literacy

Figure 13.1 The troublesome boy

This anecdote from the memoirs of Tom Prewett (1848-1944) relating to the period c.1825, gives a tantalising glimpse into what may have been Alderbury's earliest day school.

'...My father, as a boy, was a very troublesome one. His mother told me she caught him on one day bird-nesting. She took him under her arm and carried him to his Aunt, who kept a dame school in the village. My father said as soon as his mother had gone, he was told to stand on a stool, a tall paper hat with the word DUNCE written on it was placed on his head and he spent the afternoon making the other children laugh. Thus ended his schooldays...'

Wiltshire had over a hundred such privately run, cottage-based Dame Schools. Sadly, no more is known about this school or exactly where in the village it was situated.

For most poor families, low wage rates and insecurity of employment meant that education was an unaffordable luxury. A Parliamentary paper, reported in the Salisbury Journal dated 16 November 1840 said: *'Out of 121,083 couples married, one third of men and one half of women cannot write their names'*.

Yet commercial and technological advances, widespread postal communications and easier transport by road and rail required a more literate workforce able to read instructions, notices, timetables, letters, newspapers and so on.

The Anglican 'National School Society for the Education of the Poor in the Principles of the Established Church...' (1811) and the undenominational 'British and Foreign School Society' (1814) supported by Nonconformists, encouraged landowners and wealthy benefactors to provide for school buildings and teachers. From 1833 onwards, Parliament subsidised the efforts of both rival societies, with more money going to the 'National Society', despite opposition from a secular lobby which thought that the State should build its own schools.

Treasury grants encouraged a teacher-training programme (1843) and Her Majesty's Inspectorate (HMI) was set up. The Salisbury Teachers' Training College for Women was founded in 1841 by the newly formed Salisbury Diocesan Education Board (1839). Five-year apprenticeships were offered to the most able of the 13 year-old pupils as paid pupil-teachers, trained by the head teacher and examined annually by an HMI inspector. The successful ones were offered places at a training college.

It is estimated that by 1850 some three million, or three quarters of all working-class children, attended Sunday Schools offering reading and writing lessons alongside Religious Instruction, not only on Sundays but sometimes on weekdays and in the evenings.

In the 1950s a retired HMI inspector, Arnold Platts, concerned that all record of early village schools would be forgotten, collected together as much information as he could in a book entitled 'Wiltshire Schools: A Short History' (1956). In Alderbury's case his concern was justified. Prior to 1859, records are lamentably few.

Platts reports that there was

'...a day school in 1818 and a dissenters Sunday School was attended by 40 children. A schoolroom was provided in 1838, and in 1836 the two Sunday and day schools had 131 pupils, taught by a master and mistress who were paid £30 a year. Expenses were met by voluntary subscriptions and the payment of fees. The Earl of Radnor was responsible for a new elementary school provided in 1851'.

To date no more information about the earlier schools has come to light. Possibly, the 1818 school mentioned could have been the Prewett's Dame School. The 1838 schoolroom was the building we now call "The Old School" on School Hill, familiar to many generations of local children.

From 1859 more information from official sources is available. The Warburton Census, an Education Return to Parliament in that year by Her Majesty's Inspectors, investigated the provision of schools in Wiltshire. Its findings about Alderbury schools are outlined below in the order of their probable foundation.

Ivychurch Academy

'A long-standing institution in this parish, not calculated for the children of the poor or the children immediately above the poor' – Warburton.

Mr John Sopp's Academy was established around 1830 when the family moved from a school in Salisbury and leased Ivychurch House, which stood amid the ruins of the old Ivychurch Priory. John Sopp was an eminent teacher of Latin and Greek. The house accommodated at least eighteen young gentlemen aged between 9 and 15. Advertisements for the school claimed *'Ivychurch is pleasantly situated in the salubrious village of Alderbury, about three miles from Salisbury... every pupil has a separate bed'*.

From 1841 to 1847 the young Henry Fawcett was a pupil at Mr Sopp's

Academy. His biographers say that he was well-treated there. His father leased Longford Farm and Henry's diaries showed that he spent many a half-holiday there, enjoying country sports and conversing with the cottagers. This love of the country and country folk was an influence all his life. Tragically blinded aged 25, in a shooting accident, he went on to have a remarkable career in politics, becoming Postmaster General. His statue in Salisbury's Market Square is a memorial to one of the city's most famous and best-loved men.

Figure 13.2

Ivychurch House

(thought to have

come from the

school prospectus)

IVY-CHURCH.

At the death of John Sopp, in 1856, his son George succeeded him as headmaster. Only six years later, George died suddenly of a heart attack and the Academy closed, never to reopen. Many of the Sopp family are buried in Alderbury Churchyard.

Alderbury Union School

'Thirty to forty children, mixed, instructed by a mistress holding a certificate of competency, 2nd division. Mr Ruddock (October 1858) reports that the desks, furniture and apparatus are "good and efficient" and the methods and discipline "satisfactory"' – Warburton.

Although Warburton listed this school under Alderbury, it was actually situated at Harnham Hill, in the parish of Britford. It was the Workhouse School for the pauper children of destitute families of the 20 or so villages

128

that were part of the Alderbury Union, established by the Poor Law of 1834. Education was compulsory for workhouse children until they were apprenticed to a trade at about 10 or 12 years of age and perhaps boarded out.

The first School Master, appointed in 1837, was paid £20 a year and his duties were to teach the girls for three hours in the mornings and the boys for three hours in the afternoons during weekdays, and both girls and boys two hours on Sundays. There were no school holidays except for special times such as Christmas Day. Life was very restrictive, with a meagre and unvaried diet. Like the other inmates, the children were allowed no personal belongings and they wore workhouse clothes. In 1839, the Board of Guardians reprimanded the school teacher for *giving oranges to his scholars without the Master's permission*.

At first, the school was housed in the chapel but in the 1850s a new school room was built and Alderbury ratepayers shared in the cost. Inspections of the school took place regularly and were apparently favourable.

A Committee in 1874 reported on the duties of the School Mistress and her assistant. They shared four hours free time each day. They were expected to oversee the mending of 69 children's clothes in the evenings, help in the cleaning of dormitories, and take turns in accompanying pupils to church on Sundays. However, there were some compensations; the School Mistresses were entitled to an allowance of gin and wine!

Alderbury School, January 1858

*'Three rooms (1) 42 x 20 x 8¹/2 (2) 27 x 20 x 8¹/2 (3) 12 x 20 x 8¹/2 . 115 scholars, mixed, under Master (certificated) and sewing mistress who teaches the little ones in an upper room. Three pupil-teachers; desks parallel, floor boarded. Mr Hughes said "The discipline and instruction were very good." '–*Warburton.

The land on which the school was built was acquired by the Radnor Estate as a result of the Enclosure Award in 1809. Part of the mediaeval hall-house was extended to form a schoolroom: the rest of the house accommodated the master and his family. An 1838 date stone was subsequently found in the north gable. The archives of the Alderbury Women's Institute contain a statement from the Countess of Radnor, the grandmother of the present earl, that the school began in a converted barn in 1832. There is a local belief that a handsome barn was once demolished on the site. An entry in the third earl's diary, dated 31 December 1840 says, *'Visited the school at Alderbury and pleased with what I saw there'*.

The 1841 Census , though imprecise, indicates that Thomas Macintosh was the master living in the schoolhouse. (This census shows two other teachers in Alderbury – Thomas Prewett aged 39 and Martha Pearce aged 84! Could this be another connection to the Dame School?). In 1848 Kelly's Trade Directory listed John Frost and his wife as the master and mistress of 'the Alderbury National School', its new designation. Significantly,

129

perhaps, the vicar at that period, the Rev. Newton Smart, was a member of the Salisbury Diocesan Board of Education, a strong advocate of the formation of National Schools. An extension was added to the north-east corner of the schoolroom so that by the 1850s the school consisted of a large schoolroom, an adjoining classroom, and an upstairs room for infants.

Until the last decades of the ninetheenth century, attendance was not compulsory nor was it free. Pupils paid their 'school pence' every Monday morning. Sometimes, in cases of hardship, they were paid by the vicar's wife.

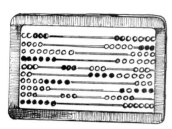

Figure 13.3

Victorian

school abacus

After the death of schoolmaster John Frost in 1851, the post went to the 18 year-old George Burden, who stayed until 1865 when he left to take up the mastership of a Salisbury grammar school. The first school log book of 1862 was started during his time. In that same year, the government introduced the 'payments by results' system. Grants to schools (including teachers' salaries) were paid according to the success of pupils in the '3Rs', tested annually by an inspector, and a satisfactory level of attendance. The classes were arranged from the seven year-olds upwards in the 'standards' of their attainment. The inspections, and the weeks leading up to them, were times of great anxiety for teachers and an ordeal for the pupils. The daily boredom of rote learning, strict discipline, and crowded classrooms that were unbearably hot in summer and numbingly cold in winter, make school life in the those days seem very unappealing.

Children in rural schools knew very little about the world beyond their own villages and gradually the curriculum was widened to include many more subjects. In 1866, Thomas Bunston was appointed as headmaster, assisted by his wife as sempstress. It was usual for the wife of the Master to teach the infants and take the older girls for needlework in the afternoons.

Absenteeism was a problem for rural schools; haymaking, beating for rabbits, potato picking, collecting acorns, child-minding and 'keeping birds from fruit' were all too often responsible for keeping pupils from their lessons. Regular and virulent epidemics of infectious diseases swept through villages and towns. Closure for weeks or even months at a time were frequently reported in the school log books. Measles, mumps, scarlet fever, typhoid fever, diphtheria, and whooping cough were chiefly responsible. In 1842, the three young daughters of the Rev. Newton Smart and his wife Frances de Bernière died at Farley within the space of one week.

Mr Bunston was succeeded in 1871 by Richard Knight, who became the longest serving headmaster, staying for 29 years and taking the school into the twentieth century. Improvements continued to be made, financed by the Earl of Radnor. In 1867 the floor of the upstairs infants' classroom was removed, leaving a gallery. A new classroom was added downstairs. In 1887, the school was improved and enlarged to accommodate more children. In

1890, to the relief of many, the government abandoned the payment-by-results system in favour of a basic grant dependent mainly on regular attendance. By this last decade of the century, elementary education had become free of charge and compulsory for children aged up to 11 (1893) and 12 (1899).

Richard Knight was succeeded in 1900 by his son, Edward LS Knight. Sadly, only seven years later, in 1907, he died aged only 47.

It was not until 1903 that a trust deed was drawn up for Alderbury School although it had been founded by the 3rd Earl of Radnor about half a century earlier, as already described. The deed confirmed that the school was let to the Vicar of Alderbury and his successors for one shilling a year for the education of children and adults of the labouring, manufacturing and other poorer classes in the Parish of Alderbury according to the principles of the National Society, and managed by a nominated committee that included the vicar, the landlord's agent and Mr Fort of Alderbury House. The school took children between the ages of 3 and 13 years and the vicar attended each week to take prayers and rehearse the pupils in the catechism in readiness for the annual diocesan inspection.

The Old

School House

window

AT Freeman then became the Head for the next 22 years until, in 1929, he retired to a bungalow in Light's Lane. In 1909, a new playground was opened and the schoolroom gallery was removed in 1911.

It was over an issue of financing cloakroom improvements demanded by the County Council in 1929 that Lord Radnor made over the lease of the school to the local authority. So, for a nominal rent, Alderbury National School became a council school.

During Mr Freeman's time, and that of his successor, Mr JW Carr, the school gained a well-deserved reputation for singing, sight-reading of music, and folk dancing. Year after year the pupils won medals, challenge cups and shields at the Wiltshire Music Festivals. It is not known what happened to the shields that once adorned the school walls.

At the beginning of World War II, in September 1939, the school hosted as evacuees the whole of Portsmouth's Lyndhurst Road Junior Boys' School and its teachers, plus some girls. If Mr Carr was disturbed when his school roll suddenly jumped from 74 to 194, he did not remark upon it in the school log book that week. The Wesleyan Methodist Chapel schoolroom was hired until the numbers reduced. Some Portsmouth boys stayed throughout the war. Although two of their teachers returned to Portsmouth one, Mr Lush, stayed on until 1944.

Among its many reforms the 1944 Education Act made provision for public education to be organised in three progressive stages – primary, secondary, and further education – with separate schools for primary and secondary pupils. From 1947 the leaving age was raised to 15. However, it was not until 22 July 1952 that Alderbury saw the end of its all-age school. From then on, pupils over the age of 11 went to Downton Secondary School or, by selective examination, to a Salisbury Grammar School. Alderbury School became a County Primary School and remained so for the next 40 years. In 1952, George Edward Murray became the headmaster and in that year the school dinner service started with meals delivered by van. New table-top desks had to be brought in to accommodate them. In 1955, tentative plans by the Local Education Authority for a new village school at Spider's Island were shelved when pupil numbers failed to justify its construction.

Around 1972, the school acquired a prefabricated mobile classroom sited at the corner of Folly Lane. Soon afterwards, in 1974, George Murray retired and Anthony (Tony) Smith was appointed to the headship. He brought with him many years' experience of teaching in New Zealand, Egypt, Malaya, Singapore, and Germany. He was keen on parental involvement in the school.

With local help and grants, the Parent Teacher Association raised enough money to build an outdoor swimming pool near the mobile classroom, for the use of pupils. Mr Smith recalls

'Our pool was built during 1979 and I remember the cheer that went up on cup final Saturday when Bobby Stokes scored the goal for Southampton that won the Cup against Manchester United. Transistor radios told the story as we beaver ed away down a large rectangular hole. Over 20 men of assorted backgrounds gave their help during summer weekends, while their wives fetched and carried. Peter Riches [the village blacksmith] made a major contribution with all the metalwork and pumping apparatus but many a hero put in hours of labour'.

Figure 13.4

Victorian

school writing

implements

Figure 13.5

The Old School

After the retirement of Mr Smith in 1987, the governors appointed the school's first woman head teacher, Mrs Enid Pope. Preparations went ahead for the implementation of the new national curriculum which came into force in 1989. At about this time, the school acquired its first computers as primary schools nationwide came to grips with teaching the new and revolutionary information technology.

A new Alderbury and West Grimstead School was becoming a reality. When Mrs Pope left in 1990 to take up an appointment in a larger school, Mrs Lesley Hall led the school for two terms, also leaving for a permanent headship elsewhere. An experienced peripatetic head teacher, Jack Copping, steered the school to its closure at Christmas 1992. In the last term, visits were arranged to the new building to meet future classmates and staff. However, as the time drew near, mounting excitement was tinged with great sadness at the realisation that, for Alderbury School, an era lasting a century and a half was at an end.

The Friends of Alderbury School commissioned a watercolour painting of the school, as did the West Grimstead PTA for their school. Fittingly, both paintings hang side by side in the new school.

Extracts from Alderbury School Log Books: 1862-1955

The log books often provide a fascinating glimpse into everyday life for the village school. Here, we provide a selection of entries, chosen as much for their intriguing look into activities which may now be forgotten, as for their actual content.

20 February 1863 Mr Burden. *'The School rather thinned in the upper classes by boys going beating for rabbits.'*

20 January 1864 *'Magic lantern entertainment in the evening. Nine boys not allowed to come, for their bad conduct towards the girls.'*

26 January 1864 *'The day so cold and dark that the children could not write on paper but did sums in the morning and singing in the afternoon instead.'*

12 November 1866 *'Rev. Hutchings... addressed the children on their duty to make a point of attendance on that [inspection] day. Absence without good reason to be visited by raising the school fees for such absent child by one penny per week for the next half year.'*

14 November 1866 *'Lady Folkestone and Miss Bouverie came to the school this afternoon. Her Ladyship heard the children sing and carefully inspected the needlework, commending some girls and blaming others. Her Ladyship hoped to see great improvement on her next visit.'*

17 November 1871 Richard Knight *'Mrs Light complained to me that teachers sometimes boxed the boys and girls ears so severely as to give them headaches.'*

133

6 December 1878 *'This is the last day of A Lewis' attendance as a pupil-teacher. A manager attended and spoke of his satisfaction at her conduct during the time of her apprenticeship and presented her, in the name of the school, with a writing desk.' [She went to Salisbury Training College].*

5 December 1879 *'Many boys late for school. Several came in after registers were marked. They had been sliding on Mr Fort's pond. Mr Fort came into school and complained of boys breaking down his hedge.'*

16 June 1884 *'Took advantage of a First Class boy being ill in school from 'smoking' to give a lesson to the class on the bad effects of tobacco especially for growing children.'*

December 1902 / January 1903: Edward Knight *'Nine weeks closure due to scarlet fever.'*

20 November 1903 *'No school on Monday afternoon. A drinking fountain opened on the Green.'*

Figure 13.6
"All the
children's gas
masks have
been
overhauled"

31 July 1912 Mr Freeman *'Holiday in the afternoon. Laying of Chapel School foundation stone.'*

26 September 1914 *'Head teacher absent from school in the afternoon. Being instructor of the local ambulance corps, he was required to accompany members to Salisbury to assist in removing wounded soldiers from the station.'*

30 October/1 November 1917 *'Outbreak of diphtheria. Two little boys died from the effects.'*

11 November 1919 *'First anniversary of Armistice Day. The King's wish for two minutes silence at 11 o'clock duly observed by the scholars in the playground, followed by the singing of the national anthem.'*

26 April 1924 *Lady Folkestone... presented to the school certificates won at the Wiltshire musical competition. Her Ladyship congratulated children on winning the Challenge Shield outright.'*

7 November 1924 *'Three of the class heard a lecture from the BBC station at Bournemouth, in the Schoolhouse.'*

25 February 1929 *'The school now becomes a council school.'*

September 1938 *Forty children went to view the excavations at Clarendon Palace.'*

4 September 1939 *'The school remains closed for a week due to the outbreak of war.'*

11 September 1939 *'The whole of Portsmouth's Lyndhurst Road Junior Boys, and some girls... have been absorbed... the ordinary timetable is being adhered to.'*

15 September 1939 *'All the children's gas masks have been overhauled... and gas mask drill taken with all...'*

8 December 1941 '...*an old pupil and a survivor from the Ark Royal came into school at 3.15 pm to tell the children of his experiences during the past three years. The children presented him with 17s 0d to replace his personal belongings. Have also sent £2. 5s. 0d. to the British Red Cross for parcels for two old scholars who are prisoners of war in Germany.*'

10 and 19 September 1952 Mr Murray '*The chief meals organiser visited and said that... 18-20 table-top desks would be supplied to replace 18 very decrepit 'tip-up' type old desks... I have blocked up about 20 'tip-up' iron standard desks so that dinners won't suddenly disappear!*'

22 July 1955 '*An historic day in the life of the school as it sees its last day as an all-age school. We attended Church for a very inspiring end of term service with farewell for Canon Clayton.*'

Log Books written after this date are not available for public scrutiny until the year 2010.

Extracts from School Memories

Before the closure of the old school, some pupils wrote to the Salisbury Journal asking former pupils for their memories of the school. Mrs Flora Lampard (née Kerly), who had been at Alderbury School during the Great War, corresponded with the children. The following extracts are from her letters.

'*Our family moved [close] to Downton midway through the war. I was between 12 & 13 years old, at the time. My three younger brothers, Gilbert, Roderick and Donald, and myself attended Alderbury School. A most dreary walk in winter time – no such thing as school buses. Mr Freeman, his wife and their son were the teachers at the time but after we had been there a few weeks, the son was called up to join the forces leaving them short staffed... they asked if I was willing to help to look after the little ones. When I reached the age of 14, my parents were asked if they would allow me to stay on for a while, they paying me a few pence a week, offering to coach me towards becoming a real teacher one day. I did it for nine months but decided it wasn't what I wanted... We took sandwiches for our dinner as in those days there were no school meals or milk. We were allowed to sit round the stove in winter. As soon as the weather changed the playground was our dining room. One good thing about that: we didn't have to brush up the crumbs!*

On very cold mornings we four each carried a hot tin. My father collected four empty tins as tall as milk bottles. He bored a few small holes in the bottom and two holes at the top of each can. Then ten minutes before leaving home, he would fill them with burning coal, clamp a lid on each and fix a long wire for us to hold them. By the time we reached school they were almost out and we were allowed to empty them on the ash pits ready to collect them on going home... There was a cane in each classroom but once you had felt it, one took great care you didn't have it a second time... On the whole, if you did as you were told, our teachers were fair.'

Memories of an Alderbury Schoolboy, 1947-54

The following are extracts from a letter written to the pupils by Michael Clarke, Senior Marketing Manager at Heinz Foods.

'In March 1947 I remember moving into a Nissen Hut on an unused Army Camp at Shute End. I didn't know at the time that we would become known as squatters and my family along with a dozen or so others were living on a camp vacated by the Americans in 1945. We were to live here for nearly two years and I was seven years old. It was from here that my first journey was made to Alderbury School. There was no transport and I walked every day in those early years... There were no school dinners and my mother would pack mine in an old Oxo cube tin, complete with a preserving jar rubber ring put around for safe keeping!

My first winter at Alderbury School in 1947 was one of the coldest on record... on one occasion we went skating on a pond not far from the school. I found some thin ice, went in, and it was nearly goodbye. But I was lucky and some of the bigger boys, George Bayford and George Gray, pulled me out. I remember the first school dinners... a van used to bring them in sealed containers and the food was ladled out, and the smell was always the same, whatever it was. Most dinner and playtimes were taken up with football during the winter, played with a tennis ball, and in the summer it was cricket. In the early days the stumps were chalked on the back of the boys' toilets, but we did progress to three wickets fixed into a block of wood. For the first four years or so, the headmaster was John Carr, a Yorkshireman. Another of my memories was the folk dancing. One tune I still remember was called Brighton Camp. By 1950, my family had moved from the camp to a bungalow with a green roof and they were to live there for the next 38 years. I remember the family elation when I was one of the pupils that passed our 11-plus exams to Bishop's School... places were limited and of the six who had passed their exams only two got a place. So, I was to stay on at Alderbury until I was fifteen.

In 1951, the football team got to the final of the under 12's cup and we played against St Osmund's at Victoria Park. It was quite an achievement for the school because we were up against much bigger schools from Salisbury and district. We did not disappoint and won the match 1-0 with Brian Ling scoring the winning goal. I still have my medal plus a photograph of the successful team.

In 1953, George Murray took over... the year of the coronation. There was a competition for a poster advertising the events of June 2nd, in the village. I was lucky enough to win ten shillings and I still have the poster today. School trips at this time were a novelty, but I do remember the coach trip to London to see the coronation decorations. From about 1953 we had lessons away from Alderbury, and once a week we would take a bus trip to Downton School to do woodwork, and cookery for the girls. I believe it was also in 1953 that the school acquired a small piece of land just above the school. It was a small field to us and hard work as we cultivated it without mechanical aids into a vegetable and flower garden. Not only that, but we built a fair sized goldfish pond as well. I remember we were all very proud of our achievement.'

A Teacher Remembers Wartime

Mrs Betty Scammell (née Coombes) was a teacher at the school during World War II.

'The school consisted of four classrooms. There was a long room divided by a screen into two sections and two rooms off this, one on either side. One was the infants' room and the other the Headmaster's room. He was Mr John Carr. I was appointed in 1940 and I stayed for four years until my husband, Henry Scammell, came home from the Middle East. There was a big 'Tortoise Stove' to heat the room but as the war went on there was a shortage of fuel and it was often very cold. There were usually about 30 children in her class. Some of them walked to school and on wet days the rails around the stove would be hung with steaming coats. The names of Barbara Riches, Jeremy Freeman, Joyce Tucker, Gladys Allen, Dorothy, Marjorie and David Dyer and the Collins family come to mind.

We had a very few books and a great shortage of paper and art materials. The Reading Scheme was the Beacon Method. Each child had to carry a gas mask to school.

When the Channel Islands were taken over by Germans, a teacher from Guernsey was sent to us and we also had evacuees and teachers sent to us from Portsmouth.

One of the managers was Sir Henry Everett... One year we planned a May-day festival making a throne from Mr Carr's high chair. What could the Queen of May wear? There was no material left in the shops. I suddenly thought of Lady Everett and I called on her on my way home. She gave me a beautiful satin nightie for our queen. This happened in the middle of the Baedeker raids, when Hitler was systematically bombing churches and cathedrals. Of course, we carried on... I can vividly remember the Tuesday afternoon when a stick of bombs fell on Salisbury. We heard this, even though three miles away! On Monday mornings, I used to sell saving stamps for the war effort. All schools were expected to do this and over the four years I collected over £2,000. Summing up my war time memories – the tragedy of a father or uncle reported missing or killed and the little ones needing lots of cuddles – my own personal life disrupted with no news at times of the whereabouts of my own young husband (thankfully he came home after four and a half years away, with no leave during that time). But it was a happy time in many ways. I loved the children and got to know the parents who were very supportive. I can truly say that being an infants' teacher in Alderbury School was a rewarding time for me.'

The New Alderbury and West Grimstead CE VA School

In July 1955 Mr Murray, the head teacher of Alderbury School, wrote in his annual report to parents *'We learn that a proposed new junior and infant school at Whaddon is being discussed'*. The dream, however, was not to become a reality until 37 years later, made possible by the Salisbury Diocesan Board of Education's proposal for a new joint school for Alderbury and West Grimstead. A site at the end of Firs Road, overlooking the bypass, was negotiated with Lord Radnor. The share the two communities had to raise was £35,000. The new Church of England Voluntary Aided school opened in January 1993: Alderbury had a Church school once again.

The first head teacher, Mr Stewart Blades, took on the immense responsibility of planning, furnishing and stocking the school in readiness for the opening. Teachers from the staffs of both schools were offered, and mostly accepted, posts in the new school. The facilities were a source of wonder to the pupils, especially those from the old Alderbury School. The extra large assembly hall was bright and airy and fitted with an exciting range of physical education apparatus such as they had never experienced before. Adjoining the hall was a modern kitchen for the preparation of school meals on the premises. There were six classrooms, each named after a British animal or bird; two library areas, a resource centre and an impressive entrance hall and corridor, all carpeted. Every classroom had computers and a cooker. Furthermore, the toilets were indoors and didn't require a dash across the playground in wet weather.

Sadly, Mr Blades fell ill and had to retire early. His deputy, Mrs Sarah Tindle, took over as acting head until the new head teacher, Mrs Jennifer Pitcher, was appointed from September 1995. Mrs Pitcher has made her own distinctive mark on the school and led the staff, pupils and governors to a very successful inspection by the Office for Standards in Education in May 1997. The inspector's report summarised the school as providing '*A broad and balanced curriculum at both key stages, encouraging pupils' personal development as well as academic progress*'.

The parent teacher association, known as the Friends of Alderbury and West Grimstead School (FAWGS) has worked hard to provide many extras, including playground tables and seats, a large outdoor play fort and a portable stage used for concerts, plays, and pantomimes. In 1998, it raised almost £5,000 as the school's contribution to a design and technology extension to the buildings. Members of the FAWGS also play a valuable part in school life in many other ways, through sporting activities, help in the classroom and as members of working parties.

The school has acquired several more computers through the voucher scheme run by the supermarket Tesco and in 1998 became one of the first Wiltshire primary schools to be connected to the World Wide Web and the internet.

The school is already being enlarged by the construction of a seventh classroom to be completed during 2000. The fellowship that exists among pupils, staff, parents, governors, and the local community augurs well for the new millennium.

14
LEISURE AND CULTURE

Sports, Clubs and Societies

Alderbury is a small village which coalesces with Whaddon. It has a rich source of social life, with something for all tastes. Many people, particularly the young, consider recreation activities in a village to be limited. However, in Alderbury and Whaddon there are over 20 clubs, societies and associations, catering for the very youngest members of the community through the 'Mothers and Toddlers Group' to activities more suited to the senior residents.

The Alderbury Singers

The Alderbury Singers is a group with a long history. The first reference to the 'Alderbury Choral Society and WI Choir' is in the report of a meeting held in 1930. However, this mentions a vote of thanks to the previous conductor for two or three years service so the Society was probably in existence as early as 1927. In 1931, and again in 1933, Alderbury won the Cup and Shield for Larger Village Choirs at the Wiltshire Music Festival in Devizes. Although 'WI Choir' had been dropped from the Society's title by late 1931, rehearsals continued in the WI hut. The entry relating to the Wiltshire Music Festival in 1933 is the last in the Minute Books until 1963, when a total of 22 members was recorded. From 1968, rehearsals were held in St Mary's Hall. The Society won the Devizes Festival Cup in 1970 and it became customary to give an annual carol concert, a spring concert, and the occasional concert for charity. The Singers entered the Devizes Festival each May, winning the cup for four-part singing in 1978. The Singers have performed many important works, including those by Schubert, Gilbert and Sullivan, Maunder, Fauré, Horowitz, Bach and Monteverdi.

The Mothers and Toddlers Group

The Mothers and Toddlers Group began after the Contact Mission in 1981, when church members visited every home in the village. Many mothers of small children were new to the village and knew of no-one to look to for any help they needed. It was decided to set up a group for mothers of under fives in St Mary's Hall one afternoon per week. A rota of older women from the church was set up to make coffee and provide advice when required. It soon became apparent that the older children were too boisterous for the babies and so the time was moved to Thursday morning when the over threes could go to Playgroup. When the Sunday School moved to the

Methodist schoolroom, the toddlers moved too. This provided them with familiar surroundings for when they started Sunday School. Eventually, the Methodists sold their building to the Roman Catholics and meetings reverted to St Mary's Hall during renovations. The church has always paid for the rent, heating etc. and members have continued to make coffee.

Alderbury Tennis Club

The present Alderbury Tennis Club can trace its origins to an evening in 1980, when a small group of villagers met to discuss the idea of building courts in the village. From the outset the Parish Council was supportive and the committee initially gained planning permission to build one court on the recreation ground, beside the bowling green. However, this met with opposition from the Cricket Club and another site was sought, this time for two courts. The Parish Council made an approach to the Earl of Radnor and by 11 August 1981 the present site next to the village green had been acquired. By March 1982, planning permission had been granted: the courts were to cost about £12,000 but there was only £223 in the bank. The committee worked hard at fund raising in the community and with grant aid from various organisations, arranged for construction in March 1983. Membership now stands at 230, including 97 juniors. A wooden pavilion store was provided in 1988 and this was replaced in 1999 by a more substantial building. The courts were resurfaced in 1992. The club holds its own tournaments and has two teams in the Sarum League. It seeks to provide opportunities for the enjoyment of affordable tennis within the community and actively encourages the young to take part.

The Friendly Club

The Friendly Club began in April 1964, when a group of enthusiasts led by the late Mrs Joyce Smith, (County Councillor) decided to start a club for the over 60s. Under the chairmanship of Leonard Bowden, Amy Rumbold, Frank Moody and Marjorie Ashford, the club thrived, increasing in membership and popularity for over 30 years. It organised trips to the seaside, gardens, the Isle of Wight and the Kennet and Avon canal and arranged mystery trips and shopping trips. There were garden parties and coffee mornings, celebrations of birthdays and golden weddings, competitions for the best handicrafts, Easter bonnets, knitting and embroidery. As the time for the church fête approached, elaborate preparations were made with much hilarity for the fancy dress competitions and the best decorated float. In October 1991, clubs from all over the South of England joined together for the Age Concern concert by the Salvation Army in the City Hall in Salisbury. At Christmas, the club's President, the Countess of Radnor, is invited to join the celebrations in the village hall with candles and crackers set out on long tables and afterwards games and carol singing. Meetings are held fortnightly in St Mary's Hall at Whaddon.

The Alderbury Players

The Alderbury Players is one of the newer groups in the village. This name, however, hides its earlier origins as the Alderbury Players group was preceded by a local drama group known as the Pepperbox Players, which was active in the village from about 1964-75. The present society began in 1991, when a group interested in the performing arts was sponsored by the Village Hall Management Committee to produce an Old Time Music Hall show. A second show called 'Between the Wars' was performed in January 1992, followed by the play 'Quiet Weekend' in May 1992. The first pantomime, 'Babes in the Wood', was produced in January 1993 in Victorian style. As the group grew stronger, it was decided to form a separate organisation independent of the Village Hall Management Committee, and The Alderbury Players was formed in May 1993, with the intention of performing two plays and one pantomime or musical each year. There have been many memorable performances over the years, including several with scripts written or adapted by local writers. The number of Players has grown steadily from 15 founder members in 1993 to over 40 now, including a significant number of young people.

The Alderbury and District Gardening Association

The Alderbury and District Gardening Association, more usually known as the Gardening Club, is another of the younger groups. It was started by Bernice Allott in 1983. Founder members included Ethel Occomore, Dorothy Stevens, Edie Sargent, George and Freda Dean, George Corben, John Cotton, Cyril and Margaret Stevens, Win Occomore, Pam Perratt and David Vidler. The Methodists offered their school room for early meetings, before the club migrated to St Mary's Hall. Increased numbers eventually dictated removal to the Bowls Club. The Club promotes good cultivation of gardens and allotments, holding meetings and lectures covering just about every possible aspect of gardening lore. It also holds shows and competitions with a high standard of exhibits, light-hearted, but judged to RHS guidelines. Competitions have included invitations to all the children in the village to grow the tallest sunflower, design a garden, or take part in the Marrow Jamboree. Another annual fixture is the summer outing, not only excursions to famous professional gardens but also visits to small private gardens nearer home. Among other events have been the successful 'Open Gardens' schemes, which many people will remember with enjoyment, with the proceeds of the first going to the New School Fund.

Alderbury Cricket Club

The Alderbury Cricket Club was one of the oldest clubs in the village, being formed in 1885. There is evidence of an earlier club in the Reading Room records of 1871. From the beginning, the clergy have played a role in the club, with Canon Hutchings being Chairman in the earliest days. In the early 1900s, the Rev. CS Weallins was both Captain and Chairman of the Club. Formal club rules were not drawn up until 1906, an early example being suspension and a fine for continued use of foul language! A number of well established village families have been associated with the Club over the years, including Dowty, Eyres, Snook, Crook, Hickman, Earney, Witt, and Bayford; there are many others, too numerous to mention. One of the highest scores recorded in the published history is 273 for 3 at Sommerton, with Tom Dowty achieving the first century for the Club. The club ceased to play during World War II, although the years immediately following the war were busy ones. There have been numerous games, fondly remembered by the residents of Alderbury and of the surrounding south Wiltshire villages whom the team played against over the years. Sadly, in 1999, through lack of support, the club was forced to close.

Alderbury Football Club

There has been a club playing in the Salisbury and District League for most seasons since 1902. Tales of keenly contested local derby matches with neighbouring villages still linger in the memories of the village residents. Home games were probably played on the land that is now the Recreation Ground and when it was acquired by the Parish Council in the 1930s, the club paid £2. 0s. 0d. rental per season for its use. In those days, the matches were always played on Saturdays as Sunday games on the Recreation Ground were forbidden. The rule was relaxed for servicemen during World War II but afterwards, was reinstated for some years.

Today, the club's ground is situated off Junction Road. The club is well supported with some 200 members drawn from a wide area. The senior teams play in Division One of the Saturday League and in Divisions Two and Four of the Sunday League.

Club competition honours include the Heseltine Cup (1950-51), the Charity Cup 'C' (1972-73), the Cook Cup (1982-83) and the Kimber Cup (1982-83).

This season (1999-2000) teams for the under-15s, under-13s and under-11s play on Sunday mornings or afternoons in the Burbage League. In 1988, the under-14s team won the League Cup. Boys – and girls – who are under 10, or under 8, play in a mini-soccer league. It is clear that for the foreseeable future, Alderbury's footballing tradition is safe.

Alderbury Playgroup

In 1965, the Alderbury Playgroup was set up in the local village hall, providing a service for the young children of the village. Mrs Ruth Stacey and the late Mrs Linda Marks held the Playgroup on two mornings per week for the cost of 2s. 6d. per session! Approximately 20 children attended at this time. All the Playgroup resources had to be stored in the cupboard at the hall: this meant that before and after each session, the equipment had to be set up and put away. This was a heavy and tiresome task but remained part of the Playgroup's daily duties until 1992. Then an opportunity arose to purchase a mobile classroom from the old Alderbury School. The move to the mobile meant that the equipment could be set up on a permanent basis. The children then had access to the surrounding outside area, which was developed into a safe apparatus play area, a garden in which the children could plant things, a wild area and a pet corner housing many rabbits and guinea pigs. Alderbury Pre-school, as it is now known, remains at this site today and continues to provide an opportunity for the three to five year old children of the village to develop their social, practical and educational skills prior to starting school. The Pre-school is open five days a week, 9.15am to 2.45pm.

Scouting in Alderbury

The group was first formed in about 1911 or 1912 with two patrols; one of the first leaders was Harold Freeman, the son of the Alderbury schoolmaster. The headquarters was originally situated in a disused gravel pit halfway between Alderbury and Whaddon and the early activities included shooting, boxing and stave drill. Lord Radnor supplied a quantity of wood logs and a log cabin was built alongside the pit. In those early days, there was great rivalry between the Alderbury and Downton Groups and there were numerous rallies and spectator events where the boys competed in tug-of-war, swimming, and trek cart drill.

With the outbreak of World War I many of the older boys and the leaders left the group to enlist in the forces. After the war the troop regained its membership, a cub pack was formed, and the following year saw Captain A Angel as the new scoutmaster. Membership of the group fluctuated over the next few years and in 1926 it seemed to have disappeared. However a new group was registered in that year: it was known as the Alderbury and Bodenham.

It appears that during 1934 the Group took off with a vengeance as both the scout troop and cub pack seems to have re-formed themselves in Alderbury, as shown by a membership of about 20 cubs in 1936. The scoutmaster at that time was Fred Laney who lived in Salisbury and each week he could be seen riding to Alderbury on his bicycle wearing his scout hat! Fred Laney was also scouter for 1st Bemerton and as a result the two groups would frequently camp together at Great Yews where they would hold district competitions. By this time scout meetings were taking place at the Women's Institute Hall in Old Road.

Following the outbreak of World War II some children from Portsmouth were evacuated to the village and eight or nine boys joined the troop. At that time much was put into the war effort. The boys used to tour the village with their trek cart collecting paper; the cart was tied behind two bikes and two boys were also tasked with holding ropes attached to it; if the cart went downhill they could act as a brake! The collection round also covered Nunton and Bodenham and the paper was stored in a small shed at the bottom of Tunnel Hill where the girl guides sorted it and once sold, the proceeds were split in half.

It is recorded in the Scout Association Annual Census for 1945 that a group existed in Alderbury; but in a history of the district written in 1968 to mark the Diamond Jubilee of Scouting in Salisbury and South Wiltshire attempts to restart a group in Alderbury were described as unsuccessful. We must assume that no scouting took place here between those years and it is known that efforts continued to be unsuccessful until 1982. In October of that year the present group was begun – this time with a cub pack. The ten founder members were: Gary and Stephen Alder, Neil Armstrong, Lee Berry, John Fay, Raymond Hunt, James Sackley, Ian Sheppard, Tom Starks and Martin Studley. Meetings were held in the Sunday School room at the rear of the Methodist Chapel (now the Catholic church) but by early 1984 the pack had outgrown the space and the Guides generously agreed to allow the cubs to use their hut.

The green and purple scarf was chosen to symbolise the bond between 3rd Salisbury (who wore purple), and Alderbury. Originally the Alderbury scarf was scarlet. The group has grown and flourished since then. A scout troop, a beaver colony, and a venture scout unit were started during the following fifteen years when girls were welcomed into the venture unit and to the group for the first time. The membership returns for the year ending January 1999 show 55 boys and ten leaders made up the group 88 years on.

Guiding in Alderbury

The first guide company in Alderbury was formed in 1911 by Lady Katherine Pleydell-Bouverie. In 1916, Lady Katherine departed to do war work and the company held together as best it could. In 1917, Miss J Osmond was running the guide company, with 18 guides and one brownie 'six'. By 1921, the guide company was taken over by Lady Elizabeth Pleydell-Bouverie (Lady 'Betty').

The Company camped each year, took part in county rallies, divisional competitions and a parade in the Cathedral. An annual event was an 'entertainment' in the WI hut in Old Road, to raise money for different causes.

In 1929 a ranger patrol was formed for the older girls, and in the same year they visited Paris. The guides celebrated the coronation in 1937, joining the whole village for festivities in Alward House after a service in St Mary's church. They also took part in a parade in the Cathedral. Whist drives, dances and the 'Entertainment' continued as the years passed, and in 1940 eight guides managed to camp for five days in Lady 'Betty's' garden, having fun despite war-time rationing and the occasional air raid warning. By 1941, the guides were growing vegetables as part of their war-time activities and several evacuees joined the company. Carol singing was held at Christmas in aid of the BBC's 'Spitfire Fund'. In 1948 Sheila Clarke gained the 'Queen's Guide' award, the first of many to be earned by members of the Alderbury Company. Their camp in the Isles of Scilly in 1951 was the first of numerous visits. Other overseas trips included Denmark and Sweden, Switzerland, Eire, and Austria.

The company celebrated its golden jubilee with a party at Longford Castle. Lord Folkestone presented the guides with a site of their own at the timber yard (now Silver Wood). Their new HQ was opened by the Countess of Radnor in 1970. The Company's diamond jubilee was celebrated in 1971, at Longford Castle.

In 1973, a seat on The Green was presented to the village to commemorate 60 years of guiding in Alderbury.

At the millennium the company continues to thrive. Its headquarters is now sited in Junction Road. Despite changes, the company still promotes the basic philosophy of guiding, started all those years ago, and is still a favourite with young girls in the village.

The first Alderbury brownie pack was registered on 7 April 1922, with Lady Pleydell-Bouverie as 'Brown Owl' (leader). The activities of the brownies today are much the same as they were in the 1930s, despite changes to the uniform and to presentation. A 2nd Alderbury pack was started in September 1998 to meet demand. Over the years there have been many Brown Owls, Tawnys, Snowys and even a Fluffy Owl!

There was eventually pressure to form a unit for the younger children and the 1st Alderbury Rainbow Guides came into being under the leadership of Barbara Riches. The first meeting in Alderbury was held in July 1990, with 15 girls taking part. They chose green tabards as their uniform. Like other members of the Guide Movement, Rainbows make a Promise. The ethos of the Rainbows is to have fun and they take part in a wide range of activities both indoors and out; exploring, sharing and discovering, painting, drawing and making things. They have their own adventures and also learn to be kind and helpful to others, sharing news in 'Rainbow Chat'! They take part in Christmas plays, raise money for good causes, attend Division fun-days and, during Easter holidays, meet with the Wilton Rainbows.

In 1996, the Rainbows took part in the South West Region's 'Octopus Challenge'. The Rainbows celebrated their national tenth birthday in 1997, marking the event by raising money for the Rainbow Trust, saved in rabbit money boxes. In 1999 there was another challenge from the South Western Region, the 'Bee a busy body' challenge, with ten elements, each to do with part of the body. The commemorative badge for the Region, a bee with flowers, was designed by the Alderbury Rainbow leader, Barbara Riches.

Sunday School

It is not clear when Sunday School began in Alderbury, although the early years are discussed elsewhere in this volume, in relation to education.

145

However in the 1950s it used to meet in Alderbury School near the church, and there were two or three classes. Christmas parties were held in the NAAFI Hut and on Good Friday members went to Ivychurch Woods to pick flowers with Lady Radnor. In the 1960s, the Sunday School met in church and also in St Mary's Hall in Whaddon. The children attended the nearest place to where they lived. In the early 1970s the two Sunday Schools combined and met in St Mary's Hall. In the 1980s the Sunday School grew significantly in numbers, so that as well as St Mary's Hall the children used the Methodist Chapel, continuing to do so when it became the Roman Catholic Chapel. For a brief spell meetings were held in the village hall, whilst building works were going on at the Chapel – you can't fit 80 children into St Mary's Hall!

During the 1980s, the Sunday School became affiliated to the Church Pastoral Aid Society and the groups became known as Scramblers, Climbers, and Explorers. Teaching material was changed to that of the Scripture Union. Between the late 1980s and the mid-1990s, ecumenical holiday clubs were run in Holy Week. Since the 1980s the Sunday School has joined the rest of the Church Family once a month for the Family Service. The Sunday School was run for over 20 years by Miss Gabrielle Hunt, who stood down in 1998.

The Mini-Songsters

The Mini-Songsters group was formed in Whiteparish in 1983. There was already a group organised by the parish church to introduce pre-school children to the Christian faith. It provided an opportunity to learn through singing simple hymns and choruses. However, when school age was reached, all this ceased so a group was started named 'Whiteparish and District Mini-Songsters', with the objective of encouraging children to sing. Given suitable encouragement it is likely that any child can sing and there has been ample opportunity, through the Mini-Songsters, to confirm this. Today, the group meets on Saturdays, in Alderbury. The aims remain the same – to teach children to sing from an early age, using secular as well as religious music. The group has sung in churches, nursing homes and at the Salisbury Young People's Festival of Music. There, twice, it was invited to sing at the winners' concert. One of the members was amongst the first girls to be accepted into the Salisbury Cathedral Girls' Choir; others have become useful singers in church choirs. In 1998, there were 20 members. The children work hard, but the aim has always been to make singing fun.

The Alderbury Bowls and Social Club

The club began in 1932 with a game of 'short ends' on the front lawn of Bill Snook's Alderbury home. Bill, a footballer of some repute, was taken with the game of bowls and he persuaded some like-minded residents to form an action group. The Parish Council gave permission for a corner of rough

146

pasture on the Recreation Ground to be developed. The founder members spent 1933 digging out bracken, constructing banks and ditches and buying turf for a 4-rink green. The first AGM was held on 18 October 1933 in the old Reading Room. Rules were adopted and a subscription was agreed of £1 to cover the development years of 1934-36. Thirty members enrolled in that first year. Interestingly, a ladies' section was discussed at this first meeting but it was not until 1970 that its formation came about.

Figure 14.1

Bowls

The formal opening of the green was a match on the 16 May 1934. The Countess of Radnor was invited to bowl the first jack. During World War II the green was closed. By 1945, bracken and a variety of weeds had re-established themselves. It was not until 1948-1950 that, by tremendous effort, the playing area was re-established. In 1953 the Parish Council granted more ground to make the club a full sized one with two extra rinks. On 11 April 1974 a new pavilion was officially opened. The club has won the Salisbury and District League for a record number of times. In 1983 it celebrated its Golden Jubilee and was honoured with a visit from the English Bowling Association, an occasion the founder members would have enjoyed. In 1999, the club received further accolades after the first team won the league title for the fifth year in a row, beating its nearest rivals (Salisbury I) by some 60 points. Altogether, in the 19 years from 1981, the club has won the league 12 times and has been runners-up on five occasions.

The Women's Institute

The Women's Institute Movement was founded in Canada in 1897, to improve and develop the conditions of rural life by providing a centre for education, social intercourse and activities.

In 1915 the first Institute in the UK was formed. Alderbury branch dates from 1919, when the Countess of Radnor became the first President. Initially, meetings were held in the Reading Room and from 1920, in an ex-army hut erected alongside. The first activity was a welcome home concert for those who had fought in World War I. Apart from traditional 'jam making' subsequent activities included talks and demonstrations, competitions, produce shows and a stall at Salisbury market. Fund-raising for charity, the hut and a proposed village hall was continuous.

By 1932, every institute was affiliated to the National Federation. This enabled the movement to voice its opinion to government on matters of moment, following resolutions, discussions and votes at every level.

In 1939, the hut became a school for evacuees. Institute meetings and activities took place in St Mary's Hall and the chapel schoolroom in Folly Lane. The WI helped with evacuees, knitted garments, preserved fruit and cooked for the Home Guard. In April 1945 the hut was returned to the WI where they remained until 1964, when they moved to the village hall.

The Institute continued to add to its range of activities. It spawned a drama group and a writer's group, instituted a village scrap book, published a short History of Alderbury, and actively supported the movement's own College of Education.

Today, the Alderbury WI holds monthly afternoon meetings. It celebrated its 80th anniversary in 1999. What would the founder have made of computers, lasers, space travel and microwave ovens?

The Youth Club

The Youth Club has had a phoenix-type existence with new groups arising from the ashes of the old. First founded in 1958 by Mrs Clayton, the vicar's wife, and Jack Mouland, it met in the Reading Room. This club eventually met its demise.

At a meeting of the Trustees of the Reading Room in 1971 it was stated that the vicar was anxious to set up a youth club on the premises. The Trustees turned him down on the grounds that a youth club was not a permitted use of the room by the Act under which it had been set up which stipulated that reading rooms purposes were to be literary, scientific and educational. One cannot help feeling that the Trustees were using this as an excuse. It ignored the fact that the previous youth club had met there and moreover during the long history of the Reading Room there had been many references to billiards, darts and table tennis – at one time it had three teams in the Salisbury and District Table Tennis League. The Youth Club went to the Village Hall and bought its own equipment! This club too, eventually closed.

The most recent reincarnation of the Youth Club was in 1984 under the name of The Way Club. This lasted until 1994 when it closed due to its being unable to find people prepared to run it. At the time of writing (2000) it is understood that there have been further discussions but so far the phoenix has not emerged from the ashes!

The Alderbury Wives

A Young Wives' Group began in 1955, started by Mrs Clayton, wife of the Rev. Wilfred Clayton. The six founder members first met for afternoons in the old Reading Room and later monthly, in the evenings, in each others' homes. Since then, the group has grown rapidly and there are now over 50 members. The venues for meetings are St Mary's Hall and the Bowls Club. During the 1980s, the name was changed to The Wives' Group in order to include all women. From the beginning, the group has been associated with the parish church, with first the Vicar, and later successive Rectors, as Honorary Chairmen; but it is not exclusive to churchgoers. The group assists with floral decorations in the church at Christmas, Easter and Harvest. It supports many village activities too, providing teas at the annual village fête. Each year, a programme of talks and social activities is arranged. Husbands and friends are invited to skittle evenings, theatre visits, and other outings. The group has adopted Christian Aid as its main charity and each May has a successful fund-raising event. Many members have loyally served on the committee and some have taken a turn as leader. The continuing success of the Group owes much to the enthusiasm of Brenda Blake and Jean Walters, both of whom have willingly taken on the chores of office over long periods. Meetings are held on the first Wednesday of each month, and the Group welcomes new members, especially the younger women of the villages, so that the success of the Group may continue in the third millennium.

The Mothers' Union

It is believed that the local branch started about 1910. A parish magazine of 1911 reported that the 'Women's Union' held a meeting at St Mary's Church with tea afterwards at the Vicarage. The WU was another name for the Mothers' Union at that time. The branch's written records have survived only from 1935. The 1936 accounts record the cost of £4. 15s 0d. for making a new banner and pole. During the difficult days of World War II, attendance faltered. In 1943 it was resolved to continue meeting on alternate months. After the war membership increased and monthly meetings were resumed and have continued ever since. Mrs Edith Sargent, Mrs Lily Hayward and Mrs Ida Bunce have all been members for over 50 years. The old banner was replaced in 1995. All members contributed to its making and a list of their names was concealed on the inside.

The MU is a Christian organisation, started in 1876 by Mary Sumner, the

wife of an Anglican Rector. It brought together Christian women from all
stations in life, working to strengthen marriage and family unity. This vision
is still reflected in the mission of the world-wide MU movement today,
which is based at Mary Sumner House in London. In recent years, the
Alderbury branch has initiated and supported several projects. These
include providing gifts for children of the parish suffering long illnesses or
traumas, initiating the loop and sound system in church, and collecting
gifts each Christmas for the women's refuge in Salisbury. It organises a
weekly prayer group which is open to all. Members meet on every fourth
Wednesday in the month at 7.30 pm, usually in St Mary's Hall. Each year a
committee arranges an interesting programme with speakers, discussions,
services, outings and a Christmas party. New members, especially 'young
mums' are welcomed most warmly.

The Small Holdings and Allotment Association

It is believed that prior to the 1908 Smallholdings and Allotment Act, Lord
Radnor had allowed villagers to use some of his land for grazing and
growing food. Until the Enclosure Act, most of it had been on Alderbury
Common. Nearly all cottages had gardens and enough space to keep a pig.
Family cows would have grazed on the Common. The Act required all local
authorities to provide plots for the labouring poor at very low rents. The
Alderbury Smallholdings and Allotments Association is presumed to have
come into being around that time. It still bears that title, although the
smallholdings were all withdrawn when, in 1965, plans for the by-pass
affected those at Ivychurch and Junction Road.

There were smallholdings or allotments in Lights Lane, Junction Road,
Ivychurch, High Trees Plantation, Chapel Ground (which covered both
Folly Lane and High Street), Clarendon Road, Grimstead Road, Spider's
Island and land adjacent to the Three Crowns at Whaddon, near to Rectory
Farm, and along Castle Lane. In the 1960s some people were still taking
their produce to Salisbury market on the bus. Gradually, over the years,
plots were sold off for housing. In 1929, a plot in Lights Lane was used 'to
build a house for the schoolmaster'. This is the house now known as
'Swinfen'. In 1988, the allotments along the High Street, formerly
belonging to the chapel, passed to the council who receive the rents
although they are still run by the Association.

The Pig Club

The Pig Club seems to have been a great success, run by a very able
committee. But the only records are in old Parish Magazines.

In January 1901 there was a good attendance at the Quarterly Meeting.
The secretary reported that 50 pigs had been insured in 1900.

In March 1901 the Alderbury, Whaddon and Petersfinger Pig Club held
its Annual General Meeting, where the accounts were presented.

150

RECEIPTS	£	s	d	EXPENDITURE	£	s	d
Balance in hand	20	12	7	Club expenses and			
Hon. Members' subs	1	5	0	compensation for lost pigs	6	14	1
Members subs	2	11	6	Balance in hand	23	15	6
Quarterly new members' fees		13	0				
Insurance – sows		11	0				
193 pigs	4	16	6				
TOTAL	30	9	7	TOTAL	30	9	7

The Honorary members mentioned above were: Canon Hutchings ten shillings; Mr Hickman (Alderbury) five shillings; Mr Hickman 2s. 6d.; Mr A Aylward 2s. 6d.; Mr C Aylward 2s. 6d.; Mr Sutton 2s. 6d. The total was thus £1. 5s. 0d. The Committee members were re-elected. The June 1901 quarterly meeting was well attended and most subscriptions were paid up. One hundred pigs had been insured in the last quarter, but £4 had been paid out in compensation for the death of pigs.

The Alderbury and District Royal British Legion

The present Branch of The Alderbury and District Royal British Legion was formed on 21 September 1921. As there is no minute book recording the formation, the location of the meeting and the names of the officers are not known.

It would appear that over the years the membership fluctuated from something in the region of 174 to its present membership of 61. The early days saw activities such as tug o' war, darts and concerts. It is recorded that smoking concerts were enjoyed by the members at various times. The meetings were held in the John Barleycorn (East Grimstead), The Hook and Glove and The Farley Reading Room (Farley), and the Cadet Hut, the Reading Room and the Green Dragon (Alderbury), amongst other places. Now members meet at the East Grimstead Reading Room.

There was always an annual dinner of the Branch. Parades of the Branch Standard over the years bears testimony to the enduring image of the British Legion. Although the Branch was formed in Alderbury, it also incorporates in its membership Pitton, Farley, the Grimsteads, and people from outside the area. It is noticeable that the branch is largely made up of people who saw service in Armed Forces during World War II, with a sprinkling of younger persons.

Every Remembrance Sunday the Branch requests that it be allowed to parade and take part in the services, in rotation, in Alderbury, the Grimsteads, Pitton, and Farley C of E churches. The Branch has been selected to be represented on occasions at the annual Royal Albert Hall Festival of Remembrance. The present standard bearer, Will Northeast was in attendance in 1997 and the late Ken Whitcher also paraded the Branch

Standard in 1981. He was awarded the Legion's highest award in 1994, a Gold Badge, for 41 years service. The Legion is reviving and extending its association with local schools.

The Reading Room

In 1870, a public meeting upheld the need for a Reading Room and Working Men's Club. The Earl of Radnor and Canon Hutchings were both supporters of a scheme that would give local working men free access to books and newspapers. This was 20 years before a public library was established in Salisbury.

At first the Reading Room premises were in the former Old Goose Inn in High Street where two rooms were rented from Mr Newton Bungay. The rules were quite strict. Members had to be of good moral character and anyone using bad language, smoking, or arriving in an intoxicated state would be fined or even expelled. Chess, draughts, dominoes and other approved games could be played but not cards. The subscription was 4d per month and the rooms were open every day, except Sundays, from 12 noon until 10pm.

The first Annual General Meeting minutes of 1871 reported a successful beginning with good attendance. There was a library of 141 books 'both useful and entertaining', and members had a choice of three daily papers and four weekly ones. A cricket club had been formed and had had a very successful season. The club continued on a successful path. Smoking was eventually allowed in the 'lower' room and 'Illustrated London News' and 'Punch' were added to the reading matter. It was noted that two members had to be fined for disorderly conduct and the breaking of a bookcase!

The records inexplicably ceased between 1873 and 1910. They resumed to record the death of the founder, Canon Hutchings. In the meantime the Reading Room had acquired its own premises on Old Road, a gift to the parish from Canon Hutchings on land specifically provided for the purpose by the Earl of Radnor. The building was of timber construction and contained a lobby, two rooms and an attached caretaker's cottage.

By 1910 the most successful activities were recorded as billiards – and cards! A dart board and a table-tennis table were soon acquired. There were regular whist drives and annual outings by train.

During World War I numbers reduced as men went off to military duty but a sufficient number carried on as best they could. A company of Royal Engineers working in Clarendon Forest was allowed free use of the facilities and a smoking concert was arranged for its members. However, an Australian unit working on the road in the area, was refused permission to use the room for a dance. By 1920, and the 50th anniversary, membership had increased to 54, a good number for a small village. The club was still for men only. A suggestion that women might join an annual excursion was, after lengthy discussion, turned down. In 1935 electric lighting was installed.

During World War II the Reading Room was taken over for military purposes. A great deal of damage was done, and afterwards compensation was received from the War Office. Membership in 1948 was still good but after that it gradually declined. Club nights were eventually reduced to twice a week and then to once a week, to save money.

By 1965 only the committee and two other members remained. A decision had to be made about closure because of the capital expenditure that would be needed to modernise the attached caretaker's cottage. Thus, after more than a century of use, and after all the legal details had been sorted out, the Reading Room closed for good. The land reverted to the Longford Estate and the remaining funds were transferred to the Village Hall Improvement Fund.

Figure 14.2

The Reading Room and Women's Institute Hut, c.1978

The Village Hall

A public meeting in 1933 established the urgent need for a village hall and consequently a committee was formed and a building fund was set up. The Earl of Radnor offered a site that was part of the old gravel pit opposite Old Road, and some timber to build it. Before the project could get underway World War II intervened, in 1939, and plans had to be shelved.

For several years after the war, building materials were under strict government control because of the damage and destruction to property nation-wide. In the early 1950s it was decided to proceed with the project

153

using a local firm, REEMA Limited, who were manufacturing pre-cast concrete sections for council houses and other buildings, including village halls. By this time the original proposed site seemed inappropriate with the increasing traffic on the A36 and the population increase in Whaddon. It was eventually decided that a corner of the recreation ground, which the parish now owned, on the south side, and adjacent to the Bowls Club, was the most suitable. It also had room for car parking. Fund-raising, a grant, voluntary help in clearing the site and much hard work enabled the building to be completed in 1959 at a cost of £3,500. Improvements and repairs have taken place over the years, the most recent being in 1998 when the toilet area was extended and modernised. The hall is well used and a great asset to village activities. With the addition of the Social Club it has become the social centre for both Alderbury and Whaddon.

The Alderbury Village Hall Social and Sports Club

The Alderbury Village Hall Social Club was founded in March 1976. The club's objectives are: *'To provide amenities for members and to raise funds for maintenance, improvements, extensions etc. of the Village Hall'*. In October 1976 a licence was granted to serve alcohol at club meetings in the Village Hall at Sunday lunchtimes. In April 1978 work commenced on a club building on adjacent land owned by the Parish Council and leased to the Trustees of the Village Hall. Club activities were transferred to the new building in July 1979.

The Social Club was financed and built by the members with the aid of various grants. An equivalent sum was subsequently given by the Social Club to the Village Hall Management Committee (VHMC) as a contribution to the cost of car park development and redecoration of the hall. The small gap between the two buildings was enclosed and a communicating door constructed to provide controlled access on specific occasions permitted by the licensing laws. Today the Social Club is a thriving and financially viable social asset to the village. It has over 300 members and employs a full-time steward. Teams of members are active participants in darts, pool, and cribbage inter-village leagues, and there are regular and seasonal entertainments. The Alderbury VHMC continues to exercise a measure of control by being constitutionally represented on the Social Club Committee and by levying a rental that achieves a balance between the club's two main objectives. In October 1994, the name was changed to the Alderbury Village Hall Social and Sports Club.

The Parish/Village Magazine

It is sad that so few of our old parish magazines have survived. In a unique way they mirror the life of the locality, allowing us reflection not only on the changes in social customs and attitudes, but also on those that remain unchanged.

154

Probably, the first parish magazine was in 1893, although no copies have been found. The county record office at Trowbridge has a single copy from each of the years 1898, 1911 and 1923. There are photocopies of several magazines from 1901. The front cover shows a photograph of St Mary's church and the editors were the vicar's two daughters. In 1901 there were 125 copies sold each month for one penny each, the cost subsidised by the vicar and some local benefactors. There were reports about organisations that are no longer in existence, such as the Band of Hope, the Church Lads' Brigade, the Alderbury Brass Band, the Unionist Club and the Pig Club. The March 1901 edition, fittingly bordered in black, contained a description of Queen Victoria's funeral. From a local history point of view, the 1911 and 1923 magazines are not nearly so interesting. Parish news was confined to the inside and back covers with illustrated inserts from religious societies filling the rest of the pages; by 1923 the cost had doubled.

During the 1930s some older residents remember the Rev. Starling's news sheets containing notes about the history of Alderbury. After that, publication of any parish news seems to have ceased, probably due to wartime restrictions.

However, in the early 1960s Mr Frank Moody, former Clerk to the Parish Council, recalls that Councillors were enthusiastic about having a *village* magazine. They believed this would help to unite the people of Alderbury, Whaddon and the surrounding area. The Rev. Christopher Pooley agreed to be the first editor. Thus, in 1964 'The Fountain' was begun and continues successfully to this day. The striking front cover illustration was the work of Harold Freeman, a teacher at Bishop Wordsworth's school and a local resident. Subsequent editors have been Mrs Sylvia Wheble, the Rev. Geoffrey Rowston and currently, Mrs Jane Copley. They have always been assisted by teams of hard-working volunteers who now print and distribute 700 magazines every month.

In such a rapidly changing technological age, one can only guess at the form our village magazine might take in future decades. Will we all log on to the internet to find our own Fountain World Wide Web site? Only time will tell.

detail of writing from the minutes book of The Reading Room

15

THE PEOPLE OF
ALDERBURY AND WHADDON

Isobel, Dowager Countess of Radnor

Although Longford Castle is not within the village boundaries, the family of Lord Radnor has always employed a great many people living in the village, has always helped and supported its employees and taken a great interest in the life of the community. In 1999, we mourned for Isobel, Dowager Countess of Radnor, well known to us all and much respected for many years.

She was born in Hertfordshire, the daughter of Colonel Oakley, on 6 September 1908. She had been married to Richard Sowerby of Lilley Manor, Herts, who died in 1939. They had no children. In 1940, she married William Pleydell-Bouverie the seventh Earl of Radnor, becoming his second wife.

Longford Castle had been used by the military during World War II. Unfortunately, soon after the military left, a fire gutted the Victorian part of the castle. It did not reach the Elizabethan part and the wonderful art collection. Lord and Lady Radnor set about restoring the castle to its former state. Lady Radnor was particularly interested in Victorian furniture, the gardens and the bird life on the River Avon. When the castle was opened to the public in 1956 it was a delight, with interesting Oriental fowl living in the grounds.

Lady Radnor was president, vice-president, chairman, or patron of numerous local organisations; Salisbury Community Healthcare Council, The Nurses' League, Salisbury Museum, youth clubs, the Girl Guides, Beekeepers (she kept bees herself), the RSPB. She was the first President of the Wiltshire Trust for Nature Conservation. Nationally, she was Vice-President of The Royal College of Nursing for 17 years. Lady Radnor was also interested in the welfare of women in prison, particularly those who gave birth there or were pregnant.

She was a member of the Women's Institute, being at one time President of the Wiltshire Federation, and for a long time President of the Alderbury Institute. Her lifelong enthusiasm for embroidery led to the completion of the famous Pleydell-Bouverie tapestry carpet.

Her husband died in 1968 and was succeeded as the Earl of Radnor by his eldest son, Lady Radnor's stepson. She herself had one son, Richard Pleydell-Bouverie, who became High Sheriff of Hertfordshire. As Dowager Countess, Isobel moved across the river to live at 'Avon Turn' in Alderbury. This house stands close to the river where she watched the birds through her binoculars, particularly a rare Montagu's harrier nesting nearby. With her death Alderbury lost a charming friend. She would have been most enthusiastic about the village history project.

The Fry Family and the Salvation Army

Charles Fry was born in Alderbury on 30 May 1838, son of William Fry, a journeyman bricklayer. He was registered at birth as William Charles Fry but known subsequently as Charles William Fry. Converted at the age of 17 in a Sunday evening prayer meeting at the Wesleyan chapel in Alderbury, he soon became a local preacher. He played the violin, cello, piano and harmonium, led a small orchestra at the chapel, and formed a brass band there for special occasions. He also played solo cornet in a local military band. In the 1871 census he is recorded as being a gamekeeper, living with his young family in Clarendon Road 'near Road Gate'. He also worked as a bricklayer like his father and later established his own business in Salisbury as a builder.

In 1878 the Salvation Army (or Christian Mission as it was then called) started to hold meetings in Salisbury and, as had happened elsewhere, its members were attacked by mobs as they preached in the market place. Charles Fry and his three sons, sympathising with them, went to their rescue and linked up with the movement. The four Frys all played brass instruments and soon the quartet was standing in the market place, accompanying the singing, and thus, the Salvation Army's first band was born.

It was soon brought to the attention of the Army's founder, William Booth, and he visited Salisbury to assess this innovation. Although he recognised immediately the value that bands could be to the Salvation Army, he proceeded cautiously by inviting the Frys to accompany him to special campaign meetings around the country. This experiment proved so successful that the decision was then taken to add brass bands to the methods used by the Salvation Army to attract people.

Charles Fry was the Army's first bandmaster. He moved from Salisbury to London with his family in 1880 where they joined the staff of the headquarters, continuing to assist in meetings as a brass or string quartet. He wrote a number of songs which appeared in 'War Cry', the movement's magazine, in 1880 and 1881. Perhaps the most famous of these are 'I've found a friend in Jesus' and 'Come, thou burning spirit come'. He died shortly after, in 1882, and is commemorated by a plaque in the cloisters of Salisbury Cathedral.

Of his three sons the eldest, Frederick William Fry, also went on to achieve fame in the Salvation Army. He was born in Alderbury on 3 July 1859 and as a boy he played a cornet in the Wesleyan Chapel orchestra there. By the age of eight he played the harmonium. When he was 14 he went to work in Whiteparish but after about four years he returned to the family home, which by then was in Salisbury, to work with his father in the building trade. He helped form the Salvation Army's band with his father and brothers in 1878 and toured Britain extensively with them until his father died. He continued travelling on a number of musical campaigns and in 1883 he was appointed to the Army's newly formed Musical Editorial Department, preparing and typesetting band music. For a time he was William Booth's private secretary. In 1891 he was appointed Bandmaster of the movement's International Staff Band.

Like his father he wrote a number of hymns of which probably the most famous was 'In the Army of Jesus we've taken our stand'. After a period in Canada he returned to England and worked for many years in the Town Clerk's Department in Gillingham, Kent where he died in 1939.

Roy Pitman: a Naturalist at Home

Alderbury has a surprising variety of flora and fauna and none knew this better than Mr Roy Pitman. Born in Salisbury in 1905, he spent his entire life studying natural history, carefully recording his observations in his diaries. Although he travelled the world and wrote in numerous specialist journals, he is perhaps best remembered in Alderbury for his 1984 book 'A Naturalist At Home', about wildlife in Wiltshire, particularly around Alderbury where he once lived. He was sometime editor of Wiltshire Natural History and lectured widely. He made a memorable appearance on television in 'Kite's Country' and advised on the well-known film 'The Petersfinger Cuckoos'. Through his keen observation, one can obtain a brief but fascinating glimpse of nature in the parish which is all too easily overlooked in the bustle of modern life. He died in October 1986, aged 80, and is buried in Alderbury churchyard.

Portrait of A Family of Artists:
The Geddes - Collins - Carpenter Family

A recent intriguing discovery in an American University archive has allowed us a glimpse into the lives of an Alderbury family some 200 years ago. Among these family papers of the famous Victorian mystery writer, Wilkie Collins, lay the unpublished memoirs of his mother, Harriet Collins, written in 1853 when she was 63 years old. From the age of about seven, she had lived in Alderbury, the eldest of the six children of Captain and Mrs Alexander Geddes of Alderbury Cottage at Shute End.

Harriet's memory for detail gives substance to the names of the local people of the time. She disguised their real names but almost all have been identified by recent biographers. In 1797 her father had leased the brick and tile house, with some land, from the Earl of Radnor. It was in an idyllic position, next to the ferry, with its garden sloping down to the River Avon. The first part of Harriet's 62,000 word narrative is an account of her life there until, in 1814 at the age of 24, she had to give up her dream of becoming an actress, and leave Alderbury to become a governess.

Alderbury Cottage

Figure 15.1

Alderbury

Cottage, c.1843

Her father appears to have been a genial man, if somewhat naive in affairs of business. Her mother, also named Harriet, and the daughter of a former Mayor of Salisbury '*...but without any dower...*', strove to keep up appearances among her wealthy friends and neighbours while bringing up her large family on very little income. Mrs Geddes '*....had a great taste for ornamental gardening and the place was soon so beautified that carriages as they passed along the road stopped to admire the rose and ivy covered cottage, the soft green velvet lawn with its gay flower beds...*'

When the local gentry called '*...great was the scuffle as they were seen to approach and also great was the scramble to dispose of children as well as of the salt fish and parsnips...*'

The so-called '*Porters*' (Mr and Mrs George Yalden Fort of Alderbury House), lived just along the road, '*...they envied us the river as at their new Italian villa they had only an artificial pond...*'

The '*Hartleys*' (Henry and Mary Hinxman of Ivychurch House), arrived just as her mother was hanging out the washing and her father was wheeling a barrow full of fir cones to burn on the fire. The visitors were impressed with their economy!

It is interesting to speculate on what might have been discussed at these neighbourly gatherings. The end of the eighteenth century and the beginning of the nineteenth was a dramatic time for the nation. As a former soldier Captain Geddes must have keenly followed news of the wars with France; the rise and downfall of Napoleon, the victories at sea and the battles on land. There were important happenings in Alderbury, too. The ill-fated Salisbury-Southampton Canal was in the process of being constructed. His neighbours were involved: Mr Fort was a shareholder and joint treasurer of the company and Mr Hinxman had complained of being molested by the contractors. Captain Geddes himself received a reduction of rent in the expectation of disturbance to his land. The Enclosure Award, entailing changes in local land ownership, would also have been a subject much debated.

None of these concerns, however, are mentioned in Harriet's memoirs. She remembers the details of the dresses she wore to the dances; trips to Salisbury in their six-seater *'Irish'* car, pulled by a blind ex-cavalry horse and delightful rambles in the meadows with a posse of rustic local children and Betsy Hazel (her real surname), who had been engaged to look after the baby. She recalled the excitement when a regiment was quartered in Salisbury and her mother's futile attempts to find rich husbands for her two elder daughters.

From early childhood it was evident that Harriet's sister, Margaret, was unusually talented at drawing and painting. Her skill came to the notice of the Earl of Radnor and the sisters were given access to the Longford Castle's picture collection so that Margaret could copy the great masters. Small commissions from his noble friends helped the family finances when Captain Geddes fell behind with the rent. Margaret took lessons in oils from Thomas Guest, a London artist who had retired to a shop in Salisbury's High Street. Harriet maintained that her sister *'...rapidly outshone her master...'*. Margaret went to study art in London, staying at the home of the family's investment broker, who was shortly to bring about her father's financial ruin. When this happened, the Earl of Radnor guaranteed Margaret's expenses in London, until she could establish herself as a professional artist. In 1814 Margaret won the gold medal at the Society of Arts and during the next fifty years she exhibited 243 paintings at the Royal Academy, earning a regular income from commissions for portraits at some of the great houses around London and Salisbury.

In 1817 she married William Carpenter, who in 1845 became Keeper of Prints and Drawings at the British Museum. They had a large family, three of whom became artists themselves. But although the most prolific and acclaimed female portrait-artist of her time, Margaret was denied election to the membership of the then all-male Royal Academy. In 1993, to mark the bi-centenary of her birth, believed to have been in 1793, Salisbury Museum held an exhibition of her work.

Meanwhile, in 1822, Harriet married the artist William Collins RA. Both sisters then lived in London and were part of the circle of great artists and writers of the day. Harriet's elder son, Wilkie Collins, became famous as a writer and was an intimate friend of Charles Dickens. His mystery novels 'Woman in White' and 'The Moonstone' have become classics. They enthralled his Victorian readers just as they are still delighting people today, being adapted for television in the 1990s. Harriet's younger son, artist Charles Allston Collins, married Kate, the daughter of Charles Dickens.

After the death of her husband, Harriet opened her house to her sons' artist friends and recaptured some of the merriment of her youth. Artists John Millais and Holman Hunt regarded themselves as her *'third and fourth sons'*.

Another of the Geddes' daughters was also a painter. Catherine Esther married the Salisbury artist John Westcott Gray in 1816. She exhibited three of her watercolours at the Royal Academy. One of their sons, Alexander Gray, left England in 1869 to found the American branch of the family and his son, Percy Gray, became a celebrated painter of the Californian landscape. Alexander returned to England for a visit in 1898 and in an unpublished autobiography he described the delights of his many childhood visits to his Geddes grandparents at Alderbury Cottage. He recalls the chickens and pigs, the fruit trees and flowers, the rowing boat by the river and the pony and chaise for trips into Salisbury. It may be safely assumed that his cousins, Wilkie and Charles Collins, also enjoyed their frequent visits to this rural paradise.

Figure 15.2

The Geddes

family grave in

St Mary's

churchyard

Before Alexander Gray left the village, he walked up to Alderbury Church to see the grave of the grandparents. The tombstone is to the right of the main path leading to the church. Unfortunately the inscription is now illegible. Residents of Alderbury for nearly fifty years, Captain and Mrs Geddes died in 1843 and 1842 respectively, both aged 79.

About 70 years later, a member of the present generation of American Grays, Donald C Whitton came to Alderbury while researching the great volume of work left by his English forbears. He visited the site of the Geddes cottage at Shute End, now 'Avon Turn', the home of the late Dowager

Countess of Radnor, who contributed to his book 'The Grays of Salisbury' which includes many examples of the work of this artistic dynasty.

Alderbury residents can be glad that after Harriet Collins' autobiography came to light, further investigations of the biographers Catherine Peters (of Wilkie Collins) and Richard J Smith (of Margaret Carpenter) have illuminated this almost forgotten corner of our history.

Thomas Prewett (1848-1943) and his Forbears

'The singing gallery without Prewett is like plum pudding without suet'. So said the Rev. Hugh Stevens (Vicar of Alderbury 1813-43) during a service in church, hearing no singing and seeing no Prewett. The origin of this couplet, heard in the village to this day in various versions, is recorded in 'Wiltshire Notes and Queries' dated October 1893. We are also told that it was George Prewett, the clerk of the parish, who led the singers in the gallery.

The Prewett name was not the most common in Alderbury. However, details given below of both a 'snapshot' view (1841 census), and a survey of burials between the years 1813-1988, show that the name Prewett figured prominently amongst the four names heading both lists.

Family Surname at 1841 Census	No. of individuals so named (No. households)	Burials at Alderbury 1813-1988 (Date of last burial)
Prewett	38 (9)	62 (1957)
Bungay	68(15)	62 (1963)
England	35 (7)	81 (1980)
Fry	45 (6)	54 (1988)

Parish records show that a 'Pruet' was married in 1612, and a 'Bungey' in 1628. Other families (living in the village of Alderbury to-day), the Northeasts and the Hatchers, can claim marriages in 1611 and 1633 respectively. But an even earlier mention made of the name 'Prewitt' in 1566, when Stephen Prewitt married Eliz. Hyare at Alderbury, shows the family may have been established over a much longer period. It is fitting therefore that an account of early days in Alderbury – at the time of the Rev. Stevens' comment above – should have been written by a Prewett.

George Prewett, mentioned above, was born in 1789 and lived at Shute End with his wife Jane. He had two sisters and five brothers. One of his brothers, Stephen (b.1796) had nine children. One of these, William Henry (b.1822) had a son Tom. This Tom Prewett, born in 1848, wrote an account of his life in 1936 when he was 88. Although his family moved to Southampton when he was five years old he continued to visit his relatives at Alderbury and his memories are both vivid and informative. A number of quotes are given below.

'My grandfather's name was Stephen and my grandmother's, Martha. My grandfather was the Estate Carpenter at Longford Castle... He was leader of the Village Band, which in my younger days supplied the music for the church. He had six sons and three daughters. All his sons were musical and all except my father were members of the Band. They lived in a large house (once a Poor House) next the Church. A wall divided the church yard and the garden. The house was made into three dwellings. My grandfather occupied a living room on the front downstairs and rooms above. Upstairs lived his cousin who did the laundry work for the Castle. The wash-house was in the garden and here was a large box mangle upon which I had many a ride. Round the corner lived Granny Light. She made humbugs and other sweets. My mother, who went into service when she was aged seven, was the youngest of the six children...

My father, ...when he was 20 joined the Royal Marines. After a short time he was put on board HMS Dolphin and sailed to South America where they were employed running the mails from Rio to Montevideo and chasing slave ships... He bought himself out just before his 25th birthday, returned to Alderbury and apprenticed himself to his Uncle George, the builder and wheelwright... After a year he married and went to live in Salisbury [he continued his apprenticeship at Alderbury] in a cottage in what I think was once a part of the Brewer's Yard. My father's apprenticeship was only for three years...When I was about three years old he went to work at Southampton returning home on Sunday mornings. He walked to Romsey then took the train to Salisbury station, which was then on the Southampton Road.'

Tom moved with his family to Southampton in January 1853. He mentions festivities both in Southampton and Alderbury in 1856 following the end of the Crimean War, and a visit (in 1858-59) to board *'The Great Eastern'*, then the largest ship in the world, (propeller, paddle wheels, and six masts) fitting out off Netley. He spent many happy days at Alderbury, Salisbury, and Wishford and describes one such occasion:

'At Alderbury on Whit Monday members of the County Club from several villages met at Alderbury. They assembled on the Village Green. Headed by the Band they then walked to the church. You would be much amused to see such a procession now, many of them in smock frocks. All the older men wore silk hats and every one had a large rosette pinned on one side of his hat. The colours were red, white, and blue, and each had three streamers hanging from the rosette. After the service in church they reformed and returned to the Green Dragon where they partook of a dinner. This was generally presided over by Earl Radnor or Lord Folkestone his eldest son. On Tuesday morning they met again and if the family were at the castle they went to Longford and afterwards to "Clarendon" the seat of Sir Frederick Bathurst. I never went to Longford but I went once to "Clarendon" and very proud I was to march by my Grandfather's side and carry his flute or his fife. He told me that the first time he led

them they covered the large circular lawn in front of the house and now, if placed in single file, they would hardly encircle it.'

Tom completed an apprenticeship as a wire-maker in 1869, and retired at Eastleigh as a Water Board Inspector in 1919. He married Sarah Gurd in 1874. Their granddaughter Rosemary (b.1931) and now married to William Collis, lives at Eling, near Totton, and kindly allowed access to Tom's manuscript.

Throughout his life Tom had been an active churchgoer, a Sunday school teacher, sidesman, and a regular attender at bible classes until his 90th birthday. He recorded details of his 90th birthday celebrations (on 24 November 1938) as a postscript to his narrative, and died aged 95 at Eastleigh on 7 December 1943.

The Bungey Family

The Bungey family is one which has a long history, much of which has its origins in Alderbury. Many of the family eventually moved to Australia but nevertheless, the name is still well known in the village today. Gracie Bungey, who is now living in Headbourne Worthy near Winchester, has documented much of the family's history. She is a descendent of Walter Bungey, who was married in Alderbury in 1628.

A large number of Bungey entries can be found in the parish records of both Alderbury and neighbouring Downton since at least the early 1600s. Originally, the spelling was Bungy and occasionally Bungie, the 'e' (and sometimes an 'a') creeping in around the late 1600s. The name is reputed to have derived from Buna, a south German mercenary who around 900 took his tribe across to 'Angleland' (East Anglia) forming a settlement at Bungay, Suffolk, originally spelt Bungy. Bungy means Buna's Island or Buna's people. Later, they moved westwards following a call from King Cedric of Wessex. The largest numbers of recorded families from the early 1600s are from the parishes of south Wiltshire, west Hampshire and north-east Dorset.

Alderbury men inter-married with the well-known local families of Phillips, Sop, Seward, Abraham, Tapper, Wort, Hatcher, Bell, Garrett, Fry, and Windsor, to name a few. Some early wills have survived which give a fascinating insight to the lives of the people and their families. Walter, who died in 1679, leaves bequests to his children John, Stephen, James, Joyce, Jane, Francis Philips and Elizabeth Tynham. An inventory of his estate amounted to around seven pounds five shillings made up of the following: three pewter dishes and one flagon (four shillings); two skillets and a boiler (six shillings); wooden utensils (two shillings); two beds and bedding (one pound); wearing apparel (ten shillings); working tools (three shillings); money in house (five pounds).

Bequests included several sums of one shilling and two shillings and although Walter probably lived quite simply, he would have had enough to live on. By 1742 his descendant John, a yeoman, was much better off,

164

describing his estate as *'messuage, tenement, orchard, garden, lands and premises purchased of William Pilgrim and his mother'*, an acre in Alderbury Common Meadow, a close of arable land called *'The Seven Acres lately belonging to John Northeast'*, a close of arable land called *'Spatchursts Croft'*, a close of pasture called *'Three Halves'* and a meadow called the *'Square Three Halves'*. There are several bequests of £200 each in his will.

Later on, a William Bungey (who died in 1851) described among his assets *'the £55 pounds in the Salisbury Savings Bank'* and mentions brother Thomas, sisters Harriet Bell and Elizabeth Batten and William Mussell of Butterfurlong who *'owes him six guineas'*. Lastly, William Mortimer Bungay (sic) of Salisbury, Gentleman, a bachelor who died in 1908, bequeaths £100 to the Salisbury Infirmary and £60 to the Band Fund of the Salisbury Detachment of the 1st Wiltshire Volunteer Rifle Corps and then goes on to list the names and addresses of some 16 beneficiaries (several of whom are Hardimans) spread all over the country. William, born in 1849, was the illegitimate son of Elizabeth but neither was disowned by the family. He inherited money from an uncle William who left Alderbury for Marske by the Sea, Yorkshire and died in 1902. Uncle William mentions family members at Darlington, and Leeds. There are several surviving family gravestones in Alderbury churchyard including one for William Mortimer Bungay and next to it, one for his mother Elizabeth.

The Alderbury burial registers show that one of the earliest entries is William Bungie buried 31 August 1607. Two Bungey men held the office of Parish Clerk. These were Walter, buried 25 December 1741 (a sad Christmas for that family), and Charles who died in 1778. Stephen married Elizabeth Fleetwood (a widow) in 1753; she was buried in 1756 – did she die in childbirth perhaps? Several Bungeys lived to a good age – James who died 1806 of 'old age' was 85; Stephen (buried in 1854) was 88, Isaac died 1903 aged 89. One of the last burial entries was 1963 for Edward Philimore Bungay, aged 80, who was cremated at Maidstone, Kent. His name is inscribed on a family tomb still standing in Alderbury churchyard.

By the time of the 1841 census the occupations of the numerous families are quite modest, blacksmith, woodman, market gardener, sawyer, agriculture labourer, servant, etc. By 1851 addresses are added which show families living at 'cottage near the school', 'near the Old Road', 'near Chapel', 'near the Crown', 'near Lights Lane', and so on, as well as several families in Silver Street. As time goes by, with the previously large number of jobs in agriculture dwindling, many moved out of Alderbury to live in Salisbury and the surrounding area taking other occupations.

In 1841 Letitia (née Sop, married 1792) the widow of William, is living with her son Henry, his wife Elizabeth and seven children. The youngest of these is Newton, aged six. Newton married a local girl, Susannah Elizabeth Robey, in 1857 and in the 1871 census Newton is shown as a grocer living 'near Chapel, Goose Green' with his wife and five children; the eldest three were born in New South Wales, Australia. Sometime after 1871 he's off again, this time taking his family to New Zealand. A number of the

Alderbury Bungeys were emigrants to South Australia. At least three other families emigrated to Australia in the 1800s.

Samuel Bungey (1829-1914) was the eldest of nine children born to William and Jane (née Garrett). By the 1830s life was hard for the working man on the land and there was interest in forming a new British colony in Australia, not like those already there. They wanted no convicts and hoped to make their fortunes away from the poverty at home. By 1833, a South Australian Association had been formed. Samuel was to start his new life there in 1849, only 13 years after the settlement began. At the age of 19, he left England forever, sailing in the 'Emily' which left London at six am on 3 May 1849 and arrived at Port Adelaide on 8 August, after only three months at sea – a much quicker journey than many at that time. In 1854 Samuel purchased 103 acres for £161 At this time he was unable to read and write and signed this deed (made out in the name of Samuel Bungay) with an 'X', but by 1882 when he took out a mortgage, he was not only able to sign his name but to make the correction to Bungey.

William Windsor Bungey (1832-1865), was the first-born child of Charles and Mary (née Windsor). There then followed three brothers and three sisters. The emigration of William's second cousin Samuel in 1849 would have aroused enormous interest throughout the family. Meanwhile, back in Alderbury, William was 17 and family legend says he found himself attracted to a woman 17 years his senior. Eliza Davey's father owned woollen mills and was quite well-to-do. Eliza became a companion to a titled lady, was then jilted, and married William on the rebound. The wedding took place in Devon in 1854 when William was 22 and Eliza 39. Sister Elizabeth married Samuel Belstone at Alderbury around the same time. William's parents had been considering emigrating for some time and on 29 April 1854, Charles took his whole family, including new daughter-in-law Eliza and son-in-law Samuel off to Australia, sailing from Southampton on the 'Navarino'. They arrived at Port Adelaide on 14 August 1854.

William Bungey (1848-1923) was 19 years younger than his brother Samuel, working as a lad for Lord Radnor at Longford Castle, before becoming head gardener at Wilton House for Squire Rawlence. He had married Mary Holloway of Whiteparish at Wilton in 1865 and they emigrated with their seven children, who ranged from Laura aged 16 to Ernest just one year. They left Plymouth on the 'Berar' on 22 July 1883, arriving Port Adelaide 21 December 1883.

Although there are not many Bungey families around the Alderbury and Salisbury area today, in Australia over 3,000 descendants can be traced from the three emigrant families mentioned above. In 1994 a grand reunion and family picnic was held in South Australia.

Gracie recalls walking down Silver Street admiring the pretty thatched cottages which were probably agriculture workers' cottages so many years ago. Many would have been home to several of the Bungey families, each of the cottages standing today being divided into three separate dwellings. At the bottom of Silver Street, one may glance across the fields to see the

166

church in the distance, which would have seen so many Bungey babies baptised, numerous couples married and the final services for the departed. The registers reflect many Bungeys, including Jerard, Letitia, Josof, Madonna, Sabina, Philimore, Newton, Thirzah, and Israel. Gracie recalls feeling privileged to have brought visitors from Australia and Canada over the years to see Silver Street, the site of their ancestors' humble beginnings at Alderbury.

The Dowty Family

'*I John Dowty of Clarendon, take thee Sarah Laws of this parish to be my lawful wedded wife.*' This first record of the present Dowty family of Alderbury and Whaddon is to be found in the marriage register for Alderbury on 19 January 1778. John had two sons, the elder, also named John (1784-1848), owned the smithy in Alderbury and his brother William (1787-1869) was a shoemaker. John had no children and the smithy passed to his nephew William (1816-90).

William, the shoemaker, lived in Rose Cottage (now named Jasmine Cottage) on The Green and his second son George (1818-1910) also became a shoemaker. He started his business in Woodfalls but came back to Rose Cottage on his father's death. He it was who became a Primitive Methodist preacher, as did a younger brother Henry (1821-75) in Willunga, South Australia. Henry called his bungalow in Willunga, Alderbury Cottage and it is now a National Trust house there.

George Dowty and his wife had eight sons and three daughters. Of the sons six joined the Metropolitan Police, five of them being promoted to sergeant and of those two went on to become sub inspectors and another, the eldest, George, became an inspector. The sixth son had to retire as medically unfit after eight years but went on to join the uniformed branch of the RSPCA. One of the five retired policemen, Albert Edwin Dowty (1863-1940) eventually returned to Alderbury to live in Firs Road and later in Rose Cottage. During his retirement he served as a JP.

A further son, Thomas Dowty (1857-1950) remained in the village, living at Mount Pleasant Farm (Castle Hill House) and was at various times a builder, farmer and undertaker. He was also a councillor, served on the Board of Guardians (for the workhouse) and was local secretary for a friendly society, The Rechabites. He played the cornet in the village band. Thomas Dowty who now lives in Whaddon is his grandson.

A Dickensian Character – The Father of the Lewis Family in Alderbury?

In his book 'Martin Chuzzlewit', completed in 1844, Charles Dickens refers to a bandy-legged tailor – an habitué of the 'Blue Dragon' an inn located in a village near Salisbury. It is popularly supposed that the village was Alderbury and the inn, the 'Green Dragon'.

In 1843, in Silver Street, in a house not more than 50 yards from the 'Green Dragon' lived William Lewis, aged 52. His great great grand-daughter Edna Paxman recalls her father telling her that William was very small, bandy-legged and known as 'Titch-Titch'. He was the father of a dynasty which flourished in Alderbury for over a hundred years.

William Lewis, born in 1791, was a master tailor working in Chelsea when he married Anne Lewis around 1815. Shortly afterwards they moved to Alderbury where he worked making livery and uniforms for servants on the Longford estate. It is highly likely that his wife, who was born in Alderbury in 1792, was a child of Anne Lewis who was employed by the Earl of Radnor between 1779 and 1794. William and Anne later moved to a house in what is now called High Street to live with their son James for the last few years of their lives. William died in 1858 and Anne in 1860. They had at least eight children.

Three of the sons Abraham, John, and James trained as tailors and were the only children to remain in Alderbury as adults, Abraham and John until their deaths in 1880 and 1900, and James until the death of his wife, Mary in 1862. Abraham was born in 1816. He became apprenticed to his father and in 1834 married Mary Leach, a local girl. Soon after, he moved to London but returned after a short while. He helped his father and took over the Post Office, then in Old Road. His wife Mary ran the bakery in the High Street. In 1980-81, when in her late nineties, his granddaughter Alma Goss Parsons (née Lewis) wrote down her recollections. These have been used extensively in these notes.

By 1841 Abraham and his wife had three children and three of Abraham's brothers John, James, and Robert, were also living with them. In 1851 the family was living in Silver Street in the house identified as that later occupied until 1988 by the Light family. The 1861 census shows Abraham and Mary still living there, but later in that year the family moved to the house next to the church, now known as Court House, and which had been the Rectory as long ago as 1649. Abraham and Mary were still residing there when they died in 1880 and 1881 respectively.

They had produced 21 children between the years 1836 and 1863. Of these, seven died in infancy. Some details are known. Jacob moved to Margate where he came to own seven jewellers' shops, developed much of Cliftonville and died a wealthy man. William established Margate College and was three time Mayor of Margate. He admired his mother so much he changed his name to Leach-Lewis. Abram founded Longford College in Margate and became a Lieutenant Colonel in the Royal Field Artillery. Alma became a headmistress at Margate and married a fellow-teacher, a German, August Hartung. Three of the boys, Frederick, Isaac, and Robert, emigrated to Australia and another, Elisha, to New Zealand. Frederick married Thirza (a Clarendon girl!) in Australia. He returned with Thirza and their three sons to settle in Alderbury after the death of his father. Another son of Abraham, Arthur, remained in Alderbury for a while, probably in service at Longford Castle, until he became butler to the Earl of

Airlie. He married the head cook, Emily Westcott, in 1881 and soon afterwards returned to Alderbury to become butler to the Earl of Radnor.

John Lewis (b.1824), the brother of Abraham, had remained in Alderbury. He and his wife had five daughters. He appears to have helped Abraham in some of his enterprises and when Abraham died he and his wife Sarah helped Arthur, who succeeded his father in these enterprises, which soon included a grocery business previously run by two elderly ladies named Waterman. Arthur had several children, all born at Alderbury. A daughter born in 1893, the Alma Goss referred to above, studied book-keeping and shorthand and helped in the shop and post office – full-time after her Aunt Sarah died. In 1904, Arthur Lewis moved with his family to Burley. Alma was married eight years later.

Not all of the Lewis graves in the Alderbury church-yard have been identified but there are a number of the family tombstones, together, near the north gateway entrance. That commemorating William and Anne was 'erected by their children living in England, America, Australia, and New Zealand'. In her memoirs, Alma Goss Parsons recalls:

'Uncle John and Aunt Sarah lived on the top road (now known as the Old Road): nearby were steps leading to Ivychurch where formerly monks had a monastery, a large building surrounded by a wall. People often visited it. In my early days the house was pulled down and the high walls were replaced by low short walls. It was reported having a secret underground passage to Clarendon House. In my time it was owned by Sir Frederick Bathurst and family who attended Alderbury Church where they occupied some seats in a special part of the church. The church was used by Lord and Lady Radnor of Longford Castle who sat in the upper pews of the chancel. The front seats of the nave were occupied by Mr Fort and family: the next seats below were taken by Mr Staples and family. Their young ladies placed dainty coloured scent bottles on the bookshelf. We girls were often tempted to take a sniff. At evening service we were allowed to sit in these pews should the other seats be filled. Squire Fort lived near the church. Lucy Fort taught the boys at Sunday School, her sister Florence the girls. We were fond of her.

The Lady Radnor I first recollected was very large and brought up in a wheel chair. It was necessary to open the wide doors to bring her in, and they used the higher seats near the communion table. Their staffs sat in the back seats. The servants of Clarendon sat behind them as well.

My father took measurements of customers for grandfather – also Uncle John – and afterwards bought materials from 'Platt' in London. He also repaired flags for various houses. Bunting came from London. Longford Castle flag was so large it needed to be opened in the vestibule of the Castle.

Alma's father, Arthur, handed down an amusing story about an occasion when King Edward VII accompanied by Lily Langtry came to stay at Longford. Arthur arranged for his son Bertram to be hidden away in the palms at the foot of the main staircase so that he could see the great event.'

169

The last member of William Lewis' extended family to be buried at Alderbury was Amy Ruth Lewis in 1955. She is thought to have been the daughter of Eliza Lewis who lived with her aunts Helen Prewett and Sarah Beaumont at what is now Court House, for more than thirty years. No descendants of William and Anne Lewis bearing the family name now live in Alderbury but the current family tree shows 250 known descendants, 75 of them in the seventh and eighth generations. A 'Lewis Day' arranged by the family and held in Alderbury in August 1988 was attended by 46 members of the family.

Figure 15.3

Alderbury Forge, c.1900

son standing, A C Maidment,

father shoeing, H Maidment,

boy unknown

16

ANECDOTES, RECOLLECTIONS & CELEBRATIONS

Frank Moody remembers...

This is an extract from the correspondence of Mr Frank Moody. Now in his nineties, Frank lives in Bristol, near his son. For most of his life, however, he lived in Alderbury, working for the Longford Estate, except during World War II when he served in the army in India. He is a member of a family who (including his uncles and grandfather) have worked for six Earls of Radnor. He and his wife once lived in the cottage next to the Green Dragon, on the Longford Estate, and later, in Firs Road. He was actively involved in village life, serving as Secretary on the Village Hall Committee at its beginning. He was Secretary to the Parish Council for 25 years and Steward of the Whaddon Methodist Chapel. A local history enthusiast, older residents still remember his film shows of Alderbury. We are most grateful for his help through a long and fascinating correspondence.

The Longford Castle Fire Brigade

Frank remembers the difficulties the village used to have with a reliable water supply and the early days of the Longford Castle Fire Brigade.

'One of the problems of such a place as Longford Castle was that of fire, which itself highlights the matter of water. Drinking water itself was a problem in Alderbury, Whaddon and all around. The castle had a good supply, the source of which came from the park at the Britford end, which has never been known to fail. At the turn of the century a main was laid to Ivychurch, a reservoir built there, and Longford and the surrounding villages have never been short since. At each hydrant as well as a tap, there was a 3-ft hose connection for fire hose. In the fire station by the estate house there was kept a small steam engine which was always ready for fire-fighting and capable of pumping its own water (out of the river or a pond) or taking it from the roadside through the system. As the years went by the supply was gradually extended until the whole of the estate country from Alderbury and Whaddon to Nunton and Odstock had a plentiful supply of water. Until that reservoir came to Ivychurch in 1901, water was like the proverbial gold dust. Alderbury was one of those places that sprouted small springs early in the year and then dried up. People whom I know who lived and worked on the estate would say that it would sometimes take 20 minutes to fill a bucket. As I recall the water supply was taken over by the local authority in the 1950s.

There was a fire brigade at the castle from early times and when Stephenson invented steam-powered engines for railways and other forms of traction, there were also steam engines to pump water to extinguish fires. All members of the brigade had alarm bells in their cottages, all of which were connected to the castle and we would make haste from wherever we happened to be. We had a fairly regular fire drill at the castle for the maintenance of equipment and checking hydrants etc. but chiefly to familiarise ourselves with the castle layout so that we knew the easiest way to get out of the place and not get lost. That was a headache that was solved in 1937 by the invention of the Davy Fire Escape. This consisted of a coil of cord wound on a pulley with, at its end, body harness (like a car seat-belt) which you would contrive to fit yourself into. A hook, fixed in the wall outside a window, would take the ring at the end of the harness and you would step off through the window and descend gracefully to the ground. These were fitted at strategic windows on each floor and we all slept much better after that. To think of 20 or 30 people groping about in the darkness and smoke was a nightmare. The Davy Fire Escape was wonderful! There was never a fire at the castle in my experience. There was a fire in the north tower after the second world war. There was a public fire service on call at that time so we let them deal with it. A housemaid, having heard the dinner bell, popped her housemaid's box inside the lift shaft and ran off to her lunch. It was supposed there were hot ashes in the box and the upward draught of air in the shaft fanned the ashes into flames. I don't know if any of the "Davy's" have been used seriously but it was always a comforting thought that they were in situ'.

The Installation of Electricity

'Electricity was installed in the cottage where I lived in Alderbury in 1933. The castle went on the national grid about the same time. They had had an electricity supply for a long time before that. They generated their own by a stationary engine and storage batteries of 110 volt system. This was set up on the ground floor of the estate office building. Fred Sheppard was the electricity operator, assisted by Fred Rumbold. When, in the 1920s, horse carriages gave way to motor cars, Fred Sheppard drove her Ladyship's car and Jim Perry drove that of the 6th Earl. They had a pair of Austin Twelves.

In case of breakdown or failure of the home-made electricity supply, there was a reserve generating system set up at the mill across the park on the River Ebble (which joins the Avon just below the castle). I think I remember it being dismantled and the cable dug up in the early 1950s. The system provided only lighting. Until the arrival of the national grid, cooking and heating were done by fires of coal and wood; heating water probably by coke. At times when there were no fires, paraffin, oil stoves or bottled gas were used.'

172

Memories of Len Moody (1901-1998)
and his daughter Mrs Brenda Wort

Len Moody was born in 1901 and as a boy he lived in a house in the High Street, now Fuchsia Cottage. During World War I the family went to live at Hole Farm, Clarendon, to help his grandparents who had farmed there since the 1880s, and who celebrated their diamond wedding anniversary there. When we talked with Len he was 97 years old and lived with his daughter, Mrs Brenda Wort, at her home in Laverstock. Sadly he died a few months later. The following extracts are taken from a conversation recorded in 1998.

A pig up the chimney...

LEN: *'I remember the airship Beta coming down in the field at the bottom of Junction Road in 1910. I was out looking after my two little brothers. I left them in the pram on the High Road and ran to have a look. Someone else found them and took them home! Mr Knight was the head at school and then Mr Freeman. One day Colonel Cody came down in his aeroplane to call on his friend, Mr Butler, in the big house there [now New Hall], at Bodenham. We all dashed down to see it at dinner time but those of us who came in late for school in the afternoon got six 'cuts' with the cane. Caning was usual in those days.*

During World War I, about 1917, there was a very severe frost all winter and when it thawed out in March, the chalk under the road had broken up making it impassable for the troops on the move and needing to get to France. All the guns got stuck in the mud. They couldn't get up Alderbury Hill or Whiteparish Hill and they even tried to go by Dean. The Canadian troops, stationed on Salisbury Plain, had to dig out and repair the road from Shute End onwards. It was a rough road before that, though, and full of pot holes.

My dad was an ambulance man and whenever a trainload or shipload of wounded men came in he would dash straight off, leaving me to milk the cows on my own, although I've seen him many a time asleep under a cow because he was so tired.

Everyone kept a pig in those days. Hickman's on High Street would slaughter them and take them into Salisbury to sell to the butchers. We used to kill our own at the farm and smoke them up the big chimney in the farmhouse. Then we'd cut the fat off and eat the rashers just as they were – sweet as a nut! The first car I remember coming through the village belonged to Dr Ellis from New Street in Salisbury. He came every Saturday morning. We boys used to wait at Shute End to give him a push. Before that he came on a push bike.

Girls usually went into service at one of the big houses in the area – lots of people had servants in those days. I remember that we boys used to wait for the servant girls from Godolphin School. There were some dances at the Reading Room, too. Mr Cox, who had the cottage next to it, was the village boot repairer.

The Sunday School extension to the Methodist Chapel at the top of Folly Lane was

173

opened by Gypsy Smith, a famous evangelist. Hundreds of people came every day to hear him and he stayed for about a week. He had a big tent pitched in the field near the Clarendon cross-roads.'.

BRENDA: *'We all went to the Wesleyan Chapel although my Granddad was the organist for the Primitive Methodists in Whaddon. They never mixed. The chapel schoolroom was light and airy and sometimes we had lantern slides in the evenings. Great fun! There was musical accompaniment to the hymns; visiting preachers used to remark upon it. The chapel anniversary was a very big occasion in the year as were the chapel outings to Bournemouth. I remember my mother knitting me a bathing costume for one outing but by the time I got out of the water, it was down to my knees because the wool had stretched!'*

The Memories of Will and Muriel Northeast, and George Hatcher

Will Northeast has lived here all his life, born in 1929 in the cottage on Old Road where he lives now. The Northeasts go back a long time in this area. His grandfather was the Postmaster in Alderbury and Will's father too, was a postman.

His other grandfather, Mr Baker, was head coachman to the 6th Earl of Radnor, driving a 'four-in-hand'. With the advent of the motorcar he became landlord of the Green Dragon until 1940. Will trained as a baker and confectioner and worked for the Occomore shop in Whaddon, baking and delivering bread until he went into the army. He resumed his career after army service and married Muriel in 1953.

Muriel comes from a branch of another old local family – the Frys. She started work at age 14 as nursemaid in the Occomore household. She lived in a tied cottage in Whaddon and then in a council house on Spider's Island. Both her parents died before she was married, so family commitments meant that she could work only part-time. Will and Muriel moved back into Will's former home on Old Road in 1955. George Hatcher, a near neighbour, was born in Petersfinger in 1912 but he was brought up by his aunt and uncle in a cottage in Silver Street after his mother died when he was only a few months old. He worked for the Longford Estate as a gardener from 1927 until he retired after 42 years service. During the war he served first in the Royal Artillery in India and then with the Royal Norfolks in Burma. The following extracts are taken from a conversation recorded in 1997.

'And the blast blew Alge back up his stairway...'

MURIEL: *'My dad was a "roadman" working from the Three Crowns to Petersfinger. He pushed a wheelbarrow, gritting, weeding, clearing the paths and ditches. There were no lorries to help him. It was very hard work. When we were young the Common was our playground where all the Wimpey houses are now. The front edge was very boggy and full of bulrushes. There was a slatted wooden bridge that we used to walk over to get to a footpath leading to two cottages. They belonged to*

Mr Tucker and Mr Hazel. Mr Hazel collected adders, getting the venom out and taking it to the hospital. We used to play up at the sandpits, too, supposedly "helping" Ralph Tanner.'

WILL: *'When they re-tiled the back of the Green Dragon they found a monk's hole in the roof. I have also seen the entrance to the tunnel, down two steps, in the cellar. My dad said that when he was a lad, Lord Radnor had two workmen go up it with a candle and a canary in a cage. When the candle went out and the canary curled over, Lord Radnor said "That's it! Everyone out!" He had it bricked up.'*

GEORGE: *'Johnny Freeman was headmaster when I went to the school. He used to stand with his back to the fireplace reading the paper. Someone would sniff and say "I smell trousers scorching!" We had an airship come over one day and we all dashed out to see it.*

One of my uncles worked for Mr Hickman who had the shop on High Street. He had to kill the pigs and sheep. He lived in one of the three cottages on Folly Lane, up on the bank. They are no longer there now.'

MURIEL: *'During the war there were loads of troops in Alderbury. The Americans dug two big concrete pits where the new houses at Silver Wood are now.'*

WILL: *'That's where they serviced their lorries, airfield equipment and staff cars. They lived in old glider packing cases. They put two or three on top of one another and built some steps and slept there. I used to supply them with bread, when I was working at Occomores. They used to call me "Rusty" because of my ginger hair. They loved our English bread. They gave me candy and chewing gum.'*

MURIEL: *'The NAAFI was where the tennis courts are now.'*

GEORGE: *'And the cookhouse was by my garden. You can still see the marks the dustbins made on the wall.'*

WILL: *'The Signals had the Reading Room to store their telephone cables. They were so heavy that they ruined the floor. After the war they put a new floor down.*

The Tank Corps were here first though, and ten of them were billeted in the Club Room at the Green Dragon when my Grandfather was still there. That's when I got German Measles after they all went down with it. The tanks, armoured cars and such did exercises on Whiteparish Hill.'

MURIEL: *'Then there were the bombs!'*

GEORGE: *'That was in 1941, just before I joined up.'*

WILL: *'It was about two or three o'clock in the morning. Alge Maidment was the air-raid warden and he was standing at his front door[at the Old Post Office on Old Road]. There was a stick of them dropped by a plane that had been chased away from Southampton.*

One dropped right by the side of the NAAFI and the whole building rose up in the air and moved three inches off its brickwork without breaking anything and the blast blew Alge back up his stairway.'

175

MURIEL: *'Usually, the only treat of the year was the Sunday School outing. We went to Bournemouth, and occasionally to Weymouth, on a charabanc.'*

GEORGE: *'The first time I went was by train. The carrier vans took us to the station. After that we went by Rowlands' Coaches with the solid tyres.*

The uncle I lived with worked on the railway. When I was small you could get the 12 o'clock branch line into Salisbury from down Junction Road.'

WILL: *'You could cross the river on the punt from Ferry Cottage with Mrs Hazel and later Jack Mouland took it over.'*

GEORGE: *'The last people to cross were those naturalists, Roy Pitman and Ollie Kite, and Roy told me that the old punt was leaking like a sieve!'*

The Memories of Tom Dowty

Tom was born in 1914 at Rose Cottage (now Jasmine Cottage) on Old Road, once the home of his great great grandfather George 'Whacker Dowty', the village cobbler – a nickname earned from the way he 'whacked' the leather to make it pliable enough for shoemaking.

In 1924 Tom moved, with his parents, to his grandfather's farm, Castle Hill House, in Whaddon. They lived in a flat on the top floor but young Tom often spent time downstairs with his grandfather, listening to stories. Tom's grandfather lived to be 97 and older residents will recall the village saying 'There's Old Tom, and Young Tom and Young Tom's son, Tom' This youngest Tom became a master carpenter after many years as an apprentice and journeyman. Some of his work can be seen in Salisbury Cathedral. He served in the RAF during the war, spending four years abroad. A lover of football all his life, Tom is currently President of Wiltshire Football Association. In July 1999, he was awarded a medal by the Football Association to mark 53 years service to the game.

The following extracts are from a conversation recorded in 1997.

'I was all ears listening...'

'Now there's an interesting thing,, my great grandfather, George Dowty, had 11 children, and several of the boys joined the Metropolitan Police Force. They all did well for themselves. They were all big chaps – my great grandfather was six feet five. The two youngest boys went into the building trade.

My grandfather was the builder down this end [Whaddon], he had gravel, sand, bricks and the farm...The present Lord Radnor's grandfather [the 6th Earl] used to come to the farmhouse to visit my grandfather very regularly, as did Canon Hutchings and as a kid I was all ears listening. I can remember that Lady Radnor used to come round with her coachman just before Christmas time handing out joints of meat to people. And they were very pleased to have them.

When I built my house up here in 1938, I applied to Longford for water, as they were the only people supplying it round here and they refused me. So I had a big 4,000 gallon tank to catch the rainwater from the roof. It went through gravel filters into a tank, then it was pumped into the bathroom, where we had big tanks to retain all the water and then it was filtered again through carbon filters. I didn't have piped water until 1957.

A story my grandfather told me happened when he was employed in building the Alderbury Union Workhouse in Britford [1879]. The craftsmen used to walk from Whiteparish, pick up with more from Whaddon, meet the craftsmen from Alderbury and go down to Ferry Cottage. Old Hazel would take them across the river on his punt when the water was too high for the stepping stones. There was a series of stepping stones across the river and they could step across them to Britford and walk through the meadows to the site. The man in charge was a Mr Prewett from Alderbury. One night when they were coming back, they got to the river on the Britford side only to find that the river had risen just over the stones. The men took off their boots and rolled up their trouser legs to wade in but Mr Prewett, who always wore a top hat, wouldn't do it. So grandfather, who was as strong as a horse, offered to carry him across on his shoulders. Halfway over, however, he lost his balance on a stone and they both fell in. Whether it was on purpose or not, I don't know – but grandfather said it wasn't!

When grandfather was 72 he caught burglars single-handed stealing from Austin Parsons' garage. He had hundreds of letters of fan mail after that.

When I was a boy there was no bus service as such and I used to go into Salisbury on one of the farm carts delivering sand from the sandpits. They used to go in twice a day. Later there was a ramshackle old bus with chain-driven wheels that came through from Lockerley on market days. There was a tailboard on the back with a pig strapped on and we kids would sit on the tail board, and try to jump off when it slowed down – and that wasn't always easy! Then there was the coal lorry from Grimstead with a Vulcan engine. It had a petrol tank on top of the driver's cab with what was called 'falling feed' so that if he was delivering coal to someone up Ashley Hill he would have to go up backwards. On a Saturday he didn't deliver coal. The truck would be swept out and two forms put down either side and a canvas hood over the top. When I was ten years old I used to catch this bus at ten o'clock in the morning to go into Salisbury to my uncle's house in Harnham. After lunch we'd walk to Victoria Park to see the football match. Afterwards we'd buy some pastries at Marshall's in Catherine Street for tea and then we went to St Edmund's Club in Hale Hall. I'd catch the Coal Lorry from the Market Place at 9 o'clock in the evening to go back home.'

The Memories of Edith Sargent

Life wasn't easy for a young wife in 1934 when Edie came from Kent to live in Whaddon. Out of work, her husband, Harry had been offered a job at his uncle's shop, Occomore's General Stores, and the cottage next door was available to rent. It was one of a terrace of tiny farm cottages without gas, water or electricity. Lighting came from oil lamps, heating from an open fire and there was an old range in the living room for cooking. Edie says

'The toilet was a bucket. We had to carry it out in the garden and dig a hole... Water was not connected up for a long time. We had to carry some round from next door and put it on the table out of reach of my little boy'.

When electricity and gas came to the village, Edie recalls the fierce competition between the two companies and her determination to have a gas cooker.

'I said, "I have to have a gas cooker. I MUST HAVE A GAS COOKER". The gas people said "Well we can't put a gas cooker in if you're going to have electric..." We already had two electric lights and so I had them taken down and arranged under the floor. When I'd got my little gas cooker and they'd moved on, I took out the lights and got them going"'.

Harry Sargent was a member of the Home Guard and he was in the platoon at the Sunday morning exercise when Lt William Foster threw himself on a bomb to save his men. Harry was also a member of the parish council for many years. Edie has not escaped tragedy. In 1939, Paul, the eldest of her three sons, contracted diphtheria when an epidemic hit some of the pupils of Alderbury School. He was taken to the isolation hospital but died after just four days. In 1958 her husband was killed in an explosion at a Salisbury firework factory. Then she had to find a job to bring in some more money. She went to the department store Style and Gerrish (now Debenhams) on Blue Boar Row in Salisbury;

'I walked up and down plucking up the courage to apply for a job'.

She was successful and worked there until she was almost 60 years of age. Edie, in her 90s, a familiar figure at most village events, regularly attending church, the Mother's Union and the Women's Institute was for many years a keen member of The Singers and The Alderbury Players. Of the village in her youth she says

'There wasn't much to do'. She has certainly made up for it since!

Extracts from the written recollections of Henry Maidment

Henry was born in 1927 but he was only three days old when his mother, Ida Ann (née Northeast), died. She had been postmistress at the post office in Old Road since 1918. His father, Algernon Maidment, who served in France in World War I took over as post master and married Olivia East of Rose Cottage, Silver Street, four years later. Algernon operated the manual telephone exchange installed in 1927 and delivered post and telegrams in one of two 'rounds', the other postman being Mr Vincent of Rectory Road. Both Algernon and Henry's grandfather (also Henry, the Alderbury blacksmith from 1880 to the mid-1920s) played in the village band. On

178

Algernon's retirement, shortly before his death in 1956, the business was transferred to the Occomore's shop in Whaddon.

Brought up in the post office, the young Henry Maidment knew almost everyone in the area, some of them memorable because of their colourful personalities:

'...like Mrs Greenwood, who lived at "High Trees" at the top of Lights Lane (occupied by the army in World War II) who was notable for the large hats she wore to church, the brims laden with fruits and flowers... the Alderbury builders, carpenters wheelwrights and undertakers were the Eyres Brothers, Vick and Bill. Their premises occupied both sides at the top of Silver Street. Bill was the skilled carpenter living initially in Chuzzlewit at the top of Silver Street, while Vick, who handled the business side, lived next door. The Eyres were still making farm carts and waggons up to World War II. The Whaddon builders were the Witt family, living in Rectory Road... The Taylors ran the dairy farm lower down Silver Street on the left and the sons used to deliver the milk around the village... I can just remember my father taking pigs for slaughter by Mr Hickman who owned the general store at High Street above the steps that led down to the main road. On the opposite side of the main road was a cast iron stand-pipe serving some of the houses in the vicinity that were still without piped water... My father remembered collecting six buckets a day from the well at Alward House, using a yoke [a shaped wooden arm sitting on the shoulders with chains and hooks for a pair of buckets]... Yebbie Belstone, the village chimney sweep, lived in the thatched and beamed cottages facing down the [School] hill... Towards Shute End the house called Avon Turn was occupied by General and Lady Everett who gave me the first ever taste of ice cream, made of fruit from the kitchen garden which was looked after by Mr Mouland. He occupied the next cottage and used to operate the ferry across the Avon... At the turning into Castle Lane was Newell's butcher's shop opposite the police station... Ralph Tanner, who was quite a character, lived with his mother off Castle Lane on the track leading to Rectory Farm. He was a brick-maker with a reputation for making a thousand bricks an hour at the brickworks near the Three Crowns... There was the shepherd, Mr Etheridge, who lived in Windwhistle Farm Cottages and loved the classics. He used to talk to me about the wisdom of the Greek philosophers whenever his wife asked me to take his mail across the fields to him at lambing time. Brought up in London, he started work in a draper's shop but was advised to take an open-air job for his health... Opposite Occomore's shop was Mr Parson's garage. As well as selling petrol and paraffin, he ran a taxi service and charged wireless accumulators for the sets used in the twenties and thirties... Tom Dowty, grandfather of the present Tom Dowty, seemed to receive quantities of mail and telegrams. As a youngster he reminded me of one of the prophets, always ready to have a long conversation whenever I delivered mail...'

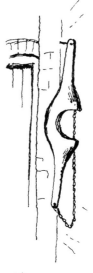

Yoke on

Old Post Office

Cottage wall

Gordon Eastman, who grew up in Alderbury, remembers...

'In 1937, for the coronation of King George VI and Queen Elizabeth, father made a wooden frame of a boat around my bicycle. It was decorated with material and paper flags. I wore a sailor cap. It was quite a push up the hill from Home Farm to the

179

Fountain where we gathered. The procession of decorated bicycles, carts, floats and people dressed up in fancy clothes went down to Alward House. This was filmed by Canon Allen with his ciné camera and shown in the church afterwards. There was a large marquee where we had tea and we were given a coronation cup and a badge. The procession winners were given prizes and a photograph was taken. We later had dancing and the maypole for the girls. Maureen Fry (née Northeast) remembers that she and her brothers and sisters were not allowed to go down to the party as they had measles and had to watch from the top of the field. It was disappointing for them but they had their cups and badges.'

Stanley Gray, a former resident remembers...

'As a tiny boy in 1935. I lived with my family at the top of School Hill. I had a little truck and when Mrs Rumbold of Folly Lane had flowers from her garden to take on the bus to Salisbury market, I took them up the hill for her on my little truck to the bus stop. I was paid two pence – no flowers no pocket money!

For the Silver Jubilee of King George V in 1935 the district nurse, Mrs Stafford, and her friend Mrs Hansford, dressed up as the "Bisto Kids". They borrowed my truck and went in the procession from the Fountain to Alward House... There was a tea tent, games and a maypole. We each had a medal of King George V and Queen Mary and also a cup with their pictures on it.'

17

MYTHS, LEGENDS
AND UNUSUAL EVENTS

'The Green Dragon', Alderbury – The Dickens Connection.

In his novel 'Martin Chuzzlewit', written in 1843-4, Charles Dickens places a great deal of the action in an inn, the 'Blue Dragon', and its neighbourhood. It has long been believed that the inn was modelled on the 'Green Dragon', at Alderbury. A passage in the novel recounts the return of Martin Chuzzlewit and Mark Tapley to the Blue Dragon Inn, from America.

It was closing time at the Dragon and the company was *'tumbling out, ...Martin and Mark were overjoyed to see these old faces... "There's the old tailor, Mark" whispered Martin. "There he goes, sir. A little bandier than he was, I think, sir, ain't he? His figure's so far altered as it seems to me, that you might wheel a rather larger barrow between his legs as he walks than you could have done conveniently when we know'd him"...'.*

At the time the novel was written there lived in Alderbury a bandy-legged tailor, then aged about 53, named William Lewis. The possibility that one of Dickens' characters had a recognisable real-life counterpart in Alderbury arouses more than passing interest and an account is given elsewhere in this book of William Lewis and the family he founded.

However, many people believe that the original of the 'Blue Dragon' was not the 'Green Dragon' in Alderbury but the 'George Hotel', in Amesbury. The rival claims have been aired over many years and it might be thought that there was little new to be said on the subject. However, it is considered that an analysis of Dickens' method of describing taverns and inns, and the presentation of additional facts based on local knowledge, provide justification.

It is known that Dickens visited Alderbury. Mr Freeman, a one-time local schoolmaster, recalled Mrs Hazel telling of having ferried Charles Dickens across the Avon at Ferry Cottage, at Shute End, Alderbury. And the present owner of St Marie's Grange, asserts that Dickens had spent some time there as a guest of the owner, after Pugin had sold the house, and subsequent to the publication of 'Martin Chuzzlewit'.

In 1922 BW Matz wrote 'Dickensian Inns and Taverns' indicating how some 40 inns, taverns and hotels – the great majority of those mentioned in Dickens' novels – were to be identified with their original counterparts. But not the Blue Dragon – an exception!

Although Dickens may have amended, replaced, omitted, or borrowed, the names of taverns, he rarely if ever invented the descriptions of those taverns or inns, or their local topography. He described what he remembered and it is found that in all of the identified inns whenever a fictional name was an altered version of that of a real-life local inn the description of the fictional inn tallied with that of the inn bearing the original name.

If, however, the descriptive and topographical evidence suggests that the 'Blue Dragon' is not a counterpart of the 'Green Dragon' at Alderbury the transfer by Dickens of the altered name of a local inn to a fictional inn with a different description would be a unique occurrence in his novels. While perhaps of some significance, undue weight should not be given to this purely statistical anomaly when comparing the rival claims of the 'Green Dragon' and 'The George'.

In the novel no concise description is given of 'The Blue Dragon' or *'the little village within an easy journey of the fair old town of Salisbury'*, but the fragmented picture given below has been built up from information given piece by piece throughout the book.

The un-named village had at least two inns and a steepled church with a vestry. The windows of the bar-room of the 'Blue Dragon' gave expansive views of pastures, brooks, hedgerows and trees. One of the bedchambers had a large sunken floor, two steps down from the door. Near to the inn were a forge, and a butcher's shop. The inn did not lie on the London-Salisbury coach route, or on the 'high road'. (These two roads may have been one and the same). On occasions journeys were made to intercept the London-Salisbury coach to meet passengers or uplift luggage, and a mail coach passed regularly each evening within easy walking distance of the inn. A turnpike connected the village with Salisbury, ten miles distant, and there was a toll-house on the outskirts of the village. The village, as a whole, was sorely stretched in providing accommodation for Mr Martin Chuzzlewit and his attendant retinue of relatives.

The 'Green Dragon' at Alderbury lies on what was the main Southampton-Romsey-Salisbury stagecoach route in the year 1839, a turnpike built more than 60 years earlier. It is a small tavern providing little accommodation. There is no bedroom with a sunken floor. However, on the first floor, at the end of a passage, there are two steps down and two small bedrooms. It seems likely that at one time this area comprised one large bedroom, as described in the novel. The view from the bar window may have been much as described. There was, and still is, a forge close to the 'Green Dragon' and there was a butcher's shop close by, in the High Street.

There was a toll-house at Petersfinger beyond the outskirts of the village but the distance to Salisbury, following the old route, was only four miles. At no point was the London-Andover-Salisbury coach route nearer to Alderbury than the distance from Alderbury to Salisbury, and to have made cross-country journeys from Alderbury to intercept the coach on its journeyings, would seem to have been neither logical nor reasonable. There is no indication that a mail-coach route passed nearby.

Alderbury church is half a mile from the inn. Although it possesses a steeple and a vestry the previous church, which was not demolished until 13 years after the date of the novel, had neither. There is only one inn in Alderbury although there is another, a mile away, in the adjacent hamlet of Whaddon.

Amesbury, with its 'George Hotel', is nine miles from Salisbury and was connected by a turnpike. There was a toll-house on the outskirts of the town, in which there were several inns and a church. The 'George Hotel' is a capacious inn. As late as 1922, when Matz wrote his book, it contained a bedroom with a sunken floor, matching the description of that occupied by old Martin Chuzzlewit. It can no longer be identified. The hotel lies on the main road along which passed the London to Exeter coaches. There is known to have been a butcher's shop adjacent at the end of the ninetheenth century and at that time the blacksmith's was about 150 yards away. The London-Salisbury coach route passed within about six miles of Amesbury, and there was a regular mail coach service from Devizes to Salisbury which passed about three miles to the west of Amesbury every evening at about 6.30pm.

Both Alderbury and Amesbury could have met Dickens' description of 'a little village', for the 1841 census return shows that the difference in population was much smaller than it was to become in later years. The figure for Alderbury was 741 and Amesbury, 1,166. There were more inns in Amesbury however, and the amount of coach traffic must have made it a 'busier' place.

The 'Green Dragon' at Alderbury would seem to have been too small for the general activity which took place in the novel's counterpart. On the other hand the size of the 'George Hotel' and the existence of other inns in Amesbury would seem to conflict with Dickens' suggestion that accommodation was limited, and the view from the George did not agree with that described by him.

Figure 17.1

The Green Dragon

1996

So which was the original 'Blue Dragon'? Charles G Harper, writing in a short paper in 'The Dickensian' in 1965, suggests that the 'Blue Dragon' is a composite picture of the two inns. But this was not Dickens' style, as has been explained above. Ernest Walls in 'The Salisbury Avon' favours Alderbury as fitting more closely the description of a little village. This would seem to ignore many of the other points of possible identification.

Matz himself was convinced that the 'Blue Dragon' was based on the 'George Hotel' at Amesbury. He found that the topography fitted the requirements of the story, and the size of the inn was more appropriate to the accommodation requirements. He gives due credit to H Snowden Ward who made a minute study of the district, ordnance maps, and coach routes, and became similarly convinced. The reader must make his own decision.

If it is thought that the 'George Hotel' fits more closely than the 'Green Dragon' the requirements of the novel, this does not rule out the possibility that Charles Dickens may have visited the 'Green Dragon', have seen William Lewis the bandy-legged tailor, and used the character in his novel.

The Great Fire of Alderbury

A 'General Gazetteer' by R Brooks, published in 1846, refers to a great fire in Alderbury in 1777 in which 200 houses were destroyed. A further mention of a fire at Alderbury, causing the loss of a factory and several houses is made in a single-sheet 'Guide to Alderbury', published from time-to-time by the Rev. Chris Pooley and his successors. This gives the date of the fire as 1770.

Both publications have reported the facts incorrectly. The houses and factory which were burnt down – in 1777 – were at Aldbourne (five miles NE of Marlborough). Full details are given in the Salisbury and Winchester Journal dated 1 September 1777. The newspaper article also refers to an earlier fire at Aldbourne in 1760. Editions of the newspaper published in 1770 and 1777 make no mention of a fire at Alderbury.

The Napoleonic Road Builders

There has, for many years, been a story that the 'new' village section of the road from Alderbury to Salisbury was constructed by French prisoners during the Napoleonic wars. It is documented in the WI Scrapbook Village History thus:

'For the main road, as we know it, dates from only Napoleonic times, when French prisoners of war made the piece of road running from St Mary's Grange (sic) to Alderbury crossroads...'

It is unclear what this statement is based upon. However, there is an early article on the ill-fated canal project in the Wiltshire Archaeological Magazine which specifically states that the road was built in 1808 by Napoleonic prisoners of war. Our research has shown that it is merely a village legend. Contemporary maps, held at the County Records Office, Trowbridge, indicate that the road was not present in 1831. The map of 1854 shows the modern-day road to Salisbury, suggesting that it was therefore built between 1831 and 1854. Napoleon was exiled to St Helena in the summer of 1815. Thus, the Napoleonic wars were over many years before the likely date that the road was built – a long time indeed for a nation to retain prisoners of war! Evidence from maps alone is not sufficient to disprove the legend, but the records for the Sarum to Eling Turnpike provide definitive evidence. The Minute Books confirm that the road was actually constructed around 1842 and the records from 1838 onwards discuss the purchase of the land to provide a suitable route for the 'new' road. Further information on this aspect is given in Chapter 11.

The Toad Hop:
A Memory, by Peggy (Eastman) Ling and Gordon Eastman.

'From at least the 1920s, probably before, there have been Toads hopping across the road at Tunnel Hill Alderbury in the Spring. This was witnessed by hundreds of school children over the years who lived by the Lower Road, on their way to The Old School further on up the hill.

In the 1930s, we used to see lots of toads hopping across the road, single and paired. Some squashed. We just picked up the live ones putting them back into the hedge or over the wall, hoping they would not come back. They seemed to come from the ditch that came from the tunnel under the road. The tunnel is difficult to see now, or the ditch and water as it is so overgrown. There were certainly toads there when we used to play there, when the stream of water coming through was low. In those days you could walk through the tunnel to the other side of the road, which was then bricked up, under the flint wall. The water came through the bricks filling the ditch when the springs were up, possibly coming from the lake at the back of Alderbury House. There was a raised area the other side of the wall in the field, that gave the impression that the tunnel was intended to go further on.

During the war 1939-45, the toads had little chance to cross the road, but some might have made it. There were so many Army vehicles around Alderbury then, some might have been taken away on their wheels, so less were noticed on the roads. We never knew why the toads hopped over the road to their deaths, or which way they were going. The wall was too high for them to jump over. It would be very interesting to know, as there have been many stories told. Our local naturalist, Roy Pitman, witnessed this 'Toad Hop' and described it in detail in his book, 'The Naturalist at Home', published in 1984. A recent description was in The Fountain April 1999.'

Whaddon's Great Storm

On the evening of 5 July 1836, a spell of hot weather was broken by a violent thunderstorm which struck Alderbury, Whaddon and the neighbouring villages. For three hours, thunder, lightning, wind and rain ravaged the

185

area. A descent of hailstones was reported, with some as big as five and a half inches in diameter. Trees were felled, sheep killed and crops ruined. Whaddon suffered the severest damage. The windows of the Three Crowns Inn were completely smashed, as were those of nearby cottages. Mr Stanford of Whaddon, a small tenant farmer with a wife and ten children, found that almost his entire crops of growing wheat and corn had been destroyed, valued at 2,000 shillings.

Farmer Mark Phillips, also of Whaddon, suffered similar heavy losses. Sympathisers from a wide area contributed to a subscription fund quickly set up to compensate the numerous victims of the storm. Within a short time, the sum of over £2,400 was raised, an enormous amount for the time. However, poor Mr Stanford, when writing to the Salisbury Press to express his gratitude for the compensation, lamented that his share amounted to only one half of what he had lost.

SELECT BIBLIOGRAPHY

A History of Wiltshire. Oxford University Press, Oxford. This series, known as the 'Victoria County History' comprises several volumes, by various editors. There is currently no volume covering Alderbury.

Albert W (1972). The Turnpike Road System in England. Cambridge University Press, London.

Atkinson RF (1992). Alderbury: An Ancient and Peculiar Parish. Published by the author, Alderbury UK.

Atkinson RF (1995). The Manors and Hundred of Alderbury: Lords, Lands and Livery. Published by the author, Alderbury UK.

Baker M (1974). From Wiltshire to Australia 1851: The Story of an Emigration. Published by the author. Easton Royal, UK.

Barron RS (1976). The Geology of Wiltshire: A Field Guide. Moonraker Press, Bradford on Avon.

Chambers J (1993). Wiltshire Machine Breakers. Published by the author, Letchworth UK.

Chandler JH (1980). Stagecoach Operation Through Wiltshire. South Wilts Industrial Archaeology Society, Salisbury.

Colt-Hoare, Sir Richard (1837). The History of Modern Wiltshire: Hundred of Alderbury. John Bowyer Nichols & Sons, London.

Gover JEB (1939). The Place Names of Wiltshire. Cambridge University Press, London.

Graham H (1886). The Annals of the Yeomanry Cavalry of Wiltshire. Marples & Co Ltd. Liverpool.

Hadfield C (1969). The Canals of South and South East England. David and Charles, Newton Abbot.

Haskins C (1922). The History of Salisbury Infirmary. Salisbury & District Infirmary & Hospital League, Salisbury.

Horn P (1989). The Victorian and Edwardian School Child. Sutton, Gloucester.

Jones DKC (1981). The Geomorphology of The British Isles: Southeast and Southern England. Methuen, London.

MacKay EA (ed.) (1948). The History of the Wiltshire Home Guard 1940-1944. Lansdown, London.

MacLachlan T (1997). The Civil War in Wiltshire. Rowan Books, Landford, Wiltshire.

Peters C (1991). The King of Inventors – A Life of Wilkie Collins. Minerva Press, London.

Platts A (1956). Wiltshire Schools: A Short History. Published by the author.

Sample P (1989) The Oldest and the Best: The History of the Wiltshire Constabulary 1839-1989. No Limits Public Relations, Salisbury.

Smith RJ (1993) Margaret Carpenter 1793-1872: A Salisbury Artist Restored. The Hatcher Review 4 (36), 2-32.

Stephen Sir Leslie (1885). Life of Henry Fawcett. Smith, Elder & Co. Ltd., London.

Timperley HW and Brill E (1965). Ancient Trackways of Wessex. Phoenix, London.

Underdown D (1985). Revel, Riot and Rebellion: Popular Politics and Culture in England 1603-1660. Oxford University Press, Oxford.

Watkin B (1989). A History of Wiltshire. Phillimore, Chichester.

Welch E (1966). The Bankrupt Canal: Southampton and Salisbury 1795-1808. Southampton City Council, Southampton.

Whitton DC (1976). The Grays of Salisbury: An Artist Family of the Nineteenth Century. Published by the author, San Francisco, USA.

LIST OF SUBSCRIBERS

We are grateful to the following subscribers
for their financial support, which has helped to make this book a reality

Doris Abbott
Carol Alder
Ted & Bernice Allott
Eugene & Margaret Andrews
Mrs Sybil Irene Andrews (née Shears)
Hazel Argar
Mrs M Ashford & Miss S Ashford
Roger & Sheila Ashton
Richard & Pamela Atkinson
Robin Atkinson
The Aylett family
Dr H Backhouse
Roger Ball
Mr & Mrs JW Bament
Mr & Mrs TW Barnett
Paul & Cherrie Barnfield
Gwen Barton
Margaret Beale
Terry Belbin
Frank & Lise Bevan
Geoffrey, Debrah, Kirsti, Stephanie & Nicki Biggs
Clive Richard Blake
David & Brenda Blake
Dr & Mrs J Boyle
David & Sheila Bratley
Josiah & Marianne Brice
Una & Peter Bridle
Vicky & Alistair Bridle
June & Dennis Brind
Richard & June Britton
Jane Broomfield
Jane Brown
LW & JQ Brown
Pat Brown
Yvonne Bryant-Simms
Mark & Fiona Bugden
Philip & Beryl Bugden

Ida Cecilia Bunce
David S Bundy
Gwenyth Bungey
Brian & Tricia Bunsell
Tony & Betty Butcher (formerly Scammell)
Andrew T Byrom
Bert & Stuart Card
Air Commodore & Mrs RAC Carter
Janice & Malcolm Carver
Len & Betty Chandler
Colin, Lara, Jack, Archie & George Chitty
Andrew & Barbara Christie-Miller
Mr & Mrs Richard Clapp
Rosemary & Tony Clark
Marion Elizabeth Clark
Graham CL Clarke
Michael Clarke
Mrs D Clements
Mrs Sue Clives
Alan & Anthea Cochrane
Mrs J Collins
Stella Collins (née Gray)
Bill & Rosemary Collis
Robert Angela Daniel & Nicholas Compton
Louise & Nicholas Cook
Mr & Mrs ME Cooke
Mr & Mrs AS Coombs
Mrs J Cooper
Jane & Phillip Copley
Sarah Corbett & Colin Campbell
John & Pam Cotton
Isabelle & Gilbert Criado
Stephen & Lesley Cross
Raymond & Fiona Crowther

John & Tracey Curtis
Chris & Katherine Dakin
Sorrel Dale
Patricia Dashwood
Mrs Susan Davies
Robert & Barbara Davison
VL de Candole
Chantal Dexmier
Shirley & David Docking
Peter Dodds
A Veronica Dodkins
Frank & Gwynneth Doran
Brenda Down
Rick & Maureen Downer
Margaret & Alfred Dowsett
Tom Dowty
Mr & Mrs B Drew
Amanda Drewett
Stephen & Margaret Dyer
Margaret Dyer (née Skutt)
Bill Edwards
Doug Edwards
Mr & Mrs Elborn
Iris & Des England
Michael England
Richard & Valerie England
Sal Etherington
Mr & Mrs RS Everett
John S Eyres
Elsie M Facer
Jo & Eric Fairall
Pat & Derek Flint
Rev'd Kim Flippance
Glenn & Angela Foreman
Joan Forrester (née Lambden)
Anne & John Foster
Keith & Jane Foster
Nicole Foulard
Jenny Gaines

Ralph & Mollie Galpin
Irene, Ted & Alan Gange
Mr & Mrs A Gates
Mr & Mrs AE Gates
Jean & Edgar Gibbs
Mr & Mrs GN Gibbs
Joan Goddard
Andy & Sasha Grandfield
Paula Gray
Rosalind Gray
SC Gray
Pauline Gray (née Guard)
Jessica Gunney & Peter Marshall
Bob & Margaret Hambling
Mr & Mrs DR Hammett
James Hammond
Jane Hammond
Muriel & Mervyn Hammond
Peter & Muriel Hammond
William Hammond
Colin & Sheila Hampton Smith
Michael & Yvonne Hardman
Richard & Elizabeth Harmon
Colin C Harris M.A.
Mrs Jennifer Harrison
Deborah & Nicholas Hart
Mr & Mrs WG Hartfall
Evelyn Hastings
Mrs Carol Hastings
Mrs Pat Haston
George & Geoffrey Hatcher
Mark & Louise Hawkins
Mary E Herbert
Mr & Mrs RM Hexter
Mr & Mrs Roger Hickman
Elaine Hicks-Arnold (formerly Hartford)
Mark Hilton
David & Mary Hinchcliff
Sue & Ray Hollingbery
Stephen Hooper
Tony Howe
KJ Hughes
Graham Hunt & family
Denis Hunter

Co Huÿbrechts
Clifford Ingram
Kathleen Ingram
Alec & Shirley Jackson
Mike & June Jackson
Natalie & Richard Jacobs
Patricia Jacobs & Newton Morton
Mrs Muriel Janes
Mrs Jessie Jarvies
Catherine & Ken Jelfs
Peter Jenkins
Cecily Jobbágy
Brian & Gillian Johnson
Bryan & Diana Jones
Ted & Phil Joyce
Martin & Wendy Jung
Jo Kay
R M & J Keach
John Kellman
Peter & Jacqueline Kellow
Lt Col J N Kelly M.C.
Martyn & Vicky Kennard
Madge, Malcolm & Stuart Keppie
John King, Lesley, Sam & Simon, Jeni & Matt
Roy & Pauline Kingett
Mrs Molly Knowles
Morgan & Anne Kruck (Martin)
Alison Andrew Nicki Jonathan & Steven Larkham
Mark & Helen Lello
George & Marion Light
Dave & Ann Lock
Robert & Rosalyn Lucas
Don & Grace Mabey
Colin & Pat Mackenzie
Mrs I MacPherson
Henry Maidment
Mr & Mrs C Malcolm
Mr & Mrs J Manning
Christine & David Marr
Mike & Stephanie Marsh
Christine Martin

Jim & Sue Mason
Mr & Mrs N R Mattinson
Barbara McAlpine
Bill & Valerie McCarthy
Peter McConnell
Neil & Jacqueline Meaden
Peter & Doreen Meek
Isobel Menzies
Mr & Mrs G Mills
Rosemary Milner
Rev'd & Mrs Gordon Mitchell
Charles Frank Moody
Mrs Elisabeth Moody (née Bennett)
Audrey Moore
Min Morgan
Mrs Elsie Morris
Rachel Mowling (née Trewhella)
Audrey & Barry Munday
Mr & Mrs WP Murray
Mrs Hilda Murray, Christine & Helen
David B Muspratt
Pauline & Gerald Naish
Bob & Glen Newman
Jeremy & Glynis Newman
David & Clare Nicholas (Martin)
Rosemary & Gerald Nicholls
Philip & Barbara Nicklen
Iain & Karen Norrington
Dr & Mrs Keith Norris
William & Muriel Northeast
Beryl Nutton
Richard & Jane Olden
Beryl Oliver
Mrs I Othen
Irene Palmer
Edna K Paxman (nee Lewis)
Colin & Barbara Payne
Brian Pearce
Colin & Jennifer Pearce
Mr & Mrs H Perkins
Michael & Pamela Perks
Mr & Mrs H Pferdmenges
Mr Ian Phillips

Mrs Jennifer Pitcher - Headteacher A&WG School
Andrew & Margaret Poole
Angela Potter
Harold & Daphne Potter
Michael Potter
Stephen & Carol Poulton
Katie & Stephen Press
Michael & Julie Press
Iris & Rod Prew
Terry & Elena Priestley
Ross & Megan Pritchard
Quality Lift Products Ltd
Graham & Maria Quinn
The Earl of Radnor
Pam Rainsley
Bill & Bernice Range
Rev. George & Mrs Nancy Razee
Elaine & Graham Read
ED Rendel
Jim Ridd
Robin Rimmer
Mrs S E Ritchie
The Robinson family
Anthony F Rogers M.B.E.
Jim & Elsie Root
Patricia Rowland (née Lewis)
Mrs Monica Royle
John & Claire Russell
Mr & Mrs WA Sanders
Ted & Joyce Sansby
David & Jackie Sargent
Edith I Sargent
Justin & Rosalind Scott
Peter Scrivens
Kathrine Sealey
E & L Shaw
Andrew & Catherine Shears
Alan & Pat Sheppard
Hector Sheppard
Mrs M D Short (Bartlam)
Jeanette Silver
John & ClaireSimpson
Martin & Karen Simpson
Vera & John Singleton

Mrs M Sinn
Ann & John Smallbones
Bertha Smith
Peter & Julie Smith
Mike & Jo Smith
Veronica Smith (née Foot)
Karl & Catherine Smith (née Hinchcliff)
Nancy D Steele
Sally Steward (Hardiman family)
Ron & Brenda Stokes
Mr & Mrs JP Sutherland
Gladys Symes
Edith & Arthur Syrett
Audrey & Michael Tapper
Keith & Jean Taylor
Margaret L Templeman
Brian & Jan Thomas
Richard & Caroline Thomson
Brian John Thorne
Nigel Wilfred Thorne
Wilfred & Mina Thorne
John & Frances Tighe
Rosemary Tivey
Mr DW & Mrs FA Tomblin
Anne Tompson
Mr & Mrs R Treadaway
Martin Trewhella
Vivian & Onaway Trewhella
Stanley & Kathleen Trickett
Anthony & Gillian Turner
David Vidler
Arthur, Rosemary & Joanne Vincent
Barry & Carol Vincent
Christopher & Helen Vincent
Doreen Vincent
Mr & Mrs D Walker
Jean & David Walters & family
Canon & Mrs Michael Ward
Denis & Barbara Watson
Nigel J Watson
Gordon, Rosemary, Alistair & James Watt
David & Tricia Webb

John & Shirley Webb
Alan & Sarah Weeks
Bob & Delia Weeks
Rose & Pete Wells
Ken & Gina Whale
Mr & Mrs G Whaley
Richard Wharton
Mrs Pat Whines
Hilda A White
Jessie Mussel White
Keith & Jenny White
Stephen & Doreen White
Sarah & Bill Wickham
Henry & Caroline Wilkinson
Brian & Liz Williams
Roger E Willis
Frank Denise Katie & Amy Wilson
Susan & Kenneth Wiltshire
Ken & Rosemary Witt
Mrs L Wood
Kay & Derek Woodgate
Mrs M Woodley, Mr B Woodley
Robert Woodward, Lesley & Emily Knowles
Mrs Brenda Wort
Sue & Nigel Wyatt
Christopher Yates
Daphne Young

INDEX

Bunce, Ida, 149,

Bundy family, 67, 162,

Bungay, John, 46,

Bungay family, 90, 95,

Bungay Lane, 78, 90,

Bungay, Newton & Susannah, 85, 152,

Bungay, Stephen, 90,

Bungey family, 164-7,

Bungey, James & Letitia, 106,

Bunston, Thomas, 130,

Burden, George, 130, 133,

Busby, Mr & Mrs, 73,

business, car repair, 18.

business, four-wheel drive, 18,

bus shelter, 120,

Butcher, Thomas & Sarah, 85,

cadet hut, 151,

camping & caravanpark, 18,

Canal House, 96,

Canal Lane, 18, 89,

canal reservoir, 110,

Canal, Salisbury & Southampton, 89, 94, 105, 108, 110-1, 160,

canal tunnel, 185,

canal wharf, 110,

Carpenter, family, 160-2,

Carpenter, William, 160,

Carr, John W, 52, 53, 131,

carriers, 93, 107-8, 111,

Carter, F W, 74,

Castle Hill, 90,

Castle Hill House, 96, 167, 176,

Castle Lane, 78, 90, 96, 115, 179,

Chapel Row, 57,

chapel, Primitive Methodist, 15, 60, 171, 174,

chapel, Roman Catholic, 15, 60,

chapel, Wesleyan Methodist, 15, 57, 58, 77, 131, 174,

Charity Farm, 97,

Cherry Tree Cottage, 92,

Christie-Miller, M V, 74,

Christie- Miller family, 13, 14, 100,

Church choir, 52-3,

Church Lads Brigade, 155,

Church, St Mary's Alderbury, 15, 49-51, 68,

Civil War, 62-3,

Clare, Edwin, 90,

Clarendon, 50, 85, 122,

Clarendon brickworks, 86,

Clarendon Estate, 13, 69, 86,

Clarendon House, 68,

Clarendon Park, 101, 110,

Clarendon Palace, 100, 134,

Clarendon Road, 60, 78, 86, 89, 96, 101,

Clarendon, Constitutions of, 14,

Clarke family, 58, 136,

Clarke, Sheila, 145,

Clarke, William, 58,

Clayton, Canon Wilfred T, 135,

Clayton, Mrs, 148, 149,

clinics, dental & medical, 58,

Clubmen movement, 62-3,

Coal Club, 58,

Cobbett, William, 63,

Coleraine, Lord, 63,

Collins family, 137, 158-162,

Collins, Wilkie, 158, 160, 161,

Collins, William, 160,

Common Plantation, 24,

conservation area, 80, 81,

Cook, Henry, 56,

Cook, John, 56,

Cook, William, 65,

Co-operative store, 18 96,

Copley, Jane, 155,

Copping, Jack, 133,

Copse, The, 49, 112,

Corben, George, 141,

Corbyn, Johannes, 48,

Cotton, John, 141,

Court House, 45, 94, 115, 168,

Cox, Mr, 173,

Cricket Club, 141-2,

Cromwell, Oliver, 63,

Crook family, 142,

Crook, Mrs, 58,

Crouch, John, 48,

Cub pack, 143,

Garden Machinery Centre, 18,
Gardening Club, 141,
Garrett family, 164,
gas supply, 124, 178,
Geddes family, 158-161,
geology of Alderbury, 22-4,
Gilbert, Emma, 38,
Glass, Edward, 81,
Godfrey, Richard, 53,
Goldstone family, 45,
Gorges, Sir Thomas, 17, 99,
gravel pit, 71, 143,
graveyard plan, 53-4,
Gray, George, 95, 136,
Gray, John Westcott, 161,
Gray, Percy, 161,
Gray, Stanley, 180,
Great Fire of Alderbury, 184,
Green Dragon, 14, 36, 39, 56, 64, 91, 97, 151,
     163, 168, 174, 175, 181-4,
Green, the, 14, 75,
Greenset House, 49, 89, 93,
Greenwood, Mrs, 179,
Grimstead Road, 25, 112, 122,
Groundwell, James de, 61,
Grout, E G, 74,
Guides,, 144,
Gumbleton, Mrs, 118,
Gumbleton, S, 74,

Haines, Thomas & Sarah, 56,
Hall, Lesley, 133,
Hall, Westley, 56,
Hand family, 102,
Hansford, Mrs, 180,
Hardiman family, 165,
Harper, Frank, 67,
Harris, George, 56,
Harris, John, 83, 91,
Hartford, Herbert, 87,
Hartford, Thomas, 87,
Haskard, Col. D, 73,
Hatcher, A W T, 74,
Hatcher family, 67, 162, 164, 174,
Hatcher, George, 174,

Hatcher, H, 120,
Hatcher, Samuel, 65,
Hatchet, Mr, 111,
Hayter, Susannah, 57,
Heyward, Lily, 149,
Hazel, Betsy, 160,
Hazel, Mr, 175, 177,
Hazel, Mrs, 176,
Hazel, Sidney, 67,
Herbert, E A, 88,
Herrington, Henry, 65,
Hibberd, Samuel, 93, 108,
Hickman family, 142, 151,
Hickman, W, 120,
Hickman's store, 173, 175, 179,
High street, 18, 75, 95-6, 123,
High Trees, 179,
Hilliard family, 55,
Hilliard, Richard, 55, 56,
Hilliard, Robert, 56,
Hinxman, Henry & Mary, 38, 159,
Hogg, Alison, 53,
Hole Farm, 28, 74, 75, 100,
Holly Tree Cottage, 93,
Home Farm, 63, 68,
Home Guard, 70-3, 75, 101, 148, 178,
Horner, Douglas, 73,
Howe, Alfred, 67,
Howe, Mr, 92,
Hunt, Gabrielle, 146,
Hunt, Holman, 161,
Hunt, Raymond, 144,
Hutchings family, 52,
Hutchings, Rev. Robert S, 48, 58, 93, 120, 133,
     142, 151, 152,
Hyare, Elizabeth, 162,

Idmiston, 64,
Ingram, William, 67,
Iron Age settlement, 29,
Ivy Cottage, 93,
Ivychurch Acadamy, 127-8,
Ivychurch Copse, 68,
Ivychurch Farm, 39, 68. 100,
Ivychurch House, 38,